# GET OUTTa ‹
# › MY WaY

## A STORIED LIFE

### CHARLOTTE SCHIFF-BOOKER

BOOKSIDE Press

BOOKSIDE Press

BookSide Press
877-741-8091
www.booksidepress.com
orders@booksidepress.com

# Contents

I dedicate this memoir

- to my sons David, Richard and Paul;
- to my grandchildren, Kaylie, Mickey, Henry, Elliot, Augustus, and Ruby;
- to my great-grandchild, Edie Lou; and
- most assuredly, to the love of my life, Hylan Bernard Booker.

I am grateful

- to Donald Freed, whose masterful genius made it possible for me to tell my story;
- to the brilliant writer and dear friend Marsha Berke for guiding me through the process;
- to so many students in the Freed writing class who were and remain family;
- to my darling best friend, mentor, and husband for his collaboration at every step of the way;
- to Judith Coppage, my literary agent, whose advice and counsel were profound and are what made publishing possible.
- to Toby Rafelson, a dear friend who provided enlightened input.

• All human beings have three lives: public, private, and secret.


—Gabriel García Márquez



STRONG WOMAN



You may encounter many defeats, but you must not be defeated. In fact, it may be necessary to encounter the defeats, so you can know who you are, what you can rise from, how you can still come out of it.



—Maya Angelou

# Commentaries

*Get Outta My Way* is a compelling tell-all memoir by Charlotte Schiff-Booker that chronicles her amazing life spread over the tapestry of American history in the changing social and political landscape during her lifetime in which she was an amazing proactive participant. In reading her page-turning novel, I felt like I was watching a great movie biography. She tells her personal tale that leads the reader through sexism, feminism, civil rights, the growth of television, cracking the glass ceiling, and, through it all, being a concerned and devoted parent. Her candid admissions about her failed marriages, sexuality, a woman trying to strive in a man's world, and surviving it all are lessons in endurance and profound strength. I found myself cheering for her when she finally found the love of her life to share in her third act. Charlotte has been a well-kept secret except for those in the early stages of broadcast and cable. *Get Outta My Way* will undoubtedly change that, and I look forward to hearing her interviews on NPR and other media outlets and receiving the attention she and her memoir rightfully deserve.

—*Carl Borack*, Olympian in fencing, 72 Munich Games,
filmmaker and documentarian

A dazzling trailblazer of a memoir, written by Charlotte Schiff-Booker, takes the genre of memoir writing to a new level. Nonlinear in its structure, it takes us on the journey of her first eight decades, often circling back, retelling, and reexamining parts and pieces of her extraordinary life. Her remarkable trajectory takes quantum leaps from her modest upbringing to the top of the skyscrapers, where wood-paneled executive suites were off-limits to women. Charlotte's love of dancing shared ground with an emerging sense of the inequities in the world. She fought for racial equity, social justice, women's rights. She cared before feminism had a name. As vice president at *Time Inc.*'s cable TV division, her presence led to an executive MBA at Columbia at Time's expense. She'd talked about fiber optics years before anyone else, convincing media moguls that cable TV was the next best thing, but not for long. She warned that new technologies put all media formats and devices at risk. Appointed associate publisher of *People* magazine, just as Schiff-Booker was rounding the fifty-year marker on the Sisyphean odyssey that is her life, an event derailed her. Recovery took three years, but she survived. She's shared personal experiences with the celebrities she knew, some revealing romantic intimacies. Now in her nineties, Schiff-Booker is thriving more fully than ever with the love of her life met at JFK thirty-eight years ago. She is healthy, happy, strong, proud of her three super sons, their divine wives, and children. *Get Outta My Way* is a must for those born in the last century or the current one. She's the real deal.

—*Lyn Lourie*, MSW, CSW

# Preface

It was a glass-ceilinged time. It was a time when men went home every night to *the little woman*. It was a time when most *little women* weren't even aware that the roof over their heads was a glass ceiling. But it was also Charlotte's time to start getting obstacles *outta my way*. Until one day, tragically, it wasn't. On that day, this larger-than-life life was ripped apart, had to be fitted back together, piece by painful, jagged piece, like a giant jigsaw puzzle. Sometimes resembling most a Picasso, out of joint, surreal, unreal, too real. A fight. And finally, victory. She hoped to find the answers by writing a memoir.

But looking back can be a madness of recall—glimpses etched in half- remembered words. She dug into hard truths long-buried. Doors opened to full sentences and memories that felt true. Philip Roth proclaims, "Memories of the past are not memories of facts but memories of your imaginings of the facts." Trying to know her life's nexus, it boiled down to a deep sense of the future. This is the coming-of-age story of *a woman of a certain age*. It is a life story, a love story. A singular woman's experience with history, melodrama, sex, and glossy high society in a fast-moving plot—set against a backdrop of the quintessential American industry: television, primetime broadcast television, and the budding of cable television into a billion-dollar industry, as told by one of its pioneers. An American story about the power game. Very Harold Robbins.

Charlotte led a life of celebrities and kings of industry, glittering parties, sexual passion, sweet romance. Famously, she was a warrior on the front lines for the rights of women, civil and political rights, human rights, free speech. It was a life of *the first woman to…* A big important life. Too big to abstract in a page or two. These are the crib notes. The real life is in the moments. Marriages, not all of them made in heaven, to three renowned and remarkable men. A mother of three renowned and remarkable sons.

A social revolutionary in the great struggles for human rights and a player in practical telecommunications. She played a key role in revising New York State rape laws to make conviction of perpetrators possible. She testified before Congress on obscenity and the just-then created phenomenon, public- access television. She produced cable television coverage of the first National Black Political Convention that played in seventy-eight cable systems across the country. She engineered *Time* magazine's coverage of the first National Women's Conference in a hundred years. And she had exquisite time outs, like being ringside at the Rumble in the Jungle in Zaire, to watch her friend Ali fight the undefeated heavyweight champion of the world and take back his title by knockout in the eighth.

After a three-year recovery from a bad accident, she busted through one cage after another in politics and television. The crash happened when she was fifty and at the top of her game, only catastrophic loss... She'd earned big bucks in a career she'd started late and at the bottom. Two disappointing marriages had cost her every which way—and then a near-fatal broken skull. When her mind began to come back, she asked herself, "What does it mean to be the key that started this engine? Not a damn thing." She told a friend she felt like an old snail hidden at the bottom of an aquarium, forgotten, invisible, irrelevant.

Three lost years later, ever Hammerstein's cockeyed optimist, she opened a window, felt the breeze, sucked in its freshness, and said aloud, "I have to find a way to pay the rent." And long years of fighting her way back physically, emotionally, and financially—surviving.

The beauty of a long life is that you can see a world, particularly a woman's world, in all the raw details of an ever-changing universe of values, rules, and limitations. The arc of this memoir is that journey. It is a uniquely American Jewish woman's journey where she must pierce the veils of the *male mythologies* about her place in the world of ideas, visions, and customs, be that home, the bedroom, the office or the board room, and against all the "you can't go there" nonsense. This frank memoir is how Charlotte Schiff-Jones-Booker did it. She lived the high life and made it through the right and wrong turns faced at every step.

Reading this book, you'll travel from the mid-twentieth century to the twenty-first but not sequentially. You'll be able to see through dreams, dead- ends, dismissals, delights, failures, and successes. You'll see how the feminist community is changing—the family, the children, the husbands, the lovers, the friends, the bosses, and the villains, creating this magpie nest of a woman's tense and complex adventure in the landscape of male vanities.

"My story is a tapestry woven in the first thirty years with classic female threads. But in 1963, the pattern began to change. The journey from a crib too small found itself in the halls of Congress in a battle to protect the new cable television industry. I walked away from theater and television to master the cable world with insights into the future of the media universe. Somehow the big changes in the communications world gave me a sense that I might transverse the American crazy quilt of race, sex, women's rights, male shallowness, and their desperate need to be in control all the time. Reading my story, you get to see great ideas rise and sparkle, and then get shot down. I entered a new world at the height of my career. A crash broke my skull. You'll feel the weight of love, the lightness of despair, and the sadness of defeat. When you enter my world you'll feel everything."

# PART 1

# Women Set Me on Fire

## Fire Island, 1962

It was the sixties, the time of liberation and contradiction—women, civil rights, the death of heroes, and a senseless war. In a way, it was my real beginning. Girlish fantasies were evaporating like beads of water on a sunny day. We were getting a taste of the future—the Soviet Union put the first man in space while the Bay of Pigs tarnished the legacy of JFK, our hero president. And then he delivered what he'd promised. Alan Shepard was America's first man in space. I felt the gravity profoundly.

What moved my career dreams into the real world were the free-spirited, accomplished women on an enchanted, puckish place called Fire Island. The sandbar began as a whaling center dating back to the eighteenth century. Later pirates came, then slave traders, a lighthouse, and a hotel. There were storms, rough waters, and bad winters, yet for a few months each year, it has become a summer retreat for many.

The great hurricane of 1938 devastated the island, its homes, and people, except for the Duffy Hotel in Cherry Grove. Gays began to come there, and soon Christopher Isherwood and W. H. Auden, dressed as Dionysus and Ganymede, were carried on followers' shoulders to anoint the Grove as a safe place for the ostracized to enjoy sun, surf, sand, sex, and even some serenity. The rest of the island's communities began to be scattered along a long stretch of sand.

My suburban friend Edna had invited us to her island summer home for a weekend. At the pier in Bayside, there was an odd mix of mortals. They were piling bikes, bagels, books, beach chairs, small appliances, pets, and kids onto the ferry. The purposeful chaos made me feel there'd be no rules on the sandbar between the Atlantic Ocean and Long Island Sound. We stepped up to the top deck to enjoy the sun and sea, hair blowing in the wind—well, others' hair. My Jewish Afro never moved. I saw a crowd of sun-tanned happy people standing on the Ocean Beach community's pier, their arms outstretched in readiness.

Wives, husbands, boyfriends, girlfriends, and children were waiting for loved ones. Some carried martinis in a thermos under one arm and two wine glasses in a free hand. Most onboard had kicked off their shoes by the time the ferry nosed into its slip. I took mine off, too, and didn't put them on again until we headed home three days later. Ed and I walked to Edna's house led by a boy pulling our bags and my four-year-old Paul in a red wagon, his brothers David and Richard on either side. We passed a barefoot bride and groom taking their vows, the couple and guests in a wild assortment of beachwear and bare skin—like a living Matisse painting of assorted patterns and semi-nudity.

As we drew closer to Edna's house, the roar of the sea grabbed my attention. When we arrived, our acerbically witty, stylish, very blonde hostess was standing at the front door. There is a story behind our friendship. We shared feeling stifled by the sterile suburbs. We'd found each other at the Baldwin Bridge Club, both of us there to conquer the vapidity of suburban life. The game of Bridge shuts the door on all other thoughts or worries. It fills the empty spaces. We liked each other at once, but who knew she led a collection of women who would liberate my hidden aspirations? Edna's vintage house wrapped its shingles around me as I sensed that I was headed for something special.

She introduced me to what seemed an endless cascade of inspiring women—artists, actors, novelists, journalists, doctors, lawyers, painters, composers, psychoanalysts—all achievers. They raised a spark that fired up unknown truths from the past. There were feisty, talented women in this astral world of lively discourse. Marlyn Brill became a friend instantly. She was a kindred activist; both of us had worked on Jesse Jackson's symbolic campaign for president. I swam in a sea of female energy and courage. For me at that time, the notion of a career showed up only in dreams. My extra-domestic focus was mainly on human rights projects, political campaigns, Bridge games, and paddle tennis. But these savvy women knew their onions, a mix of brainy broads, young, old, and in-between. I was astonished by the teamwork and their embrace of me, a stranger. The women were bonded. One talked of reframing her ambitions inside male power. A new dynamic for me, the innocent among them.

The next night I walked barefoot to the ocean, sat in the damp sand, the crescent moon squinting at me, my heartbeat in sync with the rolling waves. In the dim light, I saw only white foam, my mind fizzing with the island's female power and beauty. I'd met Dorothy Carr, an old broad with a teenage appetite for adventure. She embodied the intertwining of old and young, her curiosity ranging from the arcane to a belief in science fiction coming true in the future. She became the landlady for our first full summer on the island the following year. Books and memorabilia from global travels filled the crusty beach house. Dorothy mixed pain and wit with an existential truth that kept her life brilliantly satisfying, like my sister Judy. Dorothy became a favorite Bridge partner, mentor, and ageless, sexy friend. No longer alive, she's still a spirit that inspires me when I need it most. On the first day of our full season, I awoke in her house to sun-rays poking up from the horizon. Walking to the sea, I felt a soft, chilly ocean breeze. My bare toes curled into the welcoming sand as I listened to sound and fury revert to calm and quiet in a rhythm that eased my senses.

Traversing the island on naked feet roused a sense of freedom that spilled over to my children. David and Richard biked to a funky day camp on their own. And after supper, they'd do the same for ice cream cones and sometimes a film in an old building converted to a makeshift movie house. My older boys' appetite to be freer was whetted to the hilt. Maybe it was the absence of city traffic, scary strangers, and rigid schedules that enhanced the spirit of independence on the island.

Four-year-old Paul often disappeared on the beach. The first time brought panic. He was found finally in a police hut licking an ice cream cone, nonplussed at having scared us half to death. On his first movie night in the funky theater, we walked home under a star-filled sky, Paul looked up and shouted, "Look! Look! The planetarium." You see, it was the first real starlit sky my city boy had ever seen. He was a regular at the planetarium, just a few blocks from where we now lived.

One day on a bench waiting for a ferry, I eyed a tall male body striding toward me in khaki shorts, his caramel skin glowing from the sun, shirt unbuttoned to the waist. My right leg began to quake as he closed in. He was the man on TV with whom I'd fallen in love at age fifteen, a crush that haunted my dreams. When Harry Belafonte offered his hand to say hello, I reached up to return the clasp and pressed hard with my other hand to stop the leg from shuddering. I was fifteen years old again, my crush standing over me. I went stupid. Mercifully, the ferry came.

Dolores Autori, a new friend who'd been a Katherine Dunham dancer, had been close to the Belafontes for years. She persuaded them to rent a house on the bay. On their deck one day, I watched a Cypress Gardens-style spectacle. Bronzed bodies in sexy bikinis kicking up high waves on water skis, slaloming in graceful curves and turns. I tried to look indifferent to disguise my envy and discomfort. Harry did exactly what I was afraid of. He beckoned me to try. I declined. He promised to set me up to soar away firmly on the skis. Everyone joined in the pressure. "Don't be a scaredy cat." "What are you afraid of?" I am a strong swimmer, so how bad could it be? I eased into the water behind the boat. Harry put his arms around my waist to put me in the correct position. Then, oh no, an underwater hand grab!

I punched him in the mouth with my clenched fist and in full view of family and friends. Everyone, even his wife, Julie, and my husband, Ed, applauded, laughing. Was this some kind of test? If it was, I guess I'd passed. He was fresh. I socked him. The memory of that punch and the friendship that grew were what empowered me to visit his dressing room at the ABC studio a couple of years later. Our first Fire Island summer had been full of fun. There were marvelous parties with terrific people, and Harry was almost always around. One afternoon after a few hours of crazy poker, we walked together to the beach.

Still overwhelmed that a fifteen-year-old crazy crush was my new friend, I said, "Isn't it great that everybody here loves you so?"

I thought he was going to punch me back as he shouted, "Love? You call that love? Where the hell was love when I needed it? Why do the people who slammed the door in my face now hold it open? It makes me sick."

I felt stupid. Was it the teenage crush that mucked up my thinking? Or maybe I wasn't as hip as I thought I was. You'll soon find out more about why I abandoned the young black students in Red Hook and felt awful. It didn't help that it was the racist Brooklyn public school system that caused me to quit. That cowardice and my blunder with Harry drove me back to all the writers my Brooklyn College professor had turned me onto. I'd angered a man I adored and respected. What the hell was that about? As close as I'd been to the Black experience from childhood on, I knew I had never come close enough to really know a world that was not mine. I knew I didn't belong, but it's what I wanted. I needed to know and respect the boundaries. Marlyn and I planned a fundraiser for Dr. King at a friend's grand home.

The very idea of meeting the man who sparked the movement for African American rights had me on the edge like a leaf in a storm. When he entered with Andrew Young, I hid behind an antique screen and sucked in a breath so deep it was hard to exhale. I stepped out from behind the screen, lifted my head, straightened my back, and walked toward a giant who had brought profound change to our world. Dr.

King's kind attention turned my shyness into chutzpah. We dove into a rich conversation that moved me to tell him about the racism in Red Hook. We talked so long that the restless crowd formed a circle around us to capture his attention. I decided to get out of their way.

The event was a success that smudged the color and gender lines on Fire Island far more than we'd been able to do up to that day. I shall never forget my private conversation with the man who continued to use his oratorical gifts and brilliant mind to urge an end to racism until the day he was shot to death.

What didn't fit my perception of the progressive minds and lifestyles on this vibrant strip of sand was a place called Point O' Woods. A collection of Charles Adams-like ghoulish houses restricted for anyone not white, Anglo-Saxon, and American-born. It made no sense for this free-spirited island to have a cloistered community of folks more likely to burn a book about slavery than read it. It would be a waste of time and energy to bother with the impenetrable. Then something happened when I was on the beach with friends and my younger sons on a very hot day. A boy rushed over to inform me that David and his buddies' bikes were confiscated by the Point O' Wood's "sheriff." Their crime was to go through a rarely open gate to get to Sunken Forest, a historic preserve.

It was a long walk for me on a hot day, the blazing sun burning the sand, and my bare feet. I jumped from blanket to beach towel, from grass patch to grass patch to find relief. No hat, no parasol, not even sunblock—whoever heard of sunblock in 1964? On my blistered feet, I reached the iron gate with its menacing padlock and shouted to be let in. I begged the shy young man to open the barrier, but he refused to summon the sheriff. I left without the bikes. My feet rescued by cooler ground surfaces, I plodded back to where Edna had taken my boys. A memory flash reminded me that David's guest was his black school friend, Freddie. Where was my head? A bunch of "Jew boys" and one they'd surely refer to as a "nigger kid" were mistreated by those bigots for invading their sanctuary. It had better been only their bikes that had been assaulted.

Ah, but I worked for the *Fire Island News*, my name on the masthead next to Nat Hentoff. His jazz column in the *Village Voice* was a favorite read. Knowing him was a treat, proximity to his name in print a bonus. This was my first scoop. The headline for the article was "Attack on kids for visiting a national treasure." The first line in the article was "The confiscation and late return of boys' bicycles by Point O' Woods was considered an outrageous insult by many Fire Islanders." I ended the piece with a demand that they build a bike stand for those seeking to observe a natural wonder situated near the Point O' Woods community. They came up with a stand to hold eight bikes along with a new rule that the gate be locked only after dark.

Point O' Woods did not have a monopoly on prejudice. A stunning and charming Dolores and her handsome white husband with two mixed-race daughters were the first persons of color to build and occupy a house in Seaview, our community's name on the sandbar. Their welcome was mostly a giant cold shoulder. Marlyn and her husband, Sidney, took some heat for selling them the site, but it helped when they built their own new house next door. As members of the Law Center for Constitutional Rights, the ACLU, and antiwar everything, we soulmates waged a campaign for our new friends, along with a series of political events we'd produced, like the ones for Martin Luther King, Eleanor Roosevelt's biologist, Blanche Wiesen Cook, and civil rights attorney William Kunstler.

The tide turned on the Autori saga when their fun parties became a hot ticket. To hang with guests like Carmen McRae, Ben Gazzara, Diahanne Carroll, and Miles Davis, the color line got smudged further, if not erased. Harry and Julie Belafonte had upended the equation when they showed up in a house on the bay. To mend my misperceptions on race issues, I waffled through saved *New Yorker* excerpts from James Baldwin's *The Fire Next Time*. I came upon a letter Baldwin wrote to his nephew urging him to "show naïve and ignorant white folks how to live right and see the truth." I found it striking that an incredibly brilliant black barrier-breaking mind would urge his fifteen-year-old nephew to save white Americans from our false ideas and persuade African Americans to forgive our ignorance. And then his letter went on to say that if we didn't all find a way to build a future together, we'd face destruction. No right mind in 2021 can deny the shrewdness of that prophecy. What were we to think when the Voting Rights Act was gutted by the Supreme Court in 2018—their rationale, "Racism is over." Really?

I found solace in women friends, new social connections, and the great book *Feminine Mystique*. Betty Friedan's counternarrative was like an x-ray vision of my inner life. All the women interviewed in the book were speaking for me. They were me. Betty's moment of truth was to put me into the world with "work is the call to arms." I was told by my new friends that I was looking radiant. That must have come from a sense of self that arose from knowing inspiring women. And there were other moments worth telling, first, this one:

On a rainy day, I was at the offbeat fish store at the bay water's edge. A woman entered in dark glasses, a yellow slicker, and a kerchief-wrapped head under the hood. She and I left the store with our purchases and walked together under my umbrella. A light rain turned torrential as we reached my place, and she agreed to come in for a cup of tea until it subsided. I chatted away as I turned up the kettle and put muffins on the table. She seemed shy, so I rambled on. "The island makes me feel so alive…and how about these terrific women?" She giggled when I heralded the beauty of bare feet, her body finally relaxing under the rain gear. I'd stripped to my shorts and tank top, but she hadn't removed a thing, not even her sunglasses. Then the timid flower leaned forward, looking intent on saying something important. I leaned toward her to hear her bashful whisper. She sipped tea, cleared her throat, and nervously positioned herself to say what I could tell would be significant. "Charlotte, what I want to…" Edna barged in and yelled, "Oh my god, Marilyn Monroe!"

How did I not know? She hugged the slicker to her body and sped to the front door, looked back to say a quick "Thank you," and left. I'd been up close and personal to my most adored female actor. Enamored of her talent, ravishing beauty, and intelligence, I hated that she was a female victim, her life distorted and abused. It made me crazy that the studios sadistically exploited their valuable sex symbol. I was drawn to her pain over the men whose love and respect she craved but almost never received. She became my Medea, with only herself to kill—no children. When she died, it was as if a member of my family had passed. What was she about to say looking so intent? Would she have said that she "stopped feeling she existed in the human race?"—her words to mentor and friend Lee Strasberg just before she died.

Marilyn gave men what they wanted and got little back. I knew about that. She tried hard to be taken seriously. I knew about that too. I understood and connected to her innocence, her vulnerability, her yearning. She'll always be lighting up the screen, warming our hearts. For my eightieth birthday, my granddaughter Kaylie gave me the best book devoted to Marilyn. No gift ever meant more to me—until I helped deliver her daughter, my first great-grandchild, on my birthday in 2016.

There's another sandbar story, this time with a fascinating man that began when I was on the empty beach reading some old classic I'd found in Dorothy's house. I was on my movable chaise, a straw hat tilted over my face to hide my disgrace for missing the protest and block the sun. I had overslept and woke too late to make the boat to fight Robert Moses's plan to build a road from end to end, allowing cars to invade our sanctity. In shame, I tried to stay unseen. Checking the ocean's mood, I saw the only other person on the beach walk toward me. He handed me a new book, smiled, and walked away. What the hell, at least he walked away. I opened the book and laughed for an hour over the originality of whacky, acerbic humor inside a hilarious yet disturbing diatribe.

I spotted the stranger again headed in my direction. He asked for his book. I said, "Tell me where you live. My son will return it." He demanded that I give it to him. I resisted.

He said, "Walk to the shop in Ocean Beach and buy one."

I thought, *What's with this guy?*

I turned the book over and saw a photo of the writer's face. It was Joseph Heller's face. His dry wit led to a friendship I still cherish. In our house, he'd set up verbal combat and then sit back to enjoy the fight. I came to realize that *Catch-22*'s principal character, John Yossarian, was Joe. I enjoyed discovering that. Then I read his *Something Happened,* a novel in which the main character, Bob Slocum, lives in a zone of desolation and wonder as he abides by the demands of magazine hierarchy. I knew that Joe had written *Catch-22* while writing for *Time* and *Look* magazines, so Slocum might have come from the other side of Jo's consciousness.

These anecdotes are just two samples of how profound it was for me to spend summers on Fire Island. I got to know and be known by people I'd admired from afar, and they didn't disappoint. Over fifty years later, I can still recapture the utopian mood of Fire Island in any season or place—even while throwing snowballs and wearing fur-lined boots.


# First Job

A new beginning came to life when we moved from the Long Island suburbs to Manhattan with our three sons. I decided to make a big move myself. My restlessness and growing discontent with full-time housewifery was validated by *The Feminine Mystique.* Like the hero in a fairy tale, I set off from our apartment on the West Side of Manhattan on the BMT subway to seek my new future. I looked over the heads of the tightly packed mass of people and spotted a concave ad on top of a window that said, "f u k rd ths u k gt a jb w hi pa"—if you can read this, you can get a job with high pay—a speed-writing course that promised easy shorthand. I was thirty-one years old and had never held a full-time job. It seemed secretary was the only way to begin, so I enrolled in the course and finished in record time. The job search began and didn't take long.

I didn't want to work too far from home or my sons' schools, so I walked over to ABC, the American Broadcasting Company, and promptly flunked the typing test. Before the nerdy personnel guy could say a word, I said, "I'm not the fastest speed demon on the Olympic typing team, but trust me, I make up for lost time with spelling and grammar." He turned out to be a kind man. He set me up for an interview with Harvey Jacobs, advertising and promotion director for ABC Television International.

I stepped into his office and saw a grown man with the pockmarks of a teenager seated behind a cluttered desk. A cigarette dangled from his lips, ashes dribbled down his chest, and a snowfall of dandruff coated his shoulders. I wanted to clean him up, but not being his mother, I decided to win him over by promising to spruce up his office, his files, his appointment schedule, and his agenda. With hopes high but anxiety higher, my instinct was to take the cigarette out of his mouth. Instead, I apologized for my poor test results and revisited my earlier sales pitch, adding, "You'll be getting more than ABC is buying." My look at his blue eyes was meant to be read as "Trust me... I'm a quick study with ambition." He hired me on the spot at $90 a week. Okay, Betty! I have my first real job. Now what?

My desk was in a row of desks for secretaries. Their mean age was about nineteen. I wasn't old enough to be their mom or young enough to be one of the girls. With fake nonchalance, I took long walks on the secretary corridor's lonely aisle, like a wasteland. I was looking for a welcome sign, a feather in the nest, a friendly face. I peered into eyes that looked away. Attempts at conversation fell flat. When I made eye contact, I saw "Please keep walking."

At the aisle's end, I saw a young woman who looked like an idol in my dancing days. I said, "I bet everyone says you're the spitting image of Anne Miller, don't they?"

She looked as if she'd seen a hornet on my nose. "Who's Anne Miller?"

I raised my hand to block another blow as if I'd been punched. My desk looked a football field away—the place where I was supposed to belong was no place at all. I was an outsider, again chasing after Iris and Janet, who tried to lose me when I was six. But I put the best face on it. I was dealing with what felt like a generation gap that happened in just a bit more than a decade!

The watercooler was a collective cold shoulder of cliques, with rankings, and gossip that were closed to me. One day I overheard disgruntled words about the Frug, a new dance none of them knew how to do. Could that be a passport for one well versed in the dances of the day? With a Natasha- inspired leap into the middle of the huddle, I said, "I know the Frug!" They looked baffled, surely in disbelief that an old broad, a thirty-something, could know the Frug. I took a few turns right there and said, "If you want to learn how, let me know." I must have lost years in their eyes when they learned the dance, yet still not one of the girls, I was at least tolerated.

I found a love poem on my desk entitled "Next Year in Guayaquil." I asked Harvey what he knew about it. His answer was a shocker. He'd been at the same Catskill Hotel where my brother Sammy waited tables. My parents and I spent two weeks there in 1944. I tap-danced in a show and crashed into scenery that came tumbling down. Harvey had seen it all. He confessed to hiding behind trees, cars, and whatever would conceal his obsession to follow his love, twelve-year-old me. He said the poem was his way to deal with the coincidence. All too much for me, I declared, "Sorry, Harvey, I have to quit." He assured me nothing would come of a teenage crush. He was right. The job was great, and we stayed friends for years after I moved on. He and his wife were at my sixtieth birthday party. His crush is in his novel, *Summer on a Mountain of Spices.*

My hunger to rise was fed by writing press releases, organizing marketing events, and shooting from the hip to reach targeted goals. When Harvey was overseas, I was told by his agent that he'd sold one of his short stories for $25. I read the love story. At the end, the couple turned out to be two huge computers. Something had to be done. The story was a knockout ahead of its time, worth a whole lot more. I took the liberty of canceling the sale and then sent the story to *Playboy* with a clever cover letter. They paid $2,000 for it. I fantasized about starting a literary agency and naming it Jabberwocky, but I never did. In less than a year, Harvey and his boss created a job precisely for me, with a promotion and a raise. Personnel director Maggie Maguire disallowed the promotion. I assured my embarrassed bosses that she'd change her mind once she knew me. They arranged a meeting. I walked to her office feeling fine, but she greeted me with an icy stare. I started to speak.

She cut me off. "Our policy limits promotion of secretaries to one grade at a time, but listen, Mrs. Schiff, you can resign and come back in two months, and no policy will stand in your way."

Was I dreaming? Could it be that a woman had punished me for being a woman? Betty's "problem with no name" would not be understood by a woman living in an airless void. Maybe coming to a workplace late led me to an arrogance youth doesn't afford. I expected empathy and support from her, but she messed me up.

I said, "No point trying to change your mind. Arguing with a fool makes me feel foolish." I stomped out, slammed the door behind me, and told Harvey that I'd have to leave ABC for its hideous personnel policies. I was not aware that corporate culture's misogyny was not just in ABC. It would be everywhere.

To give me time, Harvey suggested I work on a one-week trial run for Les Crane as host of a new late-night show. Mel Brooks co-hosted. His mom was always present and laughed with pride at every joke, most at her expense, like a willing victim at a Friar's Club Roast.

I was to deliver celebrities, and I came up with Carmen McRae, Robert Ryan, and Johnny Desmond. My appetite for television production was whetted. Home at dinner time on one of my late nights, dear Ed threatened to "put an end to this nonsense." My wonderful helper, Enid, took care of his dinner, but his fury was not about food. It was what it was, a deep decline, but I stopped caring about the grumbles of a man emotionally and physically absent most of the time. What I cared about were his absences from our children even when he was home.

Now a working woman, I wanted to believe that making time spent with them special counted. We did theater, movies, concerts, hung out listening to and singing Sgt. Pepper's Lonely Heart Club Band with the Beatles, or seeing *Blazing Saddles*, my boys cracking up at the farting scene. I attended every school event and teacher conference and played all kinds of games with them, including bowling, biking, and even softball. I hoped my boys had as much fun when we were together as I did.

What trickled down from the centers of power at ABC was all manner of gossip, facts, and fancies. One day I soaked up a particularly juicy bit of news. A taping in Studio A to honor Black History Month, with Harry Belafonte, Sidney Poitier, Ossie Davis, Sammy Davis, Ruby Dee, Piper Laurie, and Roddy McDowall. My intention was to find a way inside. The civil rights struggle had found me a long time ago. I'd produced a forum for the Television Academy on Racism in Television. The all-Black panel I chose included Ossie Davis, Percy Sutton, and Charlie Kenyatta. I had no invite for this one in ABC, but I had to be there. A nobody secretary on my way out, I talked my way into the ninety-minute taping. I was in awe as they talked about the Black experience in America—something I thought I knew better than most white people.

Maybe so, but James Baldwin said that when we know better, we need to act better. Until that happens for me, I'll continue to honor the connection I feel as a Jew whose ancestors survived murderous pogroms by Cossacks in Pinsk. My grandma's stories of omnipresent danger and my love for the black family I knew well as a child gave me a sense of belonging to both worlds, one of them not mine. It came to me that as often as I felt part of the music, the vibrant energy, and the culture, what was special was feeling welcome in a world I loved.

When the taping ended, I strode over to a well-guarded backstage door, told the manager my name, and asked to see Mr. Belafonte. In minutes, pulling a sweater over his bewitching body, the beautiful man showed up happy to see me. This time my leg didn't shake like it had when we first met. I hoped he didn't hear my heart quivering. I did my best to appear casual, alone with him in his dressing room's tiny space. We parried small talk, and it stayed small. We did not touch on the rich substance of the program I'd just seen. I slid into his rhythm and brought up the crazy no-limit poker games on Fire Island. My role had been to observe as the stakes were way too high. He changed the subject with "Join me and Sidney for Sammy's last show at the Copa tonight." I wondered if he'd forgotten my public punch when he grabbed me underwater? Hell, that was two years ago. I'd go.

# The High Life

Eddie was out of town. When he was a naval officer, he spent months-long stretches abroad. I tried hard to keep our marriage afloat. He was rarely home, even as a civilian. And when home, he'd meet my deepest feelings and opinions with contempt and derision. Even our sons couldn't get from their dad what they enjoyed so much with mine, their pops. After Ed "allowed" me to get a job, I hoped it might balance the books a bit, gain his respect. Instead, it made him more disdainful and me stronger.

For the Copa, to look casually gorgeous, I chose a salmon-colored silk dress and jacket and high heels. My sons were on my bed while I "put on my face," a ritual. It was always a good time to find out what was bugging them, what they were proud of or needed. Often, I'd share my work with them. This night I told them about the Black History Month event and that all but two of the expected speakers were black and why that made a difference. I couldn't let my sons grow up not knowing the true story of slavery, how and by whom America was built, and at what human cost. They were cool about me going out with Harry. They'd known him on Fire Island.

The buzzer announced his arrival. A gleaming limousine idled at the curb. Poitier was inside sipping wine. I climbed in next to him, and Harry slipped in on my other side. We were off, my head in the clouds. We pulled up to 10 East Sixtieth Street. The doorman took my hand as I stepped onto a red carpet with a gilded "C" under a gold-tasseled canopy. Harry held my right hand, Sydney clasped my left, and we entered the nightclub side by side. I felt like Dorothy skipping down the yellow brick road, the lion on one side, the tin man on the other. My feet never touched the ground. People stared at us, and I hoped they were trying to figure us out. The women wore furs and jewels and the men's outfits were more varied. The star-studded saloon was in Art Deco Brazilian motif, metal palm trees with blue and pink lights coloring their leaves. Waiters wore tuxedos. The barstools were dressed in dark velvet cushions.

We joined Harry's compatriots next to their large table. A small one for us was carried and placed at its end. The music started, and gorgeous showgirls in mink bras and panties matching their hair colors high-kicked their way onto the stage at our feet, their bodies making me jealous. Sammy tap-danced in and sang "What Kind of Fool Am I?" He ended his act with "All of Me," and all of him was what we got. An amazing performance.

Then we went up to a midnight party in the Gotham Hotel in the same building. In a grand room of pretty people who all knew each other, I felt like a gate crasher and wondered how I might sneak away. Harry found me hiding in the corner of an adjoining room. We talked away from the crowd. Hoping to impress him, I recounted the painstaking backstory of my battle to produce a forum on Racism in Television, including how appalled the board of governors was by the very idea of serving such a meal to an all-white TV Academy. I enjoyed Harry's smile when he said, "Well done. You're a gutsy girl." I hoped he hadn't heard my gasp.

We continued to talk about so much that mattered to me, and Harry treated me with respect and appreciation for my commitment and activism in the movement. He suggested we move to a higher floor. He promised it would be less noisy. When he opened the door of a suite, my eyes fixed on a still life— a bottle of champagne in an ice bucket, a platter of cheese and crackers, fresh flowers in a lovely vase.

At the Copa, I'd noticed a stream of gorgeous women stroll by flirtatiously, making their desire to be with Harry known. So why me? What made the guy I'd punched two years ago so sure? Having been an innocent nineteen-year- old when I married Ed, here I was, high as a kite in a hotel suite with the most beautiful man I'd ever seen, a man of charismatic sensuality impossible to resist. He asked what I would like him to do. What did he mean? Was there a menu to choose from—one from column A and two from column B? My inexperience and wonder brought jitters I could not hide. He looked perplexed.

"Haven't you read Fanny Hill?" he asked, the paperback in his hand. I'm no Fanny, but he told me he'd been wanting me since our first meeting. Aware of his reputation, I didn't believe that.

But hey, it was fun to find out that my teenage crush on Harry was no longer an air castle. I was a married mother of three wanting an identity of my own, not just mother, daughter, sister, or wife. I could blame what happened next on the Scotch whisky I'd been drinking for hours, but I must admit that the man I married was still a stranger to me, and I was in a suite with a superb person I'd admired on multiple fronts. For years I'd followed his devotional support of Dr. King and the whole struggle on many levels and dimensions. Harry was a hero.

I was open to the tender and knowing way he made love to me. Our mutual pleasure inspired more times with this splendid man, but it didn't take long for me to end it. Harry made me feel alive, but the absence of deep feeling remained a gaping hole. My life with Ed grew more painful with every passing day, but I was still married and had a family to protect. To feel better about breaking a cardinal rule, I thought of the deal that I'd accepted so long ago to keep the romance alive during the courtship. Ed promised to stop pressing me to give in if I'd allow him dalliances with other women. I wondered what in the world got me to agree to such a bargain, and it made me think he might still be at it. Maybe not, but I exploited the possibility as a good conscience copout. For some reason, I came home feeling fine, with no guilt.

It was the Copa itself that kept me awake, like a delicious dinner that's hard to digest. In a swank nightclub, I'd seen how people change in different settings. DuBois wrote about "double consciousness." It made sense to me, a woman with multiple identities. One came when my suntan and bushy hair had folks taking me for Black. Each situation called for a response that suited the setting and the players. Sometimes I laughed. Other times I awkwardly alerted them to the mistake. Often, I enjoyed the fun of passing.

I awoke feeling there'd been no sleep. When I was drifting off, images from *Cabaret* were swirling in my brain—sinister, dark, and dangerously cruel images. At the Copa, the glamour was there to see, and fun to be inside. Who wouldn't want to go to a Gatsby party—all glitter, glamour, and gorgeous release from reality? Or step into a Fellini movie brilliantly dramatizing the ennui of a life without meaning? I tried to shape a narrative out of a montage of empty moves. I wanted to think of the Copa as Rick's Place, but it wasn't, and there was no Humphrey Bogart to convince me that there could be redemption in a watering hole where unreconciled creatures strived for the brass ring at all costs. My hope was that I was just another tourist too far outside to be swept up by the sweet smell of success into a kind of death. I didn't like that place. And it clearly was a place to which I had no desire to belong.

# PART 2

# A Devil's Bargain

I'd met Eddie Schiff in 1948 at his Club Soda's cellar hangout. I was sixteen. The tall nineteen-year-old strikingly handsome guy's hazel-green eyes brightened as he headed straight for me. I was wearing a yellow cotton dress, my bushy hair hidden under a newly contrived coiffure. I liked his laugh, his kisses, his challenging intellect. He was vexed to learn I was a committed virgin. Yet that very night, I wrote in my diary that I'd met the man I would marry. He didn't call.

Months later, we met again at a party and started dating, but my take on sex was the same.

Ed kept pressing. Crazy about the guy, I didn't want to lose him. My head in my heart, I agreed to a Faustian bargain. The pact went like this: he'd stop challenging my chastity if I would free him to periodically satisfy his libido elsewhere. What in the world could I have been thinking? The deal with the devil stares back at me as an original sin that would carry long-term consequences. His cracks about my politics unsettled me too, but I was sure I'd bring him around on that score—a fatal female flaw in those days. We shared a somewhat romantic time for a few months, but ornery shortcomings kept mounting. I called it quits, but missing him was excruciating.

I started digging for excuses for his main shortcomings. I knew my antiquated adherence to chastity had been and would still be my shortcoming. Yet he went along with reviving the courtship, knowing I was stuck to righteous innocence—a rule my own libido was aching to break. The only way to fix the impasse was to make this thing legal with an engagement to marry. What was I thinking? My folks had a fit. Dad's critique was, "He stands by the door like a convict looking for a way out." Mother's pistol whip, "An egg candler? His father looks at eggs one at a time to make sure they're kosher?" My parents wanted me to have in-laws who played Gin Rummy and didn't live in the place they'd escaped and wanted to forget. But they gave in. Dad was excited about a wedding.

Ed was in law school, and I was a junior at Brooklyn College. After school, Ed and I headed toward Magistrate's Court for a marriage license. I carried our books so they'd think at least one of us was working. We chuckled nervously as we climbed the steep steps. At noon on Sunday, April 27, 1951, at the stately Union Temple in Brooklyn's Grand Army Plaza, at age twenty- two and nineteen, Ed and I married as I'd prophesied. I loved this man.

The hunt for a bridal gown became a family legend. It started with the *handel,* a Yiddish word for "bargain." Here's the rundown: in the first of a phalanx of discount bridal shops on Christie Street near Chinatown, the proprietor heard mother's Yiddish translation of my design essentials, walked to the back room, and returned with a price scribbled on a scrap of paper. In Yiddish, Mother said, "Oh, too dear. Never mind," and marched out, dragging me behind her. The routine was repeated in two more bridal shops. It looked to me like mother knew this game—she must have played it a thousand times. She was at home with peddlers. In the last of a series of similar scenarios, the Yiddish version of a Kabuki drama seemed over.

There'd be no beautiful bridal gown. I followed her out of the last shop, sobbing. The owner ran after us yelling, "Vait, vait. I'll take anudda look." A little man with Mr. Magoo eyes, a belt buckled under his big belly, and a few strands of gray hair spread out across his bald head, bent over a wrinkled paper in his palm and adjusted spectacles with lenses so thick I couldn't see his eyes. He spread out the paper and gave it to my mother. The price was right. A deal was struck. I'd witnessed a rite of passage centuries old. I was not aware then that my grandmother Bubbi and the grandfather I never knew had dragged pushcarts up and down alleys yelling, "*Alta shmatas* for sale!" I found out that to survive in America, my immigrant grandparents peddled old clothes. Mother had learned from them. I learned a lot about her that day.

She was intimidated by her uppity, smart-ass kids, but more at home on Christie Street. She wielded power there. In a subway car headed home, I thanked her for what would be a more wonderful wedding dress than we could ever have afforded at Saks Fifth Avenue. She didn't wipe the smile off her face this time. My mother became Mom. In wonderment for what had enlivened a relationship so long in the shadow of indifference, my best guess was that once married, I'd no longer be her responsibility. At the wedding, she looked absolutely gorgeous in a blue taffeta ankle-length dress, matching jeweled shrug, and stylish hat tilted to one side, her classic chignon at the back of her neck—really stunning! I thought maybe now she'd come to love me, really love me. Simone de Beauvoir's *Memoirs of a Dutiful Daughter* moved me to do what I could to love and be loved by my mother—or if love was asking too much, I hoped we'd be friends.

My brainy big sister Judy knew my life intention was to be taken seriously and make a positive difference. We sat side by side on our bed, my hands in hers, our foreheads pressed together. She whispered, "Little sister, be sure to make time for what matters to you." Judy must have been conditioning me for the feminist thinking and action that was our manifest destiny. She liked Ed. Although getting married was not in her playbook, she was excited and happy for her little sister, calming me during the pre-wedding *Sturm und Drang* in a way no one else could have done. And then with her broken ankle in a cast, Judy leaned on a cane to carry her oversized body down the aisle, a beautiful maid of honor. My dapper brother Sammy led the ushers, all in tuxedos. My best friends graced the aisle in their bridesmaid costumes. The ceremony and reception were marvelous. Two large families and my elementary, high school, and college friends filled the room with their beauty and happiness for me, the first to marry.

Ed's family came, and the complete Club Soda crowd was in the mix, cheering their pal.

# Where Were the Stars?

Dad drove us to the airport for the flight to our honeymoon in Miami. I sat in the back seat, but I heard him whisper to my mother. "I can't believe that my cheerful little earful is on her way to sleep with another man." I didn't pick up on the Oedipal side of that gaffe until I was old enough to laugh at its absurdity. Or was it? In the myth, I spent the flight fantasizing. A knight in shining armor was sweeping his virgin bride into the marvel of sexual ecstasy. Legend had it that bells ring and stars come down bringing heaven with them. But on our honeymoon, what did I do—or not do? I felt a failure. It had to be my fault. Yet Ed fell asleep smiling. Utterly unprepared and too embarrassed to talk to him about it, I decided to be patient. I didn't know then that a woman is responsible for her own orgasm. I should have informed myself. I should have been ready to help the first steps in a life together be taken with finesse and understanding. I hadn't done that. The next mistake was to just wait for the stars.

I decided to make the first meal in our basement apartment a knockout! I followed an exotic recipe meticulously, covered the metal card table with linen, set it with wedding gifts and tulips. My sexual fantasies in full flourish, I wore my bridal peignoir, lit the candles, opened the red wine to let it breathe, put Frank Sinatra records on our secondhand turntable, and waited for my darling husband's surprise and warm praise. He arrived. I made a toast to us and then set down his beautiful plate. It was worthy of a photo if we'd had a camera. He asked, "Any ketchup?" I brought the bottle to the table, asking him to at least take a taste. He grabbed it out of my clenched fist and poured red goop all over everything.

After dessert, his appraisal was, "Good bread... thanks for going to so much trouble." I was reminded of a limerick I'd written when I was about seven:

> *There once was a pretty young bride,*
> *Who wiped her sad eyes as she cried.*
> *You can't learn to cook by eating the book.*
> *I tried it and I nearly died.*

I squelched the hurt and ended up doing in the kitchen what I did in the bedroom. I gave him what he wanted and shut up about it. It was my secret. One evening, his friend Seymour came for dinner. He waited for a bitter argument about Shakespeare's *Richard III* to end. Ed and I fought so loud and long, Seymour sneaked away. Spirited arguments were my favorite times with Ed, but he'd not allow the subject to be personal. And if I dared raise a political issue, he'd sneer at my concerns about racial prejudice, low teacher salaries, and the awful Korean police action that would accomplish nothing but kill and wound innocent people with no idea why they were there. He'd ask nastily, "Are you from the Pentagon with all the facts? You don't know what you're talking about."

Nevertheless, when Ed finished law school, he applied to a ninety-day program for potential naval officers. His goal was to stay out of Korea, a plan I endorsed. He had to wait for security clearance from the FBI. Newspaper headlines were shouting about Senator Joseph McCarthy's anti-Red rampage. He named the organizations I had joined as "subversive." They were not, but I was terrified Ed would be rejected because of me.

The fifties were strange even before McCarthyism. The white housewife was on TV and in the commercials among the stoves and refrigerators in flared skirts and aprons. There was Lucille Ball, who made sure we'd not forget our place. My sense of social justice came to the fore with concerns about racial prejudice in America and apartheid monstrosities in South Africa.

# A Trip to Haiti

With Ed's acceptance delayed, he was free to serve his very first client. I was to fly with him to a country about which I knew nothing. *All Souls' Rising*, by Madison Smartt Bell, told me that the colony was freed in 1804 in a revolt against the French. The slave hero, Toussaint L'Ouverture, led the most significant revolution by an enslaved people in the history of humanity. Bell's words hit me with the force of a strong wind as I'd already joined the struggle to gain equal rights for people of color.

I was on the flight still reading *All Souls*. It struck me with reports of massacres and rapes happening under the current dictator Baby Doc, son of Papa Doc Duvalier, deceased dictator. My tongue twisted at the thought that descendants of the slaves who'd beaten the French with their bodies and cannonballs were now victims of tyranny from their own.

My mind filled with dark imaginings as the plane descended, my entire body quivered.

I tried to be calm through a few unsettling bounces on the runway. But we landed safely and deplaned. On the way to collect our luggage, a short, skinny, weird-looking man rose from the tarmac and headed for us like a weed on speed. Bowing as if in a king's court, he said,

"Greetings. I'm Obelain Joliceuer, society columnist for the *Haitian Sun* at your service." He ushered us to his car, two men following with our bags, and drove us to our hotel—strangely knowing which one. The Hibolele was on the top of a mountain overlooking a turquoise sea, waves splashing white foam against the rocks. He escorted us to the front desk, his presence clearly upgrading the reception process. We followed the bellhop to our room, eager to escape Obelain's fawning flattery. He made sure we'd know that he'd be waiting in the lobby to take us to a special place. His tone was more a command than an invitation. His behavior made me think of the leech that once attached itself to my thirteen-year-old leg at Loch Sheldrake in the Catskills. I feared he'd be just as hard to shake.

We took an hour to unpack and freshen up, hoping he'd be gone. But there he was, chomping at the bit to take us to Le Grand Hotel Olafson. We entered a battered building in Petionville, apparently favored by artists, writers, and musicians. It was seedy, quaint, and as intriguing as Manhattan's Chelsea Hotel, a nineteenth-century brick building that has always housed the famous and infamous artists of one kind or another. Their historic guest list is long and wide, from Andy Warhol to Susan Sontag, the famous drawn to the freewheeling atmosphere.

The ambiance at Olafson's felt as if it were Chelsea's parallel universe with an accent. We did try to break away to dine alone. There was no chance. The strange man insisted on taking us to "Haiti's best restaurant." I thought, could it be that all this was somehow connected to Ed's purpose for being in Haiti? His mandate was to assess the legal issues his client faced to build a resort hotel. Obelain may have been assigned to keep an eye on Ed.

The restaurant food was ordinary. What came next was anything but. A band played a blend of Cuban, French, African, and Brazilian sounds. The mix was Haitian music that I found enticing. A handsome Haitian asked me to dance. He was so smooth I felt I'd danced this dance before. I belonged to the music and to the grace of a voluptuous movement. I introduced him to Ed, who invited him for a drink. Another hunk asked me to dance, then another, and another. The music put me on my toes all night long, effortlessly, sensuously, in a trance. It helped that Ed enjoyed a grand old time with his new friends.

Obelain slipped away during the dance marathon, but subsequent efforts to avoid him failed. He knew always where we'd be until we met the man we were told was Theodore Roosevelt's bastard grandson, Jean La Fontante, a fine painter. He begged me to pose for a portrait.

Ed and I liked his work, so I spent mornings in his musty old house listening to the disquieting noise of rats scurrying above among the beams. His underground rebel friends came by and spilled the beans about Obelain. He was a spy assigned to find out what Ed was about and what bribes might be up for grabs. We managed a few pleasures under the spook's radar. At Le Pension de le Clerke, we saw Katherine Dunham and her dance troupe perform a manqué voodoo ceremony, replete with animal sacrifice and drinking goat's blood.

Draped in ethnic garb with multicolored voodoo beads cascading down her neck, the exotic fifty-year-old diva's moves as a witch doctor or belly dancer were captivating. I yearned to know this woman, the founder of the first Black Dance Company in the US, a goddess who presided commandingly over every space she entered. Her fascination with Voodoo was deep and abiding. She performed and lived it. Her dancers were obliged to do the same. Van, a dancer with a haunting face and body, noticed the hypnotic influence Dunham's ceremonial performance had on me. He arranged to escort me secretly to the real deal in the hills. As my presence was forbidden, he placed me behind a large boulder. I stared at the women draped in long, flowing white gowns, their heads wrapped in red scarves, eyes wide and turning black as a shark. The drums were beating a rhythm that built in intensity and speed to an orgasmic pitch. One by one, their glaring eyes turned color and glazed over as they threw themselves into a pit of rocks, possessed. While trembling, my inner self was transported to a mystic state of being. I felt possessed but stayed crouched, the drums louder and faster—louder and faster. Van pressed his strong hand down on my thigh to protect me from myself.

I told the portrait artist my secret the next morning as he proceeded with the painting. He disdained "silly nonsense" and disavowed the mythologic domain into which Haitian history is enmeshed. He was upset. But I knew I was meant to be in this place. I didn't say a word about it to Ed, who'd been happily drinking with a newly arrived British tourist named Crosby Erving.

When we saw the finished portrait of a beautiful Haitian me, we were stunned. Ed asked the price. Jean stammered, "No, no, no. It's not for sale. It's for my show in Mexico with Diego Rivera. I'm so sorry if I wasn't clear. Please, go to Red Carpet Art Gallery and pick any one of my paintings as a gift by way of apology. After the show in Mexico, we can talk about a sale."

Post mortem, neither the artist nor the painting was ever seen again by us or any Haitian with whom we stayed in touch. One of Jean's rebel friends was murdered in the street by the brutal SS-like Tonton Macoute, another had gone to the Dominican Republic to work with a rebel named Boubé in a failed Baby Doc assassination attempt. He died too. We were never able to track down the painting. Years later, neighbors told us they were in Haiti on vacation and saw a great painting. "At first, we thought it was you… but she was black."

In Haiti, the Carnival was upon us with little warning. I wore a borrowed Haitian peasant dress, a tall, wide-brimmed straw hat, hoop earrings carrying a beggar's cup. Then I joined in behind a flatbed truck with musicians playing rhythms I'd come to love. They sang "Yellow Bird" over and over and not one time too many. Surrounded by men, women, and children painted vibrant colors or wearing costumes of mythical significance, I danced in my bare feet on the sandy road with complete abandon.

I was sweating, singing, and laughing in another world altogether. Magic isn't meant to be understood, is it? The music, the costumes, the people, and their enthusiasm toward the deeply tanned stranger with bushy hair found the way to my inner soul, deeply and profoundly.

Past midnight, I choreographed a trip back to the hotel feeling alive but spent. I couldn't help waking Ed. I begged him to "Get them to stop the music. I can't sleep." He rubbed his eyes, saying, "What music?" It was still playing in my head. I slept the entire next day until time for André Sassine's party. As a rich Armenian, he was at the top of the Haitian world; his sister, queen of apparel; his brother, owner of duty-free shops. No doubt about it. They'd made a deal with the devil Doc.

I savored Haitian and French delicacies like crispy, creamy accras and chicken paté puffs and washed them down with excellent champagne in Sassine's mansion at the top of a small mountain. I asked André if there was a phone. "Of course," he said as he opened a drawer in a gilded French Provincial desk to dig out an antique telephone. I envisioned Gloria Swanson as Norma Desmond holding the phone to her ear. But there were no wires.

I asked, "How does it work, André?"

He answered, "It doesn't. Messages are picked up and delivered by drivers."

I wondered how the rest of Haiti's population communicated. Maybe the drums I heard from the hills were sending messages.

The next day, a driver took us up the long, steep road from Port-au-Prince. My eyes were fixed on the women walking down. They carried baskets on their heads filled with melons, mangos, and fresh-killed chickens—headless ones moving jerkily as if alive. As they managed the steep, dusty road to the marketplace, how straight their backs were! I was touched by the grace and apparent ease with which they bore heavy weights, barefoot, smiling, and humming tunes to set the pace of their trek. Men along the road loitered in small groups.

Uniformed officials wove in and out menacingly. I wondered how overworked, underpaid women could carry the burden of existence under a murderous dictatorship. I felt a sisterly anger—feminist consciousness not yet fully raised in 1968. Unwittingly, I started resisting the feminine mystique even before Betty Friedan's breakthrough book defined it, a kind of thought unknown that had been feeding my unconscious. My subliminal thoughts hovered around what later was famously coined by Betty as "the problem with no name." These strong, brave Haitian women mattered. But Ed faced bribes. He decided to test Cap Haitien. Our drive cross-country was stopped at checkpoints by armed militia demanding identification, destination, and purpose, each stop threatening to be the last. It was the paradox I'd found reading Bell's book about Haiti on the plane. I was torn by opposing forces: the beauty, music, and mythology captured my heart. The cruel oppression was revolting.

Our only way to the Citadel up high was on the backs of horses. The creatures assigned to us were emaciated. Two men per horse were needed to support their bony rumps as they climbed up on the edge of the mountainside's sheer drop to infinity. Although my experience in the saddle started at Prospect Park when I was twelve years old and continued for years, terror ran through my veins. I wrapped my arms around the horse's neck, trying not to look down. We made it to the top and saw the staggeringly impressive fortress that was engineered and built to fight against the return of Napoleon's army. That was an exquisite irony. Haitians had finally been ready to fight to keep their freedom, but the French never showed up. In Cap Haitien, children as young as five and old people barely able to walk wore the same haunting look on their gaunt faces. When I'd give so much as a coin, a stampede of outstretched hands followed

Their desperation created a pressure in my gut and a burning sensation in my chest. How could I love a country whose starving people are ignored? How and why are there so many places in the world where monsters have inescapable power over innocent people? Writing this in 2021, I can't deny that my country, the one I've been devoted to all my life, appears headed in that direction. On every passing day, the poor promise of the mettle and political skill to stop the gut punch to our democracy was not succeeding, but I try to keep hope alive.

Ed advised his client that with corruption rampant and limitless, it made no sense to build and operate a resort hotel where even personal safety was questionable. The drive back to Petionville was less eventful. We encountered no threatening checkpoints. That evening I eased into the ritual of dining and dancing with the bevy of partners that kept adding to Ed's conversation cabal. Back to Olafson's for nightcaps, we went on to a late party hosted by other Haitian friends. Just for me, they'd invited the amazing Ms. Dunham. She and I hit it off quite naturally, and more so in Miami when she was eighty-two on a hunger strike against grotesque treatment of Haitian refugees. Living in Miami then, she and I were on the same page.

On our last Haiti evening, the tireless pest we'd been able to avoid for days asked me to dance. He held me too close in a disturbingly sexual way. He was so short I needed to remove my breasts from his head. Then I felt something hard just above my knee. I thought it must be a gun, him being a spy and all. It was not a gun. How would I get away without a scene?

I pretended pain, said I felt sick, and sped to the restroom. The next day, our airplane coasting on the runway, I wrestled with a bizarre feeling. With no appetite to stay where people are maltreated by a tyrant and his minions, I felt a powerful sense of connection as if from a former life. One day maybe I'll figure this out, find out why I was drawn to Afro-Cuban music as a small child and never let go. To belong or not to belong, that was my question, always my question. It is the haunting refrain that rings in my brain every time I walk into a room that is new or into a group of men already formed. Yet as a small child in dear dark janitor Stanley's basement home, or the college lounge dancing with Afro-Cuban Americans, or Sylvia's Kitchen in Harlem, the Urban League, or the Negro Ensemble Company as a member of the board, my welcome was never in doubt. In Haiti, the paradox of not knowing where I belong deepened.

# PART 3

# What's It All About, Eddie?

I now see this as a movie. On December 21, 1968, the opening scene spans a grand old West Side apartment. The windows are frosted from bitter cold air hitting steaming radiators. I, the hostess, peer proudly at a recently redecorated home now set for Ed's fortieth birthday celebration. With great pleasure, I view our spacious apartment with its art-filled foyer, walls covered in elegantly stenciled linen, a Chinese dragon rug on a parquet floor, and flowers everywhere to mark the occasion. As Ed refills his glass, Billie Holliday sings "I'm a Fool to Want You." Guests dance in and flow through the party rooms. My jazz drummer friend, Chico Hamilton, happy to find a piano, starts to play. Guests gather around and sing in harmony.

At midnight, glasses are raised for toasts. Judy is first in a stream of warm, funny, affectionate salutes to the birthday boy. Others follow in a wide variety of tone and substance. Then Ed stands front and center and swallows the last of his drink, the veins in his neck throbbing, his eyes glaring icily at me. "My beautiful one thinks she's a hotshot. Dresses up every day to turn on the guys at work. That damn *Feminine Mystique* book has been the death of me."

The movie's over. I can't recall any more of his verbal bullets, but I remember feeling angry enough to slap his face. Our guests were stunned. Only their eyes moved. Then, suddenly, the apartment emptied, my final farewells at the door were stammered gibberish. I remember telling myself that it's not the end of the world. The party was great until the last scene. But looking at the besotted Ed passed out on the couch made me want to scream and hit him for humiliating me. But he was in another world or no world at all. What was I to do with my violent thoughts? I picked up my high-heeled shoes and dragged my tired body to the bedroom. I looked in the mirror and saw my hairdo falling down, stains on my yellow gown, eyes red and blackened from tear-smudged mascara. I turned away in disgust, changed to a flannel nightgown, and crawled into bed. I listened to the silence, relieved that David was at a friend's and his brothers were asleep before the debacle.

Ed went to work the next morning, and our boys were off to school. I focused on how I might get Ed to move out for a trial separation. My boys, ages eight, twelve, and sixteen, were already asleep in their rooms that night. Expecting Ed home late, as usual, I fixed a pitcher of martinis. Then I looked back at the living room for a final check. The front door opened. Ed came in, took off his coat, and dropped into his favorite chair, looking like the morning after. I poured him a martini. He was studying me, a worried look on his face. It was time he faced the truth.

I drew a deep breath and said, "Eddie, as you know well, I've been unhappy for a long time. You allowed me to go to work but have resented every minute of it. It was dumb to host a party at an uneasy moment. We need time apart to figure out what to do." I fixed myself a minor drink.

Ed said, "So you're carrying on with Jones, is that it? I saw how he looked at you."

I bit my lip, thinking it must be that he couldn't swallow that it was being married to him that made me miserable. His ego needed to believe an affair with a man I'd never even seen before, brought by our friends to the party.

It so happens Clarence Jones had whispered in my ear, "You are gorgeous. I can't take my eyes off you." Hushed flattery from a stranger was the sum and substance of the so-called affair.

I insisted, "Let's stick to the subject, Ed. We've been arguing about my career, my activist politics, money, the kids, your drinking, your blackouts, your late nights. You keep promising to change. You do, and then you don't. I need you to move out for a few months, and then we'll see."

He refilled his martini glass from the pitcher and took a sip, scowling. I said, "I'm truly sorry, Ed. We were kids when we met and when we married. We've grown in different directions. I loved you very much and wanted us to be happy. I tried to make it right. It isn't. I've changed. The world has changed. Your attempts to change have been short-lived."

I could not hear what he was saying as he walked out. He slammed the door. The boys were safe with Enid, so I ran the few blocks to Marge Wallis for calm wisdom from my psychoanalyst friend.

I said, "Margie, I feel awful. I've done what no one I know has ever done. I've ended my marriage. I made Ed move out under the guise of a separation, but it's over."

She reacted, "You've said that before, Charlotte. Are you for real this time? Did he move out? Or are you just talking about it again?"

I said, "No. It's real. He thinks I mean a trial, but it's done. The guilt. The kids. Hell, I'm breaking up a family. I can't stand it."

Margie challenged me, "You feel guilty? Take this glass, sit down, and listen to me! For years Ed's been fucking anyone who'd let him. In my profession, it's called Don Juanism, addiction to conquests that are just hostile fucks. He's been so blatant about his hit-and-run adulteries on Fire Island, everyone knew but you. Take that word 'guilt' out of your vocabulary."

Feeling faint, I pleaded, "Margie, why didn't you tell me this was going on under my nose? Were you laughing at me too?"

Sweeping my arm to make my point, I knocked over the glass of red wine. A huge stain spread on her precious Oriental rug. I found salt and club soda and lots of paper towels in the kitchen. I was on my knees scrubbing in circles. The stain kept spreading under portraits on the wall of her mom and dad staring at me disdainfully.

"Charlotte, stop… listen to me. Even your boys knew. I'm a shrink. I know the danger of breaking up a marriage when someone isn't ready for it to implode. I'm telling you now because you're ready to hear it. My silence was out of love. I need you to know that."

# Even the Boys Knew

As I walked home on Central Park West, an inner voice kept repeating, "Even your boys knew—even your boys knew." I walked along the park on a winter night, the trees stripped bare of leafy protection, like my boys who knew. Shivering from the cold air, I felt alive on the first night of the rest of my life. As I opened the front door, "even your boys knew" changed that.

The morning loomed heavy. It would be hard for me and worse for them. In a tidal wave dream that night, the boys and I were together on the top of a dune, trying to keep from drowning.

When the wave rose too high and too close, I woke up shaking. I knew pancakes on a school day would tell them something was up. I foolishly hoped it might raise their spirits. "Please, darlings, don't be in a hurry. What I have to tell you won't be easy." They settled awkwardly as I choked on the truth. "Dad and I are separating to think things over."

Like three unwound toy soldiers, they sat still and silent, their eyes vacant. I wondered if the boys really knew.

Richard growled, "I heard you fighting. It sounded worse than just to think things over."

I resorted to begging. "My dear boys, everything depends on you knowing we both love you. We'll always love you, be there for you. It's not your fault. We were very much in love, but we were so young we just grew up in different directions. People change."

With his mouth full, Paul's eyes pierced through me. He swallowed without chewing. Silence filled the room until he started to cry, his hands over his face.

"Paul, my darling boy, look at me. Please look at me. You'll be spending more time with your dad than ever."

They swallowed their last gulps of milk to wash down the pain, jumped up, grabbed their books, shrank from my goodbye kisses, and slammed the door behind them as they ran to the elevator. I rushed to catch a glimpse. Too late. They were off to different places in the same pain. Would there be lifelong scars for my kids with parents in separate universes? What had I done?

Dinner that night was quiet. Later, I spoke privately with each of them in awkward discomfort.

Richard asked, "It's all about adultery, isn't it? Dad accused you of fooling around in Europe."

That was a blow. The accusation happened to be true. I ran into actor friend Robert Ryan in Barcelona. It was a business trip for me, a film role in Rome for him. My marriage was already a charade. Bob and I met by surprise. A weekend in a magical city with a magical man who shared my political values was an offer I couldn't refuse and never regretted. What did sadden me was telling Bob that Ed had found me out. He was afraid. Even our long- standing political friendship had to end.

David was home from college that summer and drove with me to Buck's Rock summer camp to visit his brothers. On the way, he told me he'd once dropped acid. My heart pounded in my chest as if it would burst out of my body. My throat closed, yet I heard a voice say,

"Really, David, tell me about it." Apparently, keeping communication open trumped wrapping the car around a lamppost. David described "pulsing walls" and "odd shapes in vivid colors that floated around as I was feeling tranquil." He called it a one-time experiment with trusted friends and said he was "not looking to escape from life like some other guys." The conversation ended when we arrived at the camp, but my painful panic did not. It was likely a gentler version of true reality and good that he shared small doses of truth even if they scared me half to death.

After touring the camp, we joined a crowd gathered around a tiny TV in a large field for the Apollo 11 landing on the moon. Its success raised a roaring cheer. Waiting for Neil Armstrong to step onto the moon, the only sound came from crickets in the grass. In the quiet, Richard's critical take on society's priorities moved him to shout, "Okay, we landed on the moon. Now can we pick up the garbage in Harlem?" I was very proud of my son for that, but on the way home, my shaken nervous system took me back to David's revelation.

How else was I to know the depths of despair we might be facing? I invited a young camera operator friend to dinner. He was a bit of a hippie who'd toured with the Beatles as a show runner. I told Steve that I hoped they'd connect and maybe move my son to confess the whole truth. David did admit that his drug exploration had reached a dangerous place. He'd tried heroin! My body collapsed, standing and sobbing. David wrapped his arms around me, also sobbing. He said he wished he could say he'd never touch the stuff again, but it wouldn't be true. He swore that he wanted to have a life, not leave it. He swore he'd quit soon, and I'd be the first to know. Six months later, his best friend died of an overdose. David called to say it was over for him.

Years later, I asked if he really was in control of the "experiment." He said, "No, Mom, just lucky."

I had been pursuing private goals and making unilateral domestic decisions that I don't think served my boys well at all. My cavalier confidence that they'd make it through the trauma and upheaval must have caused bad effects that linger. I'm eternally grateful that my sons are such fine men. If they weren't my boys, I'd want them to be my friends. And they are my dear friends, which helps me believe that at some point, they forgave me.

Ed had scared me into an awful separation agreement. He twisted it into the settlement for the divorce. If I'd been thinking clearly, I would not have gone along with no alimony, no settlement, and $250 a month per child until age eighteen. It was strikingly clear that I needed to earn a decent living on my own. And to do that meant ending my theater journey just as I was getting good at it. The high price to be free would be a financial burden, its consequence for our boys a bad upset. These and the coming years were complicated and stressful in so many ways, I'm confused about the chronology of events, and therefore, so will you be. I hope it will help that so much came together at about the same time. It doesn't really matter. There are times when it's not clear even to me. But in the end, the dividends of the marriage brought a light to my life as bright as the morning sun.

# PART 4

# The Prize Was My Three Sons

## David, 1952

While Eddie was overseas for six months during my first pregnancy, I furthered my college work at night thanks again to my folks' delight to babysit David. At the tail end of my pregnancy, Mother and I were hit by a stifling heat spell. I'd gained fifty pounds from water retention and no air-conditioning. I passed out onto the kitchen floor. My panicked mother picked me up and made sure I was alert before putting me to bed. She called an owner of a hotel in Rockaway to ask if we might stay near the ocean breeze. A smart move. One day on the porch in a rocking chair, knitting a baby sweater, I noticed two figures walking up the long path to the house. When they were close enough, I could see that they were my best friends, Bernice and Helen. Their shock that the deformed woman in the rocking chair was me stopped them short. They sobbed like two babies whose lollypops had been snatched away. "Oh my god, what happened to you?" And then, "I'll never have a baby—not ever!" In the end, we calmed down to enjoy a good visit. I'm not sure they ever got over seeing their friend in such a state.

It was on July 18, 1952, at St. Albans Naval Hospital, that my baby moved out of his comfort zone into the cold, dry world in very short order. In Demerol delirium, I heard, "A healthy boy."

The next day the nurse said I'd waved a finger to my baby's face, saying, "David, you'll learn how to be independent of me one day, and I'll learn to do the same."

Then a slim light shone on the fat face of the beautiful baby cradled in my arms. I breathed in, held the breath, and breathed out with images of the sea, quiet rain, and clouds of daffodils. I exhaled a pledge to never be a controlling mom to my boy. Enchanted by the magic of life, I kissed his every finger and every toe. I had ensconced baby David in Sammy's former bedroom as he'd married and moved out. Mom had insisted I take my infant out every day, the baby carriage in waiting.

Not me! No more mantras on baby food and diaper rash solutions, each young mom claiming she knows best. I'd open the windows in Sammy's room and put well-covered David down for his nap. Air inside or out is the same to a baby, and with Hardy's *Jude the Obscure* waiting next to the green club chair, I escaped the Smart Alec moms and found reading a classic in a comfy chair near my baby was better for both of us.

Dad held his first grandchild in his arms through the night when he felt I needed sleep. Mother kept warning that picking him up when he cried "will spoil him." At about the time Ed was expected home, he cabled that he was London and chose to stay an extra week. I felt kicked in the gut. Was my husband having a fling after a long absence from me and the three-month-old son he'd never seen? My heartbeat raced, along with every nerve in my body. I'd spent months apart from my husband, believing he was missing me. My friends teased me with cracks that Ed on the Riviera meant messing around. I laughed it off. He'd never do that. And anyway, he'd not be in any port long enough for anything serious. A reminder again, dear reader, that chronology in the sequence of my life stories follows my heart somewhat randomly.

Ed arrived just as I was bathing his son in the baby tub. He stepped up in his uniform, hat still on his head.

Our baby looked up smiling, then cried louder and longer than I'd ever heard. It must have been the hat. With David finally asleep, Ed and I were eager to make love that night in what was now our room as Judy had moved to Greenwich Village. Perhaps jet lag factored into brief love-making, after which Ed rolled over and fell asleep. I stayed awake, crying softly. A few weeks later, we moved to Boston for three months. Ed's ship was in for R&R (rest and recuperation) at the Boston Navy Yard. In a relentless attempt to keep our marriage alive, it helped to blame myself for whatever wasn't working.

When R&R at the Boston Navy Yard was over, the USS *Worcester* took Ed to the French Riviera and its surroundings for half a year once more. David and I moved back to my folks, and I kept taking night courses toward a degree. My best friend Leah Friedman returned from Silver Springs with her husband, Vic, and their first son, born five days after my David. A visit to Leah's apartment created a living portrait of my multitalented friend, whose independent spirit is in her DNA, no ism needed. She's a poet, playwright, painter, and opera fanatic.

I arrived at her flat with David at my side. The front door unlocked, we stepped in. Little Stewart toddled toward us in overalls. Leah must have heard us. She entered with her arms covered in multicolored paint, her hair splattered as well. In the living room, a pile of laundry sat, waiting for attention.

My judgmental Jewish mother's voice shot out of my mouth. "Leah, what are you doing? You're a mother now."

Leah looked puzzled. She said, "I'm doing what I do—this time a surreal painting of a comic genius."

It was a fabulous, brave piece of work that I adored. I stared in silence for a long time. She asked if I felt all right. I blurted out that I was jealous of how she followed her passions. When I lived in New York, I never missed one of her plays or readings. When Ed and I were courting, and my parents would ask us where we were going, the answer was always "Vic and Lee's." They thought it was a nightclub.

Our baby boys ignored each other, even when playing with the same ball in the same playpen. When past their first birthdays, a friendship was born and played out at home, Coney Island's kiddy Park, and the beach. When they moved far away, I missed them.

Ed returned, and we were off again to Boston and would reside in Arlington. David was a happy eighteen-month-old boy. I dressed him like a mini-man for an officer family dinner on the USS *Worcester*. He ate his dinner elegantly, didn't spill his milk, and politely asked to be excused when finished. He traipsed over to a den area and stayed there quietly for a long time. When we all entered that space, he was on the floor surrounded by magazines he'd been able to reach and remove from the shelves, turning pages as if reading every word. The scene spoke to me. It was my job to make him strong and smart enough to thrive in a rough world getting rougher. And he surely has done so as a dad, a father, a husband, and an entertainment impresario who rises higher with every passing day.

# Richard, 1955

Ed came home from the tour with orders to report to the Navy Yard in Arlington, Virginia. How close I'd come to block his chance to be a naval officer. McCarthy's anti-communist mania labeled everything subversive, including three human rights groups I'd visibly supported. I lived in fear that the FBI would not clear Ed's security for that reason and was much relieved when he was commissioned. Now ordered to Virginia, we moved to Falls Church, and I birthed a beautiful baby boy at Bethesda Naval Hospital, my parents in tow to help.

In the hospital, I'd asked where my husband might be. A nurse told me he was fast asleep on a bench in the lounge. I picked up my baby and fed him in my arms, staring at his dimples. I love those dimples. He burped like a trooper, and I set him in the bassinet next to my bed. On a stroll down the hospital corridor, I came upon the room where Senator McCarthy had been suffering from his first "sore elbow." I was there then, too, with false (Braxton Hicks) contractions. He'd used that farce to escape the hearings that challenged him. He was reviled on the very medium he'd mastered to gain Stalin-like power. And with these fake escapes, he would lose again, this time censored by the Senate. I'd been glued to the initial hearings from the beginning and until he was utterly rebuked. I felt a private vindication when the judge finally said to him, "At long last, have you left no decency, sir?"

Then came a far more personal and potentially tragic terror incorporated in its own storm. For Rosh Hashanah, the Jewish New Year, we drove to my family home in Brooklyn with David and three-month-old Richard. Ed was set to fly back to the base in a few days and return for Yom Kippur, the Day of Atonement. After morning coffee with mother, I found my baby sleeping on his back, vomit on his face. I couldn't wake him, not even in a tub of cold water.

He was asleep and gagging. I rushed him with a neighbor's help to St. Alban's Naval Hospital after alerting them to the crisis. I pulled up, my hands clutching the steering wheel so tightly it was hard to uncurl my fingers. Five doctors were waiting for me. I lifted Richard and found him awake.

After a brief exam, a doctor said, "He's fine, ma'am. You can take him home."

I glared at the doctor with stars and bars on his chest and grabbed him by his lapels with both hands, my chin in his face. Peering into his breezy eyes, I growled with a fierce intensity that rose from the pit of my stomach, "I know my baby. His expression is now vacant, his mind still asleep. He's normally alert, responsive, aware. Something is terribly wrong."

He looked at me with his soft blue eyes and generous lips in the tender half-smile of an Ally and gripped my hands more gently than I'd clutched his lapels. He whispered, "You're the mom, and moms know best. We'll keep him under observation. Maybe it was a convulsion, sometimes a warning sign."

A navy commander covered in medals took me seriously and honored a mother's instincts. I held my baby and fed him until I was made to leave at 6:00 p.m. Mrs. Altman was waiting patiently in the lounge. I'd entirely forgotten the kind neighbor who'd sewed every costume for my dance concerts, and now this. How awful! The next day I arrived at the hospital alone just as my baby's fever began to rise too high. Another overnight!

I was advised at midnight that Richard's fever had skyrocketed. I notified Ed to fly back. The next day at the hospital, he and I were told a spinal tap revealed viral encephalitis, an infection of the membranes of the brain.

"How long till he gets better?" I kept asking.

"Mrs. Schiff, we will do everything we possibly can," they kept saying.

At that moment, and in all the following days with my baby, kissing his nose, his forehead, his chubby hands, I worried about how long it would take for him to get better, never doubting he would. But more of "We will do everything we possibly can" hit me with deadly despair. A pain palpitated in my chest. They blanketed our baby in ice and fed him every known antibiotic. Time only for trial and error with a fever above 105 degrees. We drove home in silent terror. At 7:00 p.m., everyone but sleeping David went to *shul* for Kol Nedra, honoring the highest of holy days with music I adore.

I paced the floor, wrung my hands, and called the hospital again and again. Nothing. The phone rang finally. The fever had broken, and our baby was out of the crisis. But the doctor warned that we wouldn't know if he'd ever do the things his brother took for granted. An encephalitis brain infection plus super-high fever could cause all manner of cerebral damage. We faced the extended terror of the unknown—roll over, sit up, crawl, stand, walk, speak—the scrutiny yet to begin. When it did, a case of jitters took over.

He was down to his birth weight from projectile vomiting. I was instructed to keep feeding him infused mineral water by spoon and use a pacifier to satisfy his suckling needs. When able to hold down a special formula, he began to gain weight. Then came bronchial pneumonia with bouts of coughing and gagging for two years. On bad nights, I sat at his side in a hard chair to stay awake so that when he gagged, I could do what I was told—stick a finger down his throat to induce regurgitation. Globs of mucus out, he'd suck in a deep breath with me. In time my baby sat up, later crawled, and oh, those first wobbly steps brought happy tears to me and my dad.

I added Cheerios and green beans to applesauce. Richard chattered a stream of words and later whole sentences that surely made sense, at least to him. My sensitive boy was always watching and listening. I wanted to know what he was thinking—still do. I pondered on the origin of his focus on trust and his quest for being his own person. He'd refused to stay at Horace Mann High School. The football coach had told him, "To play football, you must cut your hair."

My star athlete rose out of his seat and, and without a word or backward glance, walked out of the room. He'd grumbled for months about his disdain for classmates' arrogant sense of superiority to be in one of the finest schools in the country. He even resented the faculty for the same reason. Richard had made it in but felt more lucky than special. I was summoned to discuss his "delinquent behavior." The coach asked what I would do about his disrespect.

I said, "What disrespect? How was it improper to follow instructions to the letter, sir? You said, 'Cut your hair or give up football.' He chose the latter."

I was proud of my son for standing his ground respectfully as an early teen. On reflection, I thought Richard's independent stance may very well have been a consequence of the traumatic life and death challenge he experienced as an infant; the first few years are important.

With Ed a civilian at last, we moved to a small four rooms in a garden apartment development in Queens, New York. We took turns with our neighbors caring for each other's little ones for rare nights out. Ed's real job was for a law firm on Park Avenue. His scrimpy salary didn't measure up to the fancy address. Our income needed help. I had a Saturday job in a local lab, and twice a month, I drove my boys to Brooklyn for their grandma (Nani) to babysit.

Mrs. Altman had arranged for me to buy dresses wholesale. I fought rush- hour crush to pick up my boys in Brooklyn and then drive home. I'd cook supper, feed, bathe, and put my boys to sleep. Ed home late always, neighbors came by to try on and buy dresses. I enjoyed running a household on $15 a week. It felt odd to be so happy against such odds, especially in light of my fascination with the idea of helping the world be what it was meant to be resonated in my mind, awake or sleeping. I was not sure then when or why my activist mentality began. I think spending my early life in the depression, in a crib too small, ice cream cone from the wagon in the hot summer every third day. With just enough money for one cone a day, we took turns. I waited with anxiety for him to crawl and to sit up, and then one day, he took a step and plopped down, laughing. And so did I.

# Paul, 1959

Ed's law practice was growing, and another child was on the way. My deliveries were quick and uncomplicated, so there'd be no drugs this time; I taught myself the Lamaze method. In labor and breathing in and out as the book instructed, my fingers stiffened, and my body went spastic. I shouted for help. The doctor took one look and yelled, "SOS, I need a blood test *now*!" Frantic noises from the corridor sounded like a battlefield. *Will I die? Will the baby live? Where's Ed? Must be another meeting.* They wheeled me into the birthing room. The test results arrived just as Paul showed his pretty face. The false crisis was the result of my faulty breathing. Paul was an adorable, happy baby born quickly.

We'd installed gold carpet in our new home in Merrick. Curious Paul picked up an open bottle of black ink and cheerfully poured it onto our pride and joy. He had no idea he'd done wrong, likely feeling he'd achieved a remarkable feat. I picked him up, inked from head to toe, and asked his father to bathe him so I might attack the stain. Ed declined and went off to some Navy Reserve meeting without looking back—maybe to keep from turning to a pillar of salt.

I put Paul in the tub. David was instructed to keep him safe. Then I called an erstwhile friend married to a carpet-cleaning entrepreneur. I pleaded urgently for help without even a how-do-you-do. He instructed me to blot the stain with lots of paper towels, pour a bottle of cleaning fluid on it, let it remain a bit, and then more paper towels. The stain miraculously vanished. The floors were blanketed with untarnished gold once again. I found Paul shriveled like a prune but still splashing his toys in the tub under David's responsible attention. He grew up loving complex objects he'd take apart and drawing airplanes, cameras, cars, and original cartoon characters.

Paul's passion for creating led to an early role as producer and director of music videos and promotions for MTV, and that led to leaving the hottest ticket in town to make movies in Hollywood. Don't tell me you never saw *My Cousin Vinny*, one of my favorite examples of the many films he produced.

# PART 5

# What I Remember

Raising kids takes me back to my mixed-up childhood. It was hard to remember how it felt to be four years old and way too big to be in a small crib. But one thing I can't forget is sleeping scrunched up in that teeny space. I didn't like being in it all day, peering through crib slats to watch my mother bring soup and Jell-O and carry hot and cold compresses back and forth. There was no place for a third bed in the tiny room shaped like a triangle. My sister Judy, at eleven years old, was in one real bed, and my brother Sammy, who was nine, was in the other. Both were on their backs with rheumatic fever. I stared through the bars of my crib-cage. Mother needed me to stay put day and night. It upset me not to touch or be touched, but my whimpers went unheard. It was as if I wasn't there.

Judy cried, "My head hurts." Silence. Then she added, "My legs hurt."

Shaking a thermometer fiercely, Mother said, "I'm busy, for God's sake, don't be a baby!"

Sammy wailed, "My tummy hurts."

Mother stroked his head, smiling at him. It wasn't like that for Judy and me. If we made her happy, she'd wipe the smile off her face with her hand as if to hide a mistake.

Sam and Judy recovered when I was almost five. Mother made them take care of me on Saturdays. I'd hold their hands and skip along to the Carol Theater for a double feature—almost always one film with creepy gangsters and the other a horror movie. I'd climb up and sit on my knees to be high enough, then peek through my fingers to keep out the scary stuff. That night in my crib-cage, I'd dream I was in jail. I woke thinking for a minute I was still inside some dark, eerie place. Every Saturday morning, I waged a fight with myself. My bad dreams made me want to stay away from scary movies. But this was my only chance to go out like a big girl with a grown-up brother and sister. I was glad they were ordered to take me. When Dad took me anywhere, I was more than glad. At Coney Island on summer weekends, I splashed in the waves, dug in the sand, took in the rays to get tan like my parents. I loved the ocean, its ebb and flow calming and then exciting me. Tumbling in the waves with my dad was paradise. He taught me to swim.

His powerful hand under my belly was just enough to keep me afloat. He made me feel the ocean was a place where I belonged. On shore, my habit was to disappear. In the beginning, it scared my folks, afraid I might be lost or even drowned. They learned to listen for the Afro-Cuban drum beat. They'd find me dancing in the center of a circle, hips swirling, heart beating, and shoulders shaking to the Afro-Cuban rhythm, the music hypnotizing me.

I had a special, safe place at 691 Linden Boulevard, where we lived. It was the cellar home of janitor Stanley, a cozy spot near the coal furnace. He was handsome like my dad but much darker. And he was fun, like my dad. My mother was way upstairs, so she never scolded him for spoiling me. She didn't see him fix my tricycle, play games with me and his kids, and give us pops—orange ice with vanilla ice cream inside. And there was always music. When I was with them,

I could feel the smile on my face. Maybe it was the smile that Dad raised when taking coins out of my ears and calling me his "cheerful little earful." Dad on the third floor and Stanley in the basement made me feel special. Judy and Sammy, both lawyers-to-be, constructed a contract in pencil on a large yellow pad, full of phrases like "Charlotte Grad, party of the first part."

They quarreled about things like who should have the first crack at hitting me for being annoying. When they made me mad, I'd dash down the cellar steps. One night when they were babysitting me, Judy fixed dinner. She mixed spaghetti with scrambled eggs and tons of ketchup. She put a box of Rice Krispies on the table just in case. The lights blew. She lit candles. When I leaned over to find the prize in the cereal box, the bushy mop on my head went up in a blaze. Sammy punched out the fire with his fists, hurting my head and my pride while saving my scalp. I ran down the stairs. Stanley hugged me, saying, "Thank your brother for being so brave."

One Sunday, I was dressed up in my new wine-colored woolen coat with velvet collar and matching bonnet. My mother and I would visit Aunt Rose and Uncle Willie. I watched my mother put on a green silk blouse and skirt, fix her pitch-black hair in a bun, and clip pearls on her ears. How pretty she was. And then my toes turned in, and my sweaty hands twisted a hanky into a wet ball.

Words burst out of my windpipe: "Please, Ma—can I go out to play until you're ready?"

She said, "No, it's not necessary."

This time I actually finished the question before she delivered her mean mantra. When I was in kindergarten, we moved across the street to a bigger place. Judy told me we'd have our own bedroom and share a double bed. No more triangle room. No more crib. I was free at last on the second floor of a two-family house in an apartment that was very big. Rich relatives donated old furniture to fill the large rooms.

An enormous mahogany dining table and fancy high-backed chairs were a wonder. I wanted to make this uncharted string of rooms home. There was so much empty space. I wished our relatives would stop sending furniture so I might roller-skate or dance around the rooms.

# Bubbi

Our new downstairs wasn't Stanley's home anymore. Oh, how I missed him and his snug retreat. I didn't have his safe place anymore, but I still had visits to my Bubbi (Grandma). Her house was fronted by a stoop with brick steps that led to a heavy wooden door, boots, and coats left in a tiny vestibule. She and I always sat in the kitchen. I loved her kitchen, a warm, bright place where she'd cook on the stove or bake goodies like apple kuchen in the oven. She let me help her break the eggs, mix the batter, and taste everything— mushroom and barley soup, challah bread, chopped liver, kishka—stuffed intestines, really, but thankfully she never told me.

I felt safe in my Bubbi's cozy kitchen. We'd sit at a metal table and play Pisha Pesha, a card game from Russia that always cheered me. My grandma let me win a lot, but I never let her know I knew. Bubbi was the only grandparent I ever knew; the others died before I was born.

I asked a lot of questions about them. They went unanswered as my parents never talked about the past in a language I understood. Bubbi helped me understand how hard life was for the Jews in Pinsk where she lived long ago. Her heavy-accented English was peppered with Yiddish words and expressions, but somehow I understood every idea, if not every word. She talked about *shul*, the synagogue where ladies are required to sit upstairs behind a curtain. I always sat next to my dad until a *shamas*, the sexton, shooed me away. He waved his finger as a weapon, clicking his tongue to make sure I knew I'd broken a rule at age seven, a rule I now deplore.

Bubbi turned her cards face down on the table now and then. She'd close her eyes and tell me a story about Pinsk. It was where mean men called Cossacks would stampede on their horses into the village to steal and burn homes; beat, kidnap, and sometimes kill men and boys; and do hateful things to women and girls. A Russian "Paul Revere" galloped ahead shouting, "The Cossacks are coming!" so the villagers could run for safety in the forest.

One story had lasting significance. It was the one about the pogrom that drove them out of Pinsk. The village crier shouted from his horse that the Cossacks were right behind him. They grabbed the *siddur* (book of daily prayers) and the ritual brass candlesticks and ran for the forest to hide. Bubbi said her people feared for their lives, but they were afraid also that they would find their homes burnt to rubble when they returned. My grandma's face flushed, and her hands shook as she told this story. I remember wiggling my body into the chair as if at the Carol Theater to see my first live performance. Bubbi portrayed the freedom rider.

She yelled, "*Mach schnell! Avekoyfn!*" (Hurry up! let's go!) She told me she rushed to save the candlesticks, and in her haste, she mistakenly took one from one set and one from the other, then ran to the woods with the unmatched candlesticks clutched to her breast.

Bubbi turned her head as if the Cossacks were about to charge at us this minute. I clutched the arms of the metal chair so tightly that my right thumb began to bleed. I was shivering. "Was everyone okay, Bubbi?"

She took a long sigh and said, "Vee made it, da howz still standing."

And Papa said, "Gnug, vee aeklayfn to America." (Enough, we're going to America.)

As if talking to a ghost, Bubbi whispered, in a wide grin, "I'm in America. No more pogroms"

The candlesticks she saved have been with me all my adult life. When I light them ceremonially, I wave my hands over them like my grandma did, reciting, "*Baruch atah Adonai, eloheinu melech ha'olam…*"

(Praised are You, the Eternal One, our God, Ruler of the universe, who has kept us alive, sustained us, and enabled us to reach this moment.) For me, it's the ritual that counts, and I hoped it would be so for my children. I wanted them to know their heritage. As I lit the candles and recited the *barucha*, the history of the Jews would flash before me. Tears welled up, and the prayer words got stuck in my throat. I don't have to believe in a mystical higher power to connect to my roots. I can remember trying to get my mother's attention. I tried all kinds of strategies and white lies, and they only rarely worked. But all I had to do with Bubbi was to be in the same room.

When I was in second grade and my grandma was eighty-three, her leg was amputated. I shuddered to think of my grandma with one leg. I tried to be strong about it when Mother dropped me off at her house. The aroma of chicken fricassee pulled me into the kitchen. My one-legged Bubbi was mopping the floor from her wheelchair and also baking a Rosh Hashanah/Jewish New Year delicacy with honey, a symbol for a sweet new year. She took turns, one hand holding the mop, the other pushing the wheel either to get to the next dirty spot or the stove.

When Grandma died, Judy begged our mother to let me go to the funeral. Not a chance! Judy was allowed to attend as she was fifteen. I was eight years old. The mother, who hardly ever conducted a conversation with me, didn't allow me to say goodbye to my grandmother. I sat alone when they were at the funeral. Bubbi was my queen with one leg. She took me seriously, and her house was my home. Far too young then to discern meaning in her courage, now I see a plot shared by millions. On her quest to run from the Cossacks as a teenager, she crossed the Atlantic in steerage, then pedaled old clothes in alleyways, and hand-scrubbed sheets in a crowded immigrant section of tenements. She lost her husband early, suffered diabetes, leg amputation, and cancer. My mother's mother was a protagonist of escape. It's almost cliché to talk about how her family came to their American surname, a story replicated thousands of times.

At Ellis Island, the man who would be my grandfather stood for hours on endless lines. Finally, from an official seated at a table in front of an iron- barred gate he heard, "What is your name?" No answer. "Your *namen.*"

Grandpa said, "Misheira."

He was asked, "How do you spell it?"

"*Nit farshteyn.*" Grandpa didn't have English, as they used to say. The man said, "Goldberg!" as he stamped the name on all grandpa's papers.

A symbol of the Goldbergs, Kaplans, Goldsteins, Schwartzes, Marcuses, and others entering the New World. Here's a poem to tell you some of what my grandma meant to me:

### *ANNA ELIZABETH GOLDBERG*
### *(1861–1940)*

*Bubbi, I remember you.*
*I remember helping you to cook,*
*Teaching you to read English,*
*Learning from you about life.*
*I remember you.*

*Best of grandmothers.*
*I can still smell the soup you fed me.*
*See the rooms you lived in,*
*Feel your arms around me.*
*Warm, clear memories.*
*Speak to me from long ago.*
*Tell me that you love me,*
*that your arms are still around me,*
*that I am whole*

Young life is full of surprises. And mine was no different. Some were good, some bad, some simply strange. Little girls are silly and do silly things. Early cravings have a way of superseding silly. Mine was to dance, an obsession that had me cry out for lessons when I was seven years old. But like I said about surprises. I'd become a demon when in first grade, along with seven friends. We wore blue cardigans with Demons in big red block letters on the back and a big red devil's face on the front left side. We lived up to our club's name by teasing little kids, trying on shoes with no plan to buy, and making stupid phone calls to strange numbers randomly pulled from the phone book just to make trouble. Being a pesky brat wasn't working for me. I had other plans.

# Dance

My persistent passion for dance started when I was a toddler. When approaching seven, I craved classes. Trouble was, if I asked mother, she'd refuse. All would be lost if I didn't find a way around, "No, it's not necessary," her relentless shibboleth. I couldn't try Dad. He'd been told to say, "Ask your mother." He watched me dance, smiling from ear to ear. How could I make this happen? At last, I came up with a plan. Maybe I could get my dad to pretend it's his idea, not mine. Happy day! He agreed to trick her into saying yes. Mother's approval remained our secret conspiracy—a lesson in strategy I'd remember.

The studio was at the top of a steep flight of stairs on Utica Avenue next to the Carol Theater. I stood cowed for a long time at the studio door. I opened it a crack to take a peek. At the far end of a huge room was a piano, and on two walls were railings at which little girls like me dressed in tights and ballet slippers were doing leg stretches. I wanted to clap my hands, but all I could do was sneak out to the bathroom, shaking like a dog after a bath. When I calmed down enough to slip back in, a lady named Natasha motioned me to the ballet barre. Trying hard to keep up, I lowered my head. Then I raised my chin and opened my eyes to a squint, and what I saw through sweat and tears was Natasha nodding toward me in approval!

She was a former diva from the Ballet Russe de Monte Carlo who spoke with a heavy Russian accent in a strong voice. Everything about her was grand. I stared at her graceful hands, their long fingers doing a dance of their own, a dance with dramatic power that added magical meaning to her words. Her long, slim, fluid body belied the wrinkles in her commanding face. Most of all, she was a woman in charge. I'd never known a female who owned and used authority like that, a hint that a woman's power could be a graceful thing of beauty. I love the memory of my first time with it, a thought unknown that came to me years later.

She entered my dreams as the Queen of Sheba or sometimes King Arthur. King or queen, she was the boss. I knew about them from the children's books Judy read to me. In class, Queen Natasha made me get it right. First position, second position, third position. I tried to mimic her hypnotic hands, hold my back straight and head high. One day she pulled me close as if I were a doll, muttering to herself, "Yes, this child has it. I see a crown on her curly head."

At home, in our only bathroom—a small closet with plumbing—the towel rack became my ballet barre, the mirror too small to check for correct form. I was in the studio nearly every day. Natasha was always happy to see me. Mother bragged to her friends but never took a photo or watched a class. By age nine, I was a star in our tiny galaxy, on stage dancing, curtsying, loving the applause and the flowers. Still too shy to quit the Demons, I was glad to have dance class and rehearsals as a good excuse to be absent from mean-spirited pranks.

Helen, Janet, Iris, Roberta, Shirley, Janet, and Marilyn were still my best friends. I gave them no reason to be mad at me. They had no idea that I was jealous of them. You see, Veronica Lake, the movie star famous for her "peekaboo bang," had all my friends with great hair that flowed a bang. I'd stare at them when they snapped back their heads, and the bang would fly. Not me. When I was a little girl, my mother put my washed hair into layers of rolled curls, like a Shirley Temple with dark hair. When too old for that, she used horsetail combs to get through a mass of kinky hair so huge, mean kids called me "wild woman of Borneo." What was worse was that I couldn't flip my hair. It wouldn't move. At a table doing my homework, my brain was fixed on not being able to flip my hair. A lightbulb flashed inside my jealousy. I pushed the chair back, stood up, walked to my dad's closet, found his camel-hair robe with the silk rope belt, took it out of the loops, found the scissors, cut off the tassel, and pinned it to the front of my hair with a bobby pin. I spun my head around again and again. Daddy's tassel went with it. When homework was done, my neck hurt, but I was happy.

When Dad noticed the missing tassel, I confessed. He smiled, again saying, "My cheerful little earful."

On a Sunday morning, weeks before my tenth birthday, I was in the kitchen rereading *Heidi* while Dad listened to a football game. Suddenly, silence filled the room. Upset to be missing the game, Dad got mad at the radio.

Then came the voice of CBS newsman John Daly: "We interrupt this program to bring you a special news bulletin. The Japanese have attacked Pearl Harbor, Hawaii, by air, just announced by President Roosevelt."

Dad ran to the telephone. Mother dropped a pot filled with Baker's bittersweet chocolate squares she was melting to cover a freshly baked cake. There was now brown gook all over the floor. With both hands pressed on her heart, she pleaded, "Moe, tell me what's going on." Judy came out of our room looking worried. Sammy wasn't home.

We were at war. Demon pranks grew more cruel and stupid. I did my best to escape from the devilish deeds of my friends, but I was not strong enough—until that Sunday morning when everything changed. Not much a ten-year- old could do, but I stopped doing what made me so ashamed. Now there were two more good excuses—dance class and World War II.

It upset me to see my dad scared. He'd been a teenage prize fighter and once punched through our kitchen door. Now his fists were so clenched his knuckles turned white. We sat around the Emerson radio into the night, all of us gripped with fear. War with Germany was declared two days later. We heard rumors that European Jews were in trouble. Huddled around the radio on Saturday mornings, we were somewhat comforted by FDR's fireside chats.

Dad held fast to the American dream. In the depression, he dug ditches and drove an ice cream truck. Now a respected executive, I could tell he was upset a lot. He tried to bury trouble, but that's like keeping a beach ball below tumbling ocean waves—exhausting and impossible. What was disturbing him? One day, I read *Bride of the Sabbath*, the story of the children of Jewish immigrants' who are desperate to assimilate. It brought to mind my folks cringing in the presence of Jews with accents talking loud in a public place. And there was more. He was the only executive at Columbia Pictures who hadn't graduated from high school, let alone college. He felt he didn't belong. I knew a lot about that. There was my scheme with Ma. I tried to say whatever she wanted to hear and pretend to be whomever she wanted me to be. When I grew up, taking everyone head-on actually felt fine. Daddy, on the other hand, silently suffered the bullies. When I grew up, I fought back for both of us and with a fury he could not express. I still "followed his footsteps," but with a stomping tread. The war brought weird nightmares, like. Cossacks in brown shirts and steel helmets carrying flaming torches galloping to my grandma's house in Pinsk.

My mother said I woke her yelling, "Bubbi…run!" Now the Jews were in more trouble, big trouble. I knitted scarves for the soldiers, sold US War Bonds and Stamps, and begged the grown-ups to let me roll bandages. They'd chase me away as if I thought it was a game or something. Finally, a wrinkled old lady spoke out, "It's good she wants to help. Let her." They taught me how, and every day after dance class,

I spent an hour rolling bandages at the Jewish Center. And I helped my mother with the food ration coupons.

Natasha was Russian. I was afraid she might go home. She didn't. I missed not one lesson or concert in spite of blackouts, air raid tests, sirens screaming, and drills at school where we hid under our desks shaking as if a bomb had really dropped. And then came Rosie the Riveter, who excited young women to join the workforce. My brother Sammy joined the Navy after his seventeenth birthday, and my sister Judy despaired over not joining the WACS because our parents wouldn't allow it. World War II changed everybody and everything except dance. One change that found its way into my obsession with the war was that boys were not putting my curls in the inkwells or doing other nasty stuff like that anymore. And when I was twelve years old, a boy named Billy Cranston put a Valentine card on my desk. It made me feel special. He asked me to go with him to a double feature at the Carol Theater on Saturday. My first date was standing at our front door, dark hair slicked back.

The young Cary Grant, bouncing a yoyo, asked, "Is Charlotte home?"

Dad reluctantly sent us off to see *Gunga Din* with the real Cary Grant and *King Kong* with Fay Wray. I wanted to tell Billy that I'd seen photos of Fay Wray holding hands with my dad in Hollywood, but I didn't. After sucking up the last drops of our ice cream sodas in a shop nearby, we turned toward the theater. A sign under the marquee threw us for a loop. The tickets price had jumped the day before from a dime to eleven cents. Billie was left with twenty cents, and I'd never heard of mad money. He sat me down on a fire hydrant. "Don't move. I'll be right back!" After an eight-block round-trip run, rumpled, sweaty, and breathless, he stretched out his arm, palm up, and proudly showed me two wet pennies as if they were gold coins taken from a treasure chest.

This Galahad moment stayed with me for years. I kept looking for more of the same. My dad was my hero, and Sammy, my prince. They were hard acts to follow. When I was ten, my big brother wrapped an umbrella handle around the neck of a boy who'd been rude to me. From that day on, if the poor kid found himself walking toward me, he would bolt like a sprung coil to the other side of the street, his eyes filled with fear. Sammy was a terrific big brother.

Dance became my life. For months I practiced, rehearsed, memorized, and dreamed about my first big solo. Before my thirteenth birthday, I stood center stage, Flamenco-costumed in white organdy layers bordered by a red ribbon, a black satin blouson and vest trimmed with gold coins, and a Spanish fedora with red balls dangling from the brim that I wore at a rakish tilt. I was posed in profile with my right arm arched over my head, left hand placed saucily on my hip. The curtain opened. The audience, struck by the exotic tableau, broke into wild applause. "El Choclo" chords sounded. I couldn't move, not one dance step in my brain.

I remained frozen for what seemed forever, the people in the front seats staring at me, holding their collective breath. I couldn't move. I knew I had to move. The steps were nowhere to be found. I improvised as I'd done when a toddler on the beach, shaking shoulders, moving hips Latina fashion, and twirling. Suddenly, a passage in the music connected to the part of the brain where the choreography was hiding. I picked up the dance as rehearsed and finished on the right note to applause louder than the opening roar that had terrorized me. I ran to the wings and threw myself into Natasha's arms, weeping in humiliation. She convinced me that only she and I knew. My savior's arms were like Bubbi's hug after I'd danced the Hawaiian Hula for her. I danced my way through the hard times, feeling the horror of war but not understanding it. Gearing up to pirouette for Natasha with the war finally over, another war was being waged inside my body. It turned out to be a kidney infection that put dance and nearly all else on hold. The hiatus from ballet, tap lessons, and concerts caused the worst pain.

I was to eat fish, chicken, and veggies. No ice cream. No candy, cake, or cookies. No hamburgers or spaghetti and meatballs. I became a delirious bundle of bones on what felt like a cold marble slab, my body remembering the same delirium that came over me when I'd nearly died from coal gas as a toddler. In both cases, I'd been given sulfa to which I must have been allergic. Misery and pain became my life, the world hiding somewhere else. There'd be no school, television hadn't happened yet, and my eyes were too swollen to read. Lonely, bored, and sad, I cried about ballet concerts carrying on without me. I'd found my place—the dance studio, the bathroom towel barre, all in a domicile of my mind and body. I was in bed with no sense of belonging, of having a place in the world. The feeling was gone. Would it ever return?

Able to read at last, I chose *The Diary of Anne Frank*. I was taken aback by her high spirits while hiding from Nazis in a cramped space, afraid for her life. To be safe, they were not to speak or move during the day and were in the dark at night. I couldn't put the book down until the end. It made me cry. It made me angry. It made me ashamed. How did I dare have feelings of deprivation for being under the weather for a few months? The higher her spirits, the harder it was for me. I felt a bond with Anne. I was a Jewish teenager about her age. Her diary read as if she was talking to me. She became my friend. In the reading, I wanted her to live, amazed that in abject fear, she never departed from her belief that "people are really good at heart."

Freed from restrictions at last, I ran to the studio with my ballet and tap shoes over my shoulders. I raced upstairs and bolted inside to throw myself into Natasha's welcoming arms.

From across the room, she stopped me with a booming roar, "What have you done to yourself? You have ruined everything! Even Igor Youskevich is not tall enough to dance with you. And those balloons on your chest. *Nyet!*" I thought she must be joking, probably about to open her arms and say, "Come to me, darling." She did no such thing. The other girls seemed frozen in second position, staring in silence. I turned my back to Natasha and dragged what felt like lead boots toward the door that looked far away. I went down the steps and all the way home under an unstoppable flow of blinding tears. I stomped into my room and slammed the door behind me.

I stayed there for days. Judy tried to comfort me, but I had run away from the ballerina mother who didn't love me anymore, and now I was home to my real mother, always afraid she didn't love me either. At my every downfall, she'd say, "I told you not to…" How crazy is that? Was it my fault that I grew too tall and my boobs too big for ballet? Bedroom shades stayed down. I'd fallen into a hole with no bottom, like the borderless bridge to nowhere in my dreams. My dance dream had been stolen. What could possibly replace it?

My folks took me to a Christmas party in the offices of Harry Cohn, Chairman and CEO of Columbia Pictures, my dad's boss. The idea of meeting movie stars lifted the gloom.

We walked into a huge suite of glitter and crystal. The first person I saw was my idol, Rita Hayworth, her lustrous red hair cascading through the air and onto her shoulders like a ballet. Hors d'oeuvres were served on silver trays by waiters who looked like movie stars. They were not, but they wanted to be. I could tell. A Marlene Dietrich clone sat on the grand piano, her long, shapely legs in super-high heels crossed seductively over the side, her face heavily made up, her body in a slinky black dress with plunging neckline, diamonds all over the place, topped by a silver fox boa slung over one shoulder. Another stunning lady in brown satin sauntered up to my dad. He summoned me, and she asked that I grace the party with a spin. I assumed he had told her about my dancing life. A montage on speed flashed—flamenco costume, arms filled with flowers. Since taps were still on my Mary Janes, I said I'd improvise if the pianist would give me a tango rhythm. I was not afraid to dance for gorgeous people in a gorgeous room. And holy moly! Rita Hayworth was there!

My mother was beautiful in a royal-blue dress with fake diamond clips at the corners of a square neckline and the coal-black chignon at her nape. Then a surprise—she was smiling! I liked believing it was because my dance was a hit in my wine-colored taffeta dress and newly invented Grecian hairstyle. Still no camera.

The talent scout told my dad and me that she'd like me to come west to audition for a spot in a film. She said she loved my "expressive hands." At first, I was excited. Ten minutes later, it felt too soon for Hollywood after being thrown out by my other mother. And just as my mind was beating me up for chickening out, I was introduced to Gene Kelly. Oh my god! Natasha said I was too tall for Igor Youskevitch. I towered over Kelly. Maybe being sick had saved me. But damn it, in those classes and concerts, I was somebody.

# Red Hook

Womanhood hit me like a rising tide. By the end of the Forties, I was close to being engaged, and the war in Korea would find me at Brooklyn College, still an avatar without definition. I was fretting over the decision to end the punishing war with Japan by dropping the first atomic bombs on not one but two Japanese cities. The human suffering seen in movie theater newsreels horrified me. I'd stagger home senseless. And we'd later choose the Korean War, calling it a "police action."

I was a sophomore at Brooklyn College, majoring in education at age eighteen. They assigned me to student-teach at an elementary school in Red Hook. I'd never been in that neighborhood, but I'd read articles in the *Daily News* about knifings, muggings, rapes, and wife-battering that happened a lot in Red Hook. The people who lived there were poor and mostly non-white. Well, I'd campaigned for a Brooklyn Borough president candidate when I was twelve, fought for higher teacher salaries in high school, had adored Stanley and his family downstairs, and had been in love with the music of Billie Holliday and Ray Charles for years. I thought, what's the big deal?

I was on my way to an unfamiliar locale in a taxi. Through a dirty window, I saw streets strewn with garbage and broken glass, stores fronted by cracked or bordered windows, shady characters coming, going, and loitering in the streets. The cab made it to the rundown old schoolhouse emblazoned with graffiti saying "I'm here," "Look at me," and "Your momma's a whore" and spray paintings of daggers, helmets, crowns, and body parts. Debris in a yard across the street was a kaleidoscope of broken beer bottles, used condoms, and chicken bones. I stepped out of the cab trembling, my eyes fighting to stay open.

Brooklyn College had seen it fit to place me, a teenager, in a sixth-grade classroom. Some of the boys were so huge they must have been repeaters. They towered over me. I held my breath and pressed my lips together, my body throbbing with anxiety. One dark-skinned boy with nappy hair put his muscular arm on my shoulder. "So, teach, ya wanna fuck?" As shocked as he'd hoped I'd be, I started shaking like a screen door in a hurricane.

"Don't let them see how frightened you are, girl," I whispered to myself. Yet a bigger fear was to not be up to the challenge. I searched for a way to deal with the rude ruckus. I must have done something right in high school. I tutored the football team's only Negro. He passed his grades and thanked me for "making learning fun." My brain spun for ways to spot and establish rapport with a few good apples to help in my struggle for order. The classroom door opened.

A shriveled, old white lady, osteoporosis curving her back and lowering her head onto her chest, limped over and strained to get her hand up to my shoulder for a friendly tap. "You'll be fine, dearie," said the supervisor, "just don't try to teach these animals anything…and do keep the noise from filtering into the hallway." She might as well have smacked me in the face. The force of her words was a blow harder than any punch these tough guys might deliver. Her purpose clearly was to enlist me into the Brooklyn public school system's doctrine of writing off the non-white student population. The old racist knew nothing of my attraction to the Black experience that had begun on Linden Boulevard.

An old hand at looking through the extended bars of childhood, I felt the students' anger. The supervisor's blatant racism hit me hard in a deeply personal way. So did the pupils' hostility toward me. Years later, I learned from Black Panther rhetoric that I wasn't just another white face to these sixth graders. The genes of their ancestors told them I was the face of the enemy dating back to slavery. I spent four more days uneasy and alone in a crowded, angry room. At home, safe but not-so-sound, bad thoughts invaded my sleep. It was not their boisterous behavior that upset me or drove me away. It was the school system's sanctioned bigotry. No way could an eighteen-year-old teacher-in-training change a systemic racist doctrine. I had to quit.

Was I a coward for not trying to make a difference? I craved a secret place to lick my wounds, hoping shame would pass. I tried not to think it a failure, but the cowardice of abandonment became a lasting shadow, the sword of Damocles hanging over my future. I did not know at the time that this moment was ground zero of my activist passion. I had been up close to the racial chasm that has changed very little since the halcyon days of my youth. From this spout would flow *Brown v. Board of Education*, the Supreme Court declaration that school segregation was unconstitutional. The civil rights movement began a few years later with the bus boycott in Montgomery, Alabama. I had switched my major from education to political science.

Did growing up during World War II and the Holocaust connect me to those at the mercy of oppressors? It was from Isabel Wilkerson's *The Warmth of Other Suns* that I learned about the Great Migration of millions of Negroes to the north, escaping Jim Crow slavery to a new world and hoping to be free from lynching and other abuses. The bent-backed supervisor who referred to dark students as "animals" had made it clear to me that Jim Crow was as hard to kill as the oppression of Jewish people—likely harder. I had faced a fight on the home front for permission to make that change in my major. Mother's first reaction after I quit was to ask me in a nasty, judgmental voice how I managed to ruin a student-teaching assignment. Dad wanted to fix it. Judy was glad I'd walked away. Big brother Sammy was too busy in law school to notice. I'd be in our tiny bathroom crying and thinking. Judy weighed in as always on my side. Only two ways for me to stay in Red Hook. In one, I'd be just another assembly-line proctor from hell. The other would've made me a colonial police officer disguised as a teacher, my every move or word a clown show, a mockery against the inheritance of slavery. I would not do either one. Yet biting the dust wrote "feckless coward" all over me. I would be abandoning victims of circumstance likely headed for despairing lives. Could I change anything against the odds imposed by the Brooklyn Public School System? I didn't think so.

My jail-cell-crib chimera found its way back in my dreams, but this time it was the schoolkids who were behind bars. What smacked of danger were the effects of abuse on the students, later termed by Black Panther, Huey P. Newton, as "reactionary suicide." There'd been a hostile, self-destructive energy in that classroom. I begged my parents to understand that if I stayed, my world would be a bigoted school system, versions of Red Hook recurring again and again. My parents always insisted I major in education, "the only respectable profession for a woman" in their minds. I was glad when they freed me to learn what I hoped would be the true history and politics of my country. I had made the change to political science.

I'd already been fighting Brooklyn College's red-baiting dean. As editor of a school paper, I was asked but refused to limit my extracurricular political advocacies. No force was strong enough to block out the daily reminders that power is corrupted by itself. My desire—no, my need—to try to make a difference would not be abated. I entered a crowded classroom, daylight barely seeping through unwashed windows. In front of a chalkboard stood a long-bearded, yarmulka-wearing Orthodox Jew with tassels sticking out of his old-fashioned, oversized, velvet-collared black jacket. How could an Orthodox Jew constrained by time-honored sanctions be my first political science professor? Was he the scholar to enlighten me on "postmodern secular issues"? I squirmed in trepidation, then was taken aback by his comprehensive opening remarks. I played with the idea that this educator named Mordecai was sent by the gods to validate my decision to change my major. A man clothed in the garb of unbending ritual chose an existential approach to civics. I was struck by his philosophic, global view of history, particularly on the Holocaust and its relation to slavery. His words verified what was stirring in my brain. In a few weeks, this odd-looking person seemed a soulmate—and I was having a bit of a crush.

He inspired me to read more poetry and novels by Langston Hughes. He talked of Richard Wright's *Native Son* and Ralph Ellison's *Invisible Man*, both novels I'd already relished. He felt strongly about one I'd never heard of, Zora Neale Hurston's *Their Eyes Were Watching God*. In keeping with his connection of slavery with the Holocaust, he recommended a wide range of books by Jewish writers past and present, many I'd read and appreciated deeply, especially I. B. Singer's *Satan in Goray*. Mornings I'd awake and leap out of bed—so much to look forward to. I hoped that after class, my professor and I might keep talking. It was uncanny that in spite of the differences between us in age, lifestyle, priorities, and experience, I felt safe and respected in his company. He took my life intention seriously.

Uneasy about the attraction, I said to myself, "Don't worry, you're a committed virgin, engaged at last to boyfriend Eddie. Mordecai's an Orthodox Jew, a married man. Don't be ridiculous."

The first to arrive in class, I sauntered over to my seat in the second row and took out a compact to check for smudges. I lifted my head and saw Mordecai staring at me. When he caught my glance, he looked at his watch as if unaware I was in the room. But why? Was he looking at his watch to remind himself he's old enough to be my father? Mordecai upset my equilibrium. Did he remind me of my dad? He was not handsome, although our private sessions were filled with handsome moments. Hurston's protagonist, Janie, made me think hard about what it means to be a woman— black or white. Yet when I sought Mordecai's wisdom on the myths that pigeonhole women in our society, he changed the subject like the *shamas* in *shul* who chased me upstairs to be with females hidden behind the curtain. I snapped out of that image to ask Mordecai why women were thought unworthy to pray with the men. No answer. Maybe he was as stuck in his myth as I'd been in mine. But his tethering Black history to Jewishness continued to be exciting.

He wove a literary tapestry with threads from Allen Ginsberg to Frederick Douglass, from Maimonides to the budding James Baldwin. He looked more fundamentalist than our family's Russian rabbi, yet he validated a merge with the African American plight. He still ignored my developing feminist consciousness, an embryo that would gestate in its own time with or without his help. Mordecai inadvertently aided my quest by introducing me to Janie, Hurston's fictional, self-empowered black woman character. Her slave dialect was hard going at first, but the music took over when I read it out loud. Hurston's courage to take control of her life and speak her mind thrilled me. Her Janie dismissed an abusive lover after saving both of them from a horrible hurricane.

Her final words to him were, "But Ah'm uh woman every inch of me, and Ah know it. Dat's uh whole lot more'n you kin say. You big-bellies round here and put out a lot of brag, but 'tain't nothin' to it but yo' big voice."

I wondered if Mordecai had read this book. Did he know that Janie was able to rob Joe of the "illusion of irresistible maleness that all men cherish"?

For a man steeped in an ancient theology and culture to introduce me to my first fictional female hero since Jo of *Little Women* and Nora of *A Doll's House,* and they were white. It was a great gift. Somehow I couldn't imagine him aware of the novel's political profundity, the story of female power to survive and stand alone. She became my fictional hero. In 1936 Hurston took a stance against the force of racism and misogyny—a live black woman immersed in the sounds and rhythms of fighting for freedom against all odds. She did so with a joyous energy of survival. Once fictional Janie saved herself and her man, she sent him off, never to return. Yet, raising the woman's issue with Mordecai remained futile. He'd ask me to stay after class to resolve the impasse and then just dance around it. I'd leave his office defeated but strangely aroused. Could it have been healthy combat that turned me on? Never mind. What really mattered was the effect he was having on my thinking. As a woman young and un-radicalized, it occurred to me that I was what Ralph Ellison meant by invisible.

I came upon what may be the best book on slavery ever written, *The Peculiar Institution,* by Kenneth Stamp. Bare, cruel facts spoke for themselves. The white historian replicated posters that carried stark advice for getting the most from each slave at a minimal cost. The rule was, "Maximize profit by providing bare sustenance necessary for high production levels."

I wondered why I was drawn to a struggle of such horrifying life and death magnitude. I was told in grade school that we waged a civil war so Abraham Lincoln could "free the slaves." I asked, "What's a slave?" No answer. The subject came up again in high school under the category "Reconstruction," all about Booker T. Washington. There was no mention of federal troops abandoning the South to KKK's lynching mania, grotesquely unequal schools, wage slavery, and disenfranchisement. In Hurston's words, "Booker T? He wuz a great big man, wasn't he…s'posed tuh be. All he ever done was cut de monkey for white folks. So dey pomped him up. But you know whut de ole folks say, de higher de monkey climbs de mo' he sho his behind, so dat's de way it wuz wid Booker T." Mordecai caused my heart to stammer and my mind to come alive. I was excited that a scholar found me worthy of private conversation.

Blood went rushing through my veins when with dramatic power, he read dark revelations aloud, adding graphic descriptions and quotes. My aim at eighteen was to build a political posture, but I was underinformed until Mordecai entered my life. Sensual feelings put me on the edge of I knew not what. I was aroused necking with Ed but remained a committed virgin. I was in unhappy limbo, my sexual ideation still a fantasy. Mordecai was a man of honor who helped me find ways to make a difference. A small chance to do that happened:

Ten black girls were not allowed to form their own House Plan, a format established as a democratic alternative to sororities and fraternities.

The issue was raised at a House Plan Association Board meeting: "These girls are all-black. It breaks our rules against discrimination!"

Shaking my fist Bella Abzug style, I shouted, "What the hell are you talking about? Most House Plans are all-white. Is that discrimination?"

Jaws dropped as if the hinges had snapped. The vote was to "allow" ten friends of color to form a House Plan. They made me the plan's sponsor, likely what they considered a punishment.

Maybe it was cocky to feel heroic for saving the day for ten black girls I didn't even know, but I was happy. My first task was to chaperone their celebration party. I arrived late and sidled over to a tall, thin guy with a Jimmy Hendrix Afro the size of his head. I led him to the dance floor, his eyes darting nervously to see who was eying him. La Playa Sextet's Latin beat poured out from the record player, and we samba'd away. When the music changed, he walked me off the floor with his arm around my waist and a big smile.

My activist life was born.

How could we still be stuck in the Mississippi mud after years of apparent change? It haunted me still to have been exposed to a blatantly racist supervisor. I thought of Mordecai's advice to pick where it's possible to make a difference as I'd done for the House Plan Association. His words still ring true: "We're but a speck on this globe. All we can do is touch what's near and add something worthwhile." An Orthodox Jew taught me so much. I loved his mind, and he respected mine. I never believed my genius sister Judy's symphony of praise for my intellect. Mordecai had no ax to grind and no baby sister to uplift and yet considered my mind worthy of his attention. Writing opens decades-old doors of awareness that can be staggering. I'm grateful he taught me well and raised my self-esteem. He deepened my need to make a difference.

# PART 6

# Me and My Mother

In 1963, life in the suburbs was no life for me. I loved the house, the garden, the wonderful designer furniture my generous brother had gifted us. Replicas can be seen at fine museums everywhere. The trouble with suburbs like Merrick, Long Island, was the white sameness of it all. The few friends I made were restless, like me. A favorite was Edna, whom you know I'd met at the Bridge Club. She was a maverick with a super sense of humor. The only rules Edna followed were the ones she invented. That same year my mother underwent a mastectomy. In recovery, she suffered acute back pain that worried me. I asked a doctor friend to take a look. He did, and he made a different diagnosis. My mother's breast cancer was a symptom of a more expansive and dangerous lymphoma that had been what was affecting her back. My parents moved into our new home, and I became Mom's caregiver. I was raising three kids, the youngest not yet a year old, and running a home on my own, my mother crying out for me at every turn. I had to hire live-in help. I'd suffered my mother's indifference for twenty-eight years, and now I was her angel. I liked the change of heart but could barely stay sanding up with the exhaustion. Always craving her elusive love, I grew up pretending to be the person she wanted me to be. I craved but had never enjoyed a real conversation with my mother.

When I was in the third grade, I talked her into a pact: The deal was that every day after school, I'd sit at the foot of her bed during her afternoon rest so we could talk for a half hour. I used to dread her vacant look. Not thinking of something else, just vacant. She did honor her pledge, but I could never tell if she was listening to the stories of my day. Sometimes I couldn't even tell if she was awake. She'd say nothing, even if I complained about my teacher, Mrs. English, or my friend Marilyn Dubinsky for making fun of my bushy hair. When I was seven, I hid under the kitchen table to eavesdrop on my mother and her Canasta ladies. She was telling them that in 1931, she jumped off the dresser, used a knitting needle, and tried everything "to get rid of that pregnancy." Wait a minute. I was born in 1932. She was talking about me!

Crouched under the heavy tablecloth, too scared to take a breath or move a muscle, my bottom lip tasted like blood. Having long felt ignored, to hear my mother resent my very existence stayed fixed in my mind and heart. No wonder she never took a picture of me dancing solos or sewed a stitch on a costume. I couldn't bear not feeling loved by my mother, so somehow, I managed to fling those feelings away.

On her turns back to the hospital, in and out of coma, I watched her do nothing but breathe—no movement, no expression. Once she opened her eyes and, out of the blue, said, "Things between me and your dad were not so perfect, no matter what you may think." Her body limp, the fullness of beauty gone, color drained from her face. She went out again. I sat stiffly in a metal chair, wondering why she was rewriting the loving marriage I'd grown up knowing. She reached for my hand and squeezed it as hard as she could.

She found the words to beg me to be my own person: "Be careful, Charlotte. Don't let Eddie take over your life." She took a deep breath to say, "Your dad needed me to be there for him. He was afraid." She screwed up her face and said, "It cost me to keep him feeling big. Let me tell…" Her arms at her side, her limp hands turned over. Midsentence she'd gone silent. Tubes and IVs attached to extremities and apertures, a beeping monitor with green and red graph lines tracking her vitals. My mother was dying. A sadness came over me. Then the small child inside was reliving hurts from her indifference—like the time I broke my tooth roller-skating.

I yelled from the street in terrible pain. She told me to go to the dentist next door, alone. He pierced a nerve. I screamed so loud the cop on the corner charged in, suspecting child abuse. Ma, just a few steps away, couldn't be bothered. The memory made me cry, and then guilt and shame came over me. If my mother really didn't love me, it must have been my fault. I was a smarty-pants with an undereducated mother. No wonder it was trouble talking to me or even being with me. I would not forget her gift of truth about marriage.

I told no one that her life was about to end. I knew Dad needed to hope, Judy was too furious to care, and Sam, whom I'd been visiting often as he lived near the hospital, happened to be out of town on business. When she died, my dad fell apart, his nose dripping along with his eyes. I felt relief. He needed to deal with reality. He needed to grieve, to mourn, to savor happy memories, and to live. After she was gone, my heart filled up with a riot of conflicted feelings. Out of the mix, one of them stood out. I loved her. I missed her. Sadly, I'd spent my life loving and missing her. And before she died, she gave me advice about my marriage. She gave me the courage to face the truth.

With a raised feminist consciousness, I look now at the missing pieces of my mother's love in a new way. I can respect that she came from another world at a different time. When she took ill, she trusted and needed me day and night. That was hard but healing. I was taking cautious steps toward finding my place in this world. I thought it had to be a place, unlike the one I grew up believing in—to be a good daughter, sister, wife, and mother. I wanted to be all those things and more. My mom never knew she could even dream of having an identity of her own. My heart forgave her. Facing truth liberated me, something I wish my sister had been able to do.

I wish I had reached that understanding years before she died. I live with regrets for not reaching my new understanding while I could have helped her to feel better about herself. I was never able to get answers about my mom from my dear grandma. Bubbi never said a bad word about her daughter, but then again, I don't remember her ever saying a good one. Mother/daughter conflict is a universal syndrome, and what made it hard for me was holding on to the notion that it was my fault not to be the daughter she wanted. It helps that I've come to understand the truth that she had a hard time dealing with a new world with new ideals, lifestyles, and awarenesses.

# PART 7

# Mr. Burns, Please!

In 1964, a job opportunity was arranged for me by a highly respected executive at ABC.

He was on my side about corporate discrimination. I set out for an interview with Lloyd Burns, president of Screen Gems International, part of Columbia Pictures. First, I needed to pave the way with my dad. Columbia was the company he joined the week I was born. In his thirty-fourth year of managing short subjects, he was ousted by new owners with no severance, no pension, not even a gold watch. I needed to know how he'd feel if I worked for the company that had turned my dad into Willy Loman. I'd seen Arthur Miller's *Death of a Salesman* at sixteen. The play haunted me as I witnessed Dad's status and salary at Columbia Pictures diminish. Like Loman, he left home every day dapper from head to toe, except for the shiny seat of his pants that he hoped no one would see under the jacket.

He never showed shame or embarrassment. I wanted to say, "Dad, you're not fooling me with your straight back and good face," as Loman's son said to him in the play.

I asked him if he minded my working for Columbia Pictures. "Wonderful, darling girl, take the job."

I walked through the glass doors of the Columbia building on Fifth Avenue on a Saturday morning and was bowled over by an avalanche of memories: I was a kid alone in the executive screening room, watching movies starring Paul Muni, Clark Gable, and the Three Stooges. I saw my idol Rita Hayworth in *Strawberry Blonde*, and she watched me dance when I was fourteen.

Lloyd Burns's name on the door in brass letters snapped me back to why I was there. I entered his huge office of sofas, fancy bar, and plush carpet. He rose from behind a mammoth desk and stared at me. Tall, a mustache bookended by jowls, he waved me away from the chair I was about to camp in.

"Don't sit down. I don't want to waste your time or mine. I'll ask one question. Your answer will let me know if we have anything to talk about." I waited, shifting, left foot, right foot, like a racehorse at the starting gate. "Do you cry easily?" he asked.

Without skipping a beat, I replied, "Only at basketball games."

He sat down laughing and motioned me to do the same. It was a mystery to me where that answer had come from, but he liked it. We talked and talked. He offered me a job.

I was quick to say, "Thanks, but no, sir. I haven't even left ABC yet. This is my first interview." I gave him a truncated version of the ABC debacle, and then, "To take one more secretarial job, I need a vow that there'll be no corporate policy to block my way up." I thought, maybe my history in the Columbia building as a child gave me strength. Yet I'd always lived in a paradox: on one side an intruder, on the other a long-lost cousin.

What likely empowered me is that the interview wasn't over. Mr. Burns looked pensive, and after more give-and-take, he proposed a deal. I'd spend one year to get his house in order, and if earned, no arbitrary policy would block a promotion. He stated an addendum that if promoted, I would be obliged to find and train my replacement. We shook hands on a starting date at a higher salary than ABC was in the habit of paying new employees with vaginas.

I liked that I'd be working for a straight shooter with a wry sense of humor. However, I'd heard he was a tyrant when disappointed. I learned quickly that it was in my invisible place in his inner sanctum that I learned the nuance of high-end management. It never left me. While Ralph Ellison's *Invisible Man* is not about secretaries, the principle is the same. He wrote, "It's sometimes advantageous to be unseen." He was right about that.

I was the invisible witness to Lloyd's passive-aggressive tyranny. I recognized his hard-ass behavior as a cover for his insecurities and fear. It motivated me to stay calm in his storm and to do a superb job of putting his affairs in methodical order. I even managed to convince myself that his elbow repeatedly brushing against my breast as I entered his office was pure accident. Booked on a multicountry trip, he needed extensive preparation.

He asked me to work late. I could do that thanks to Edith, my live-in housekeeper/nanny. At 7:00 p.m., after two solid hours of intense focus, he said, "Fix me a Scotch… and one for yourself." When I brought over the drinks, he patted his hand on the sofa for me to join him, then queried me about my ambitions. Oh joy! He was thinking about his promise much sooner than I'd expected. How splendid! He asked great questions about my intentions, and my full answers pleased him.

Suddenly and out of nowhere, I found myself in a viselike grip. One arm pinned me tightly to his chest. He was very strong. Shocked and angry, I punched his chest from a cramped position, but with my fists pressed to my ribs, I had no leverage. A vision flashed in my brain: a *New Yorker* cartoon of the two of us—as we were. The caption, "Mr. Burns, please," cracked me up. I cringed, blushed, and laughed out loud from the absurdity all at the same time.

He went limp. I stood up. He blustered an apology, took a pause, and then rebuked my "childish behavior." After an awkward silence, he tried persuasion. How good for my future it would be and what's-the-big-fuss kind of stuff. Perhaps it was my utter innocence that moved me to react with behavior even more absurd than his.

Standing with my arms outstretched, I stared into his eyes and said, "Okay. If it's so important to you, do it…get it over with. How long will it take? Five, ten minutes? Go ahead. Do it." He was too humiliated to budge or say a word. But to be certain, I added, "You'll never see me again, Mr. Burns, and you'll be losing the best secretary you may ever have…but if it's so important…" I'd sidestepped his assault, but had no idea how I'd found the chutzpah.

An effective professional relationship grew along with a friendship and new self-confidence. Lloyd and I even partnered at the Madison Bridge Club. The first time, desperate to hold my own with a Master Bridge Champion, I second-guessed every bid, every play, making a series of mistakes that kept us losing. He never shamed me. But we stopped at a coffee shop after the game. He reiterated my every mistaken bid or play. He went on and on, remembering every card. My confidence collapsed like an undercooked soufflé. I asked him what he thought the Chinese laborers who built our railroads in the 1860s did when the spikes they hammered again and again finally were flush with the ground. He looked at me as if I'd gone mad and nodded his head in a no. I said emphatically, "They stopped!" My witty boss apologized. I felt redeemed but deeply worried about what the next challenge would be and how I'd deal with it.

# A Bridge Too Far

When I needed escape from a fractious marriage or the corporate conundrums, I played that tricky card game called Bridge. Sometimes my cohorts were two gay friends. One was a rotund opera singer, his partner, a tall, skinny, top executive at IBM. I agreed to be his beard at corporate VIP functions to make sure his esteemed position wasn't compromised when being "queer" wasn't understood. Our dissimulation worked until his bosses started to fret that the loving couple hadn't moved on to marriage. He found a substitute beard to keep the charade going.

One night we played Bridge in their psychiatrist friend's apartment above a restaurant. My gaze was drawn to figurative and impressionist paintings on every vertical surface, all signed by Zero Mostel. The shrink confessed that the actor was a long-standing patient. The front door suddenly rattled, was pushed open, and in barged the very man we'd been talking about. I thought, *Wow, I'm in the same room with Broadway's comic genius.*

I had just taken a plunge with a hazardous four-no-trump bid, knowing I needed two finesses to pull it off. Our opponents were looking cocky, so I glared at their eyes to catch a bluff. We were all chain-smoking and focused, and the great Zero Mostel was ignored. He talked to us, but we paid little attention.

He was pissed, but I was too focused on a potential disaster if I failed to finesse the killing card. The other players were equally engrossed. So what did Zero do? He came back from the loo singing a capella, "Tradition! Tradition!" And then he sang the song about paying for a horse and getting a mule—and then shifted back and forth from Tevye to the guy who's scamming him. Zero then became many people in one ever-changing body and voice—and always loud. We were all entranced as he commenced to play all the parts in *Fiddler on the Roof.* We sat a few feet away from this human hurricane, catching his sweat spewing in all directions as he pivoted his belly and sang "If I Were a Rich Man" at the top of his voice, arms raised, facial expressions adding breathtaking dimension to Tevye's dilemma. And after singing each of the daughter's marital miasma and suffering from the elopement of the third, he's faced with Schpritzer, his fourth daughter, who was in love with a Russian! Tevye fought against the last straw.

His precious Jewish daughter marry a Russian? Nyet. Never. He switched to her as she pleaded, "But I love him."

His answer as Tevye was my favorite line from the show: "So a bird loves a fish, and where are they going to build a house?"

The four of us sat in jaw-dropped awe for three hours. I will never forget Zero morphing into each character's face, body, voice, and even gender. *Fiddler on the Roof* is one of my favorite shows. Its narrow, ethnic theme captures the universal human condition. It has been staged in Japan 1,300 times and is still playing in some sixty countries. Taxying home in the wee hours, my spirit rose even higher when I realized that he had saved me from humiliation. I could never have "made" that bid.

# Gossip

Ironically, Lloyd's new calm in the office aroused suspicion. Rumors spread that he was having his way with me. His lifted mood was in step with my arrival. Apparently enjoying the rumor, he fueled it by awarding me an office with a window—a status symbol. One day I collided in a corridor with a work friend often berated by Lloyd. I didn't think he saw what I saw during those disputes. Lloyd's insults were meant to arouse gumption in a man he admired who didn't have the gall to stick to his convictions when challenged. My friend was unaware of the traditions and tropes needed to satisfy this boss. Much later, he benefited from corporate training not offered to women, and his status did rise, his tiny office still hidden behind filing cabinets.

He congratulated me and then leaned close to whisper, "Tell me... we're friends, right?"

I said, "Of course we are."

He asked, "Who are you sleeping with?"

I wanted to knee him, but I looked around conspiratorially to ensure no one was near enough to hear my secret. I moved close, our faces nose-to-nose. I asked him in a low voice, "You mean you don't know?" His eyes widened for the scoop, and I drew in even closer, placing my hands on his shoulders. I whispered in his ear, "Everybody but you, Norman. Have a nice day."

I once gave a speech on the business of being a woman to media majors at the University of Chicago. The dean knew I was writing a memoir and asked me to read a chapter after my remarks. I chose the Mr. Burns story that I felt would resonate with eighteen-year-olds, particularly women, and also some male counterparts. The only sounds I heard while reading my first harassment experience came from birds in the trees outside an open window.

Then there was a rush of questions. Q&A lasted nearly two hours. A student from India confessed her sexual horror story, tearfully complaining of relentless despair, depression, and a sense of forlorn hollowness. She said she hadn't been able to shake feeling a victim. In the end, with a bright smile and sparkling eyes, she thanked me for having laughed my way out of it and for releasing her from an obsession with victimhood. I spoke as a mother in my thirties, not a college freshman, yet she wrapped her mind around the concept of humiliating the harasser, even if he is the boss.

Encouraged by the #MeToo movement, I can't wait for more women to know that bad behavior short of a violent assault by powerful men can be stopped in a number of ways if we stand our ground. Being strong or clever didn't always work for me, though. A time or two, I'm sad to say, filing a complaint turned out to be pointless and punishable. That's changing, but there will be times when the only endgame is to walk away. The real hope is that most men eventually will stop committing sexual misdeeds. Many already have. Male fear and resentment of women is a time immemorial reality. Now they fear exposure's hurtful consequences and their loss of power to abuse freely.

I remain grateful to Frederick Douglass for his relentless articulation on the wide subject of abuse, especially his declaration that "power concedes nothing without a demand." It is a truth evidenced in all manner of spheres and circumstance, public and personal. I wish I could have stemmed the negative effect my early steps toward a career were having on my marriage. The search for my place in the world intensified at about the same pace as Ed's antagonism toward me. It was wonderful to be moving well in the work world against misogynist winds threatening to wreck my delicate balance. At home, it was harder. And I had not as yet faced Ed with my demands, and the fights were getting nastier.

My first corporate harasser had taken me seriously when I stood my ground. And one day, he suggested I assist program coordinator Bill Wilson. We coproduced a low-budget series called *Spotlight On*, shot in Agincourt, Canada. I persuaded Mel Tormé and my jazz genius friends Johnny Desmond and Carmen McRae to appear for a pittance by bartering a video of their half- hour shows for private use—a real bonus in those early days of using that medium for the private promotion of talent. Bill and I became friends working together, and when he left Screen Gems, Lloyd proposed that I replace him. Bill warned me that Dan Enright, his boss who would now be my boss, was a depraved manic depressive. I wasn't afraid. I'd done well with a tyrant who'd scared off many before me.

Bill cautioned again that Dan Enright was a mental mess. Disgraced for a villainous scandal he perpetrated producing the quiz show *Twenty-One*, vitriolic feedback exiled him to oblivion. Eager to restore his standing, he made Lloyd an offer he couldn't refuse. He would contribute his great skill for little pay and no expense reimbursements. He hoped it would put his reputation back on track. He was not happy to learn that his new second would be someone he didn't even know, let alone a woman! We'd barely spoken when a big deal with the Canadian television network CTV was suddenly canceled. He left for Fiji to produce a TV series for Screen Gems leaving no counsel or instruction for what I was to do in his absence.

Weeks later, CTV revived the deal. "Can you handle this on your own?" Lloyd asked.

"Absolutely," I said while mentally scratching my head on how I would produce a strip of daytime programs in Montreal on a low budget.

The purpose was to satisfy Canada's quota system meant to limit competitive prime-time American series like *Bewitched.* To sell prime time series, Screen Gems had to coproduce lesser fare with Canada, employ some Canadians in the crew and talent.

The Montreal daytime strip would include an "agony pageant" about marriage, a fictional courtroom series, and a quiz show. For the quiz show, I hired a friend who was expert. For the other two, I picked brains on how to rent and equip space, set a timeline, hire staff, and create above- and below- the-line production budgets. With all that done, I flew to Montreal to hire the team for three separate daytime series.

*Magistrate's Court* predated *Judge Judy* by thirty-five years. As it was fictional, actors would be given context and attitude from which to improvise. To collect content, I sat on a hard bench in night court, taking notes for episode ideas. To gain ideas for *Marriage Confidential,* I pored over *Ask Anne Landers* columns. I needed writers willing to work for a trifle who would expand an idea to a two-pager from which the actors would improvise. My former boss, Harvey Jacobs, knocked out "script outlines" by the dozens. My sister Judy, who'd won $25 bonuses weekly by conjuring winning ideas for the *Ellery Queen* series, was eager to pitch in.

The quiz show preproduction was well under way thanks to the experienced old hand luckily available. Ed's fits got worse. His resentment of my growing stature was taking on a nasty life of its own. Even though wonderful helper Enid still lived with us, I worried that Ed was not filling the void created by my absences. I often felt I was in the center of a tug of war. From one side, my career pulled at me, and from the other, missing the boys yanked at my heart.

Not being with them enough, it mattered that time spent together be special. Of course, there was their Pops, my dad, and their idol, friend, father, and grandfather. At a summer rental in Rockaway

Beach, nothing made my boys happier than being with their Pops. And I never missed a school play, concert, athletic event, or parent-teacher meeting. At home, we all hung out watching TV or singing the Beatles' *Sergeant Pepper's Lonely Heart Club Band* album. I started taking the older boys to plays like *Hamlet* with Richard Burton and great movies like *Yellow Submarine.*

It was time to complete my work on the Canada project. I was ready to be in Montreal for final run-throughs. Dan Enright blew in from Fiji. Hot to brag about reaching goals on time and under budget, I ran into his office. He gifted me with an Indian sari of exquisitely gold-threaded green silk. I proudly began pouring out my achievements. His hand came up like a traffic cop at a school crossing. He sprayed me with a hundred-word magazine of abusive, raving insults. I can still feel the force. He stared at my gift as if about to grab it back as he raged on. I wanted to scream at the bastard, but my eyes were on the gold threads that formed a geometric design. The silk glowed in an emerald sheen. His rant sputtered its last venom and seemed far away as I gently folded and refolded the sari that had become hypnotic. I then rose from the chair and tiptoed out of the room, clutching the macabre metaphor to my bosom.

I learned Lloyd had not notified Dan that the Canadian contract had been retrieved, that he wanted to save him from worrying about it. Dan was furious that I'd taken on the challenge. He told me in no uncertain terms, "You will not be needed in Montreal. The boss is back!"

A very puzzled and upset crew called me to complain, but the programs had launched successfully. Shortly, Dan astonished me by praising me for a job well done. His accolades opened a door I'd been yearning to step into: "Time to talk about salary, Dan. I…"

Clutching his heart with his left hand, his forehead with the other, he whined, "After all I have done for you…a chance no one else would have given you…a woman with no experience…and as I understand, wasting time on African American politics, how can you be so crass and ungrateful?"

A fretful pulse sent me genuflecting backward out of his office sputtering, "I'm sorry, so sorry," to a man publicly disgraced for betraying a network, an audience, and bundles of investors and advertisers for his series, *Twenty-One*—a man who'd shut me out of a job well done. As the hire Dan never wanted, I might have to leave. But I thought Lloyd's affection and regard would prevail.

We met. Looking sad and uncomfortable, Lloyd said, "Sorry, Charlotte. I get Dan almost gratis. I warned you."

My mind wandered from his words to wondering how my dad felt when the same company sent him packing: "There were promises made… I put thirty-four years into this firm… You can't eat the orange and throw the peel away…a man is not a piece of fruit!" But Dad didn't say that either. It was again what Arthur Miller had Willy Loman say to his boss in *Death of a Salesman*.

Lloyd hugged me like an uncle and said, "Take your sweet time. You'll get a top-notch reference from me and full salary until you find what you're looking for." His kindness was comforting, but the entire scenario led me to worry about this career I'd been trying to build. And although Dan's villainy was not limited to disrespecting and mistreating women, I was certain he'd never have done to a man what he did to me. I'd learned the hard way that misogyny twists and turns its menace at home and at work. Was I meant to redefine myself to suit the circumstances of each monstrosity of bad luck?

The years 1967–1969 had been terrible years. Dad dead on the sidewalk. Martin Luther King and Bobby Kennedy murdered. Chicago police riot. Richard Nixon elected. My marriage on its last legs. Yet life does go on. Living in Manhattan was working well for my boys and for my career. I'd moved from secretary to production executive. Every win or loss was a lesson learned; every smart or even false move was somehow one more step up the career ladder. A break between jobs allowed me more time for my sons' pursuits which filled me with pride.

However, the prospect of ending my marriage gave me nightmares. What might it do to my innocent boys? It was also no help at all that my next gig was still a mystery.

# PART 8

# Life Goes On

Needing private time to think, I borrowed Edna's house on Fire Island. Bundled up against a brisk wind, I strolled on an empty beach. Two people plodded toward me in hooded jackets. I recognized them. Hell, I'd come off- season to be alone, to think, to wonder what to do next. But here were Marc Merson, theater, film, and television producer, and wife, Nina.

We stopped to say hello. A brewing storm was speeding up. We clutched one another, fighting against the harsh wind that pushed against our urgent striving to return from the water's edge. Marc shouted over nature's noises, "Hey, Charlotte, are you up for a project? I'm producing a Television Special for NBC."

I stared at the rough, foamy waves, praying the wind wouldn't blow his words into the rough sea. I held fast to his arm, "Tell me about it, Marc."

"Well, it's going to be a very special musical version of *Androcles and the Lion*, George Bernard Shaw's first play. Noel Coward, he's seventy now, will be Caesar, and Richard Rodgers, he's sixty-six, is composing the original score. Could be the last role for both of these lions."

Over wet sand, the wind had blown a metaphysical chance to me. I nodded yes but needed to know more. "Marc, who would I be? What would I do?"

He stopped me and took my face in his hands. Our eyes met. "You'll be our troubleshooter for publicity, casting, catering, and coordinating. I've heard you're good at finding holes and jumping in. We'll need that."

# Showbiz

Wow! I was taken seriously for a role in something much greater than what started me in production at Screen Gems/Columbia Pictures. Blood rushed to my head, and goosebumps tickled the back of my neck. In preproduction, I was already finding holes. I jumped in, plugged leaks, and picked brains to find out how to do whatever came next. I dealt with NABET, the television union, and network geeks, talent agents, managers, caterers, script supervisors, and operations managers. When a search for two dancers to inhabit a costume to be the lion hit a brick wall, I suggested six-foot-seven Geoffrey Holder. He could be the lion by himself. A descendant of slaves to play the wounded lion who saves two white Christians running from enslavement. That looked to me like great PR as well.

After telling Marc all of this, he said, "Okay, get him!"

I tried, but Geoffrey was missing. My wide search finally found him hiding in Spain in a huff over mean-spirited criticism of his one-man show at the Delacorte Theater in Central Park. I'd seen his performance and found it brilliant. His answer to me was an angry "I'm not coming back to racism and homophobia. Not ever!" I called again the next day. This time I commiserated with his rage and told my ABC story of promotion denied due to a corporate policy against upward mobility for employees with vaginas. He cracked up. We'd both known exclusion and insult, not for what we did or said but for who we were. To be the lion who needed a thorn removed, his final words were, "Dear girl, when do we begin?"

Weeks into rehearsal, I stepped outside for some air and spotted Geoffrey striding toward me from the end of a long block. It was easy to recognize a super tall, ebony black man with not a hair on his head and wearing a white double-breasted suit, royal-blue shirt, and Kelly-green tie.

I said, "Geoffrey, why an outfit like that for a dinky, tacky studio in a lousy part of town?"

He answered in his resounding "Cocoa Nut" voice, "With a great sense of responsibility!"—a quintessential Geoffrey Holder moment.

I enjoyed being his friend. And there was another new friend. I love looking at a photo of us captured deep in conversation—Noel Coward in his Julius Caesar costume and me with dangling petal earrings, a mini-skirted dress, and my legs crossed, revealing a bruise on my bare knee from a roller- skating fall that broke my front tooth.

We were operating with a pay or play contract. It meant that Sir Noel's absence due to illness threatened to create costs way over budget. When he returned in three days, I asked how he was feeling.

He said, "When I awake, I read the obituaries in the *Times*, and if my name's not there, I shave."

I responded, "Sir Coward, I'm shocked that you, of all people, would steal a joke from George S. Kaufman."

His quick reply: "You little bitch, I knew I was going to like you."

With that, he gave me a big hug, laughing affectionately. On the last day of shooting, Marc asked me to produce the show's album. I'd never done that before. I was nervous. But when it was finished, Sir Noel complimented and thanked me robustly for doing so well. He then asked me to join him and his aide/companion, Cole, to see a Peter Ustinov play in a new theater at the budding Lincoln Center. Excited at the prospect of hearing Noel Coward's witty ad-libs, actually more than seeing the play, I gladly accepted.

When settled in our seats, he asked, pointing, "Who pray tell is that actor three rows below us?"

I told him it was Rip Torn. He said, "Lovely, I like his work. Ask him up."

He was happy to come up to our row, and I introduced him, "Sir Noel, may I present Rip Torn."

The actor shouted, "Are you crazy? I'm Peter Falk!"

Heads turned. All eyes, front, back, and sideways, were on me, as in an E. F. Hutton commercial. Mercifully, the curtains parted, and the first act began. At play's end, I declined Sir Noel's invite to join them at Sardi's. I raced home, dove into bed fully dressed, and buried my head under the covers to bury my shameful stupidity.

But two realities saved me from woeful distress. One was Marc's call in the morning asking me to work with him on a feature film coming up. The other was my son Richard's bar mitzvah the very next day. Handsome in a Beatles- inspired suit with a mandarin collar, he chanted the Torah portion well and made a speech with provocative originality. He hadn't been keen on the demanding preparation or the event itself, but he had a ball at the party at the Tavern on the Green in Central Park, and so did I. Dancing with Geoffrey Holder made me feel like Judith Jamison, Alvin Ailey's super star. I remembered Rita Hayworth watching me dance at Harry Cohen's Christmas party. My muck-up with Noel Coward was now old news.

When Geoffrey Holder died in 2014, I pored over the book of his life as actor, dancer, choreographer, costume designer, and portrait artist. The gift of a painting of his wife, the exquisite ballerina Carmen de Lavallade, has been prominently displayed in my every home. On my last day with him in his loft on Prince Street in Soho, he showed me his storyboards for a remake of the film *The Red Shoes* with a Black cast. He asked me to work on it with him. Oh, to be part of his all-Black remake of my favorite movie! After lunch, we walked to a sound studio.

In his booming voice, he recorded tales from African myths in books for children. They were republished with the inspired illustrations he'd painted. Then he died. I still miss him. I'll always miss him.

My next gig with Marc was the film *The Heart Is a Lonely Hunter*, based on Carson McCullers's novel and directed by Joseph Strick, famous for the film *Ulysses*. My mandate was first to hunt for another Julie Harris to play Mick. The search had lasted for weeks without a win. I'd hoped to do better at the Barter Theater in Abingdon, Virginia. I was escorted by Barter founder Robert Porterfield to a Disneyland-size line of moms and daughters snaking through the grass. He apologized for not having prescreened candidates as instructed. He suggested I "just quickly say yes or no and it will be over in no time."

Did he really expect me to subject innocent fledglings on line for hours to a quick "No"? I would not be rushed! Hours later, Porterfield excitedly pointed to a mother on line. He said with notable pride, "She was set to play Scarlett O'Hara before Vivien Leigh got the role."

I pulled her aside and whispered a difficult question, "Why chance your lovely daughter with the same letdown you suffered years ago?"

Looking puzzled, she said, "Why, sugah, whatevah can you mean? Ah'm famous for almos' gettin' the paht. Ma family watches *Gone with the Wind* on my birthdays to toast me for how close ah come."

This mother supporting her ambitious daughter's desires made me jealous. Every girl on line had a mom at her side. My mother's "No, it's not necessary" never failed to tarnish silver linings. So not having found a Julie Harris clone in Virginia, I moved on to Tennessee, and there she was! Sondra Locke was perfect. Director Strick's joy over how right she was pumped me up to take what I thought might otherwise have been a risk. The thing is, he'd mentally cast the lead female role, and I pressed him to consider Thelma Oliver, a lesser-known but brilliant actor. I begged him to screen-test her. He refused, dismissing her as nothing but a dancer.

When he was out of town, I persuaded Marc and the script adapter to audition Thelma Oliver. On Strick's return, they raved rapturously about the actress from the brilliant Holocaust film, *The Pawnbroker,* who also played in *Sweet Charity.* Strick walked up to my desk, grabbed me by the elbows, and literally threw me out of the door shouting, "You're fired!" Probably the shortest film career in history.

Never mind, in spite of the weirdness of my actions, Marc was impressed with my gutsy move to do something I believed to be good for the film. He took me on as associate producer for the Off-Broadway play *Fragments* by Murray Schisgal and starring Gene Hackman. Coming up to rehearsals very soon, it was ironic that three weeks after I was fired by Strick, he was fired. I vowed to be more contained with my opinions. But when rehearsals started, holding back began to sting. I'd learned my lesson from outlandish missteps that had me shot out of Strick's cannon. And so, I kept my lips zipped as I wrung my hands, chewed cuticles, and chain-smoked.

Then trouble began to show its ugly face. The director did not understand Murray's tense comedy at all, and Hackman's frustrations mounted. In the script, his character is meant to be obsessed with an experiment to freeze a monkey for eighteen years and bring him back to life. Hackman was warned not to play the part as a mad scientist. While rehearsing the scene with a fake monkey, Gene needed help. The scene seemed quite crazy to him.

The director paced the floor for a few minutes and then said, "I got it. Just pick up the tube, put it down the monkey's throat, and speak the line."

This time, Gene seemed ready to really go crazy. He yelled, "Damn it, I need to know who the fuck I am, not what to do with my hands!"

Coproducer Edgar Lansbury called a break. Gene and I went out for a drink. I did the awful again. I broke protocol. I raised a fresh idea, and with the lead actor no less. I was out of order, especially not having cleared it with Marc or Edgar. My idea was to replace him with Ulu Grosbard. Gene and Marc gushed with glee at the idea. You see, I knew that Ulu had directed the hit *The Subject Was Roses*, which was produced by Edgar. Of course, he loved the idea too. His only worry was that Ulu might not be available. But he was. For weeks, Murray and I had been committing tobacco suicide in the back of the theater. Marc and Gene thanked me, and the change was made.

Opening night was well-received by the audience, and the reviews were spectacular. Jimmy Coco won the supporting actor Obie Award. Critical praise was no guarantee for an Off-Broadway hit in those days. A few slow weeks against an offbeat blockbuster down the block led to its close.

Gene and I became friends, and with a marriage ending, there was romance. The liaison came to an end with good feelings when he went back to Hollywood. I continued to marvel at his intelligent acting skills in movie after movie, and we were always pleased to run into one another in restaurants or parties. I found him to be a very special, sexy, super smart, highly decent person. I enjoyed most of the men I'd been dealing with on my thespian journey. They were kind and great fun to be around. About *Fragments'* fate, I was thanked, not booted out for bending rules. David and Richard, sixteen and thirteen, saw the play and were proud of their mom. It surely didn't measure up to the *Hamlet* with Richard Burton I'd taken them to see for an introduction to Shakespeare. About the drive to make a mark and "have it all," the tug of war between doing right by my boys and career demands was far from over.

It is imperative for a single mom with no alimony or settlement to search for stable work. I tried a headhunter. I peered at her angular, high cheek- boned, pale face as she read the extensive resumé behind her desk. Hopes rose with every nod of her head, every smile. And then, "Your rapid rise and work experience are impressive"—a long pause sent me to the edge of my seat—"but you've been good at too many things for too short a time in each case." Her eyebrows pinched over nondescript eyes, she said, "I'm afraid you're an unidentified object I have no idea how to market." She shook my hand and showed me the door.

I stepped onto Avenue of the Americas in a funk. I'd been called a lot of things, but "unidentified object"? I sat down in a coffee shop to think. Lady Luck had been there for me on Fire Island, with *Feminine Mystique*, on ABC, Screen Gems, *Androcles*, and *Fragments*. To serve a larger purpose and make a living, I needed a plan. One job was always the good old secretary gig, but it had to be in a small company run by its owner, not bound by arbitrary corporate rules again. I plowed through the classifieds, a tough call. An ad caught my eye. "Drew Lawrence Productions: television commercial company valued for its creative spirit seeks a well-rounded executive assistant to the president." I made an appointment.

# TV Commercials

Since men need to feel big, I decided to come off humble, efficient, and earnest. So before heading for East Eightieth Street, I deleted the prior four years from my resumé. I entered a small office of props and posters, furnished with stylish, practical pieces casually arranged for modular functionality. A man stepped out and extended his arm. We shook hands. I towered over him. Stolid, his feet spread apart like a boxer ready to pack a mean punch, he ushered me into his private office. It was large, toasty, and homey, with family pictures and kids' artwork. All the muscles in my body relaxed. I felt good in this room.

"My name is Arnie Stone. Do come in and sit down."

I said, "Thanks, I'm Charlotte Schiff. I liked your ad because it said you run a lively, creative shop. I sensed you might listen if I came up with good ideas." I handed him the edited resumé.

He said, "Yeah, you beat me to the punch. I was ready to ask why you answered this ad. What's your angle?"

I told him, "My angle is to earn a steady salary in a job that won't put me to sleep. I'm getting a divorce and have three kids. I type fast, know how to write a letter, and can keep order in an office… plus I know a kind of shorthand that works. And, oh, about the last four years? I focused on being a mom until I had to go back to work." I didn't want to scare this guy. I lied.

He said, "I'm not interested in hiring anyone who'd rather do something else. I fear you'd be that person, Charlotte."

I countered, "Trust me, Mr. Stone. I am an excellent executive assistant."

He said, "I have a good feeling about you, but I need time to think. You've got moxie and style. I like that, but I don't want to bite off more than either of us can chew."

I stood up and leaned on his desk. With our heads nearly touching, I looked him in the eye. "Well, my dream is to find a guy to work for who's a straight shooter, his feet on the ground and not giving or taking bullshit lightly. Someone I can learn from and respect who will respect me… and to be honest, who'd be open to more than he bargained for and be glad of it."

I lifted my head, straightened my back, and started to turn away as I said, "The one thing I'm most sure of is that if you hire me, you won't be sorry." The scene became a freeze-frame when halfway to the door, I stopped with my head turned toward Arnie, who was staring down at his desk.

He looked up to say, "When can you start?"

"Just a minute. What's the salary?"

"It's $300 a week with a two-week paid vacation after one year."

"Done. See you on Monday. What time?"

"Be here at nine. Welcome aboard."

I sprinted for the door and caught his smile as I turned my head once more before stepping toward the elevator. I smiled. I trusted this guy. His company was ordinary, and he was neither famous nor powerful. Belonging was clear—no cage, no bars, no exclusion. This cool guy made me feel safe and serene, as my dad always had. He was a Sherman tank kind of guy, feet and legs, a sturdy wheelbase, a man who knew his way around, his street smarts sharp. He took me seriously and with no sneaky sex vibes. Dad dead and Ed out I was alone in the man's world of business. Maybe I'd found a haven in which to recalibrate my professional life.

The very next week, Arnie's son's illness called him away. A pitch to McCann Erickson was scheduled for that day. If we canceled, we'd be out of the competitive loop. I reached him by phone and said, "Arnie, let me do it. With creatives at my side with their storyboards and graphs, I'll be fine. If we don't show, we'll lose anyway, so take a shot with me."

We won the contract. In a month, I was promoted to vice president, trained my replacement, and did well on my first crack at producing a commercial. I worked on two more commercials, joined Arnie on pitches, and with some success, sent reels to friends positioned to give us jobs. I was working for a boss raised in an orphanage who took no prisoners. I found that out on location near Orlando for an orange juice commercial. We'd struck the set at midnight. All of us starving, our hippy-looking selves entered a hamburger joint. We slid into a booth.

Suddenly, in a low, fierce whisper with powerful intent, Arnie said, "Don't turn your heads. Act normal, and keep talking. When I raise my right hand, get up, walk out the front door like horses with blinders on, and head right to the van."

I followed his orders but sneaked a glimpse of four rough guys with cigarette packs in their T-shirt sleeves, leaning on the bar staring at us, socking their fists menacingly. I was in redneck country. And a street guy had my back.

The next gig was a Burley's Cologne cheapie that needed a split-screen format to show a man on a horse, a motorcycle, a canoe in a pool, playing tennis on a court and doing parallel bars. All in one day. The Concord Hotel in the Catskills, Upstate New York, which was like a city and had everything, came to mind. I booked it. At dinner that night, Clarence and I ran into friends of his who invited us to their table. I was chatting with a guy named Jimmy. I mentioned the plan for the Concord. "The boss is my buddy. I'll take care of it." A month later, I registered talent, crew, client, agency rep, and me. When I gave my name, a line of bellmen materialized like a puff of smoke. The captain stood at attention, awaiting my orders. Conjuring a mental image of the hairy guys at that dinner, it occurred to me that I might have been sitting next to a "made guy" who wasn't kidding.

I went straight to the lobby early morning. I was taken to the horse, motorcycle, and canoe in the pool that awaited our attention. By afternoon, all segments had been shot but the one on parallel bars. The Concord had no gym in those days. Jimmy's buddy told us not to worry. Minutes later, he told me the students at Monticello High School were sent home so we could shoot the scene in their gym. Hey, I'd seen *Godfather* a few times. They'd own me.

When I asked for the bill that covered eleven people housed and fed for a day and two nights, I was told, "It's been taken care of."

I insisted, "No way! I won't leave until I've settled the bill myself."

Arnie anointed me "location maven." I felt confident that in the Catskills or any other part of the forest, I'd be good at this. Next, I was on to cast cute kids for a chocolate drink commercial.

Son Paul, at age seven, and I flew to Florida to find more kids and shoot the spot. He had fun. With money tight, I thought of Paul doing more of this. A few more commercials with stage mothers led me to not consider that abnormal world for my child. The next task was to find exotic settings, one for Shetland hairdryer, the other for its rug shampooer. My new friend Clarence's political connections had me choose the Bahamas. My idea was to shoot the hairdryer spot in a French Provincial bedroom set on an empty beach. And for the shampooer, 150 yards of red carpet would be laid out on an unpopulated island, the shot being shampooed from a helicopter. I hired a few locals for the crew.

On a dock, I greeted a small boat's captain who'd come to take us and the red carpet to "Love Island." The young Bahamian hunk leaned toward me and whispered in my ear, "Hi, they call me Satisfying Sam. Your desires are mine to serve."

I laughed so hard the young satisfier was left with no choice but to settle down to business. We wrapped on time and under budget but left 150 yards of heavy, wet red carpet on the island. We couldn't pick it up. The hairdryer scene shot on the beach made me think of David Hockney's whimsical water paintings. What amused me most was that after going through all the machinations of finding exotic locations, the drill actually was to focus mainly on the love shot (closeups of the product). Arnie, the client, and the agency were happy. The stranger Clarence, now more than just a new friend, handled the politics for filming in the Bahamas, the site of our occasional weekend escape.

On Sidney Poitier's rented yacht, we met his girlfriend Joanna Shimkus, soon to be his wife. I was taken by her inner and outer beauty. She was about to marry a kind, thoughtful man I was glad to know well. Clarence introduced me to Quincy Jones and his then wife, a lovely Swedish woman with a long honey-blond braid. Harry and Julie Belafonte were aboard as well, the Copa caper merely a fond memory. The yacht's dining crew wore red uniforms with gold buttons and epaulets. Lunch was served on fine china, champagne was served in crystal flutes, and grits was the nouveau cuisine side dish. Was that a witty counterpoint, or did they just love grits? Clarence told me Quincy thought I was Black. I worshipped the sun, never feeling tan enough. Vacation choices were always tropical, work lunch hours in LA spent in a bikini at the pool. Maybe it's a kind of identity schizophrenia. What was I in the crème de la crème mostly black universe? Did I belong, or was it just a temporary visa? I was forever trying to be part of many worlds—housewife, mother, white, black, professional—often wondering if such an overreach made sense.

Back at the ranch, I learned that at a key client, Raleigh Cigarettes, sales were down. I suggested we take a new approach. Since their smokes were purchased primarily for the coupons, I pitched Arnie that we persuade Post, Keyes & Gardner agency to give us a modest budget for a creative experiment.

I said, "What about Daisy Mae and Lil Abner types that are popular with coupon customers?"

Arnie said, "How can we do that?"

My answer: "If we get a green light in their Chicago office, we can go to Second City, the improv comedy capital, to find talents that look the part."

He said, "The suits will never go for it."

But they did, and at Second City, we singled out the best of the best—Peter Boyle and Louise Lasser.

The end result was spectacular. We screened the spots to them proudly. Their first words were, "Are you out of your minds? Those people are ordinary!"

I said, "But that's the point, sir. Raleigh smokers will be looking at themselves feeling honored. Besides, they are wonderful-looking people, just like Raleigh smokers."

Flat-out rejection. Too bad Norman Lear's *All in the Family* was not even an idea back then. When Norman's risky series became a blockbuster and a template for gutsy humor with purposeful meaning, bigotry was challenged with satire, viewers laughing while gaining decent ideas subliminally. The agency was the loser, and I knew they'd feel silent shame when watching Archie Bunker. It would surely upset them for their mistake. The next idea was AT&T Long-distance Telephone; J. Walter Thompson was the agency.

We sold them on Jimmy Coco. His improv genius put all of us in stitches. He ad-libbed plots. "Ma, what do you mean I never call. I'm on the phone!" It was great to work with Jimmy again. The showstopper's improv in *Fragments* is what won him an Obie. We edited thirty- and sixty-second spots out of hours of gold. We dealt with a different agency, but the rebuff was the same. Arnie's regard for me hadn't tarnished. He knew I was onto something, even if they didn't.

The rejection of our edgy efforts hurt more when regulation pulled tobacco out of broadcast, taking half our cash flow with it. Sad for me, but worse for Arnie. His firm would fold. I had had enough with commercials anyway, especially for cigarettes. My son Richard was the one who shamed me into giving up the deadly habit. The way it happened is worth noting.

A dialogue began with David's lucky escape from messing with drugs. I was compelled to talk Richard out of any notion to test that water. I sat him down for a serious talk, my first words something like, "Drugs are dangerous. I don't know enough to enlighten you specifically, so all I can do is beg you to love yourself enough to avoid doing anything stupid, with the jury still out on how damaging it can be to your life."

He said, "Your credibility is seriously impaired. You caution me to take care of myself and not be stupid, just as you puff yourself to death."

I never smoked another cigarette and am grateful to my darling son. I tried to return the favor, but Richard, like so many addicted smokers, stopped and started again and again. I told him the key was to become a nonsmoker, thereby eliminating the stop-and-start syndrome. It didn't work, but at least he stayed away from drugs. I was sorry to leave Arnie after three good years. It frustrated me that my ideas seemed forever ahead of the curve. I left that world feeling refocused. I thought there must be a way to weave social justice into my work life.

# PART 9

# My Dad

I was in a dream. The phone rang so loud it woke me. "Is this Charlotte Schiff?

"Yes. Why? It's the middle of the night!"

"Is Maurice Grad your father?

"Yes, why do you want to know?"

"I'm sorry to tell you, ma'am. Your father is dead."

My breathing stopped. The telephone hum filled up the world. The cop added, "He was found not breathing,"

My hands shook. I scribbled his number on a scrap of paper. My voice was still talking, and all I heard was white noise. My fingers stiff and my knees buckled, I crumbled onto the rug and sat in a blank stare for a long time. With crippled hands, I gripped the phone and managed to dial.

"Judy. A cop called. Dad's dead. Oh my god, how will I tell the boys? They love him so."

My head was pounding. My chest hurt, and the nerves constricted in the back of my neck. Judy waited for me to continue. I gave her the police phone number, and then my throat closed. She said she'd call the cops to get the full story and call me back.

# Nobody Cared

Dad fell on the sidewalk on his way home at 10:30 p.m., right after he'd phoned me. He was lying under a tree until three in the morning. He died about an hour before they found him. I imagined my dad sprawled out on the sidewalk alive for hours, people stepping past him one by one without a glance. It's hard to remember anything but the shock. Judy and I were told to go to the morgue to identify his body. We scrambled out of the cab and walked into a gray building with cracked windows and an odor that made me gasp for air. A man in a lab coat took us into a room so cold I saw my breath. He pulled out the trolley with a tag on his bare foot that read "Maurice Grad." I covered my eyes.

"I don't want to see my dad dead."

He said, "Please, ladies, let's get this over with."

I looked at a colorless version of the face I loved. When the man in the white coat pushed my dad back into the metal wall, I nearly fainted. Outside we tried to recover our senses to place a call to our brother in Los Angeles. He said hello. I moved my mouth but made no sound.

"Who is this? If you don't talk, I'm hanging up."

I said, "It's me, Sammy. I have bad news. Dad suffered a heart attack! No, no, it was really bad. He died on the sidewalk at about two o'clock this morning. How will I tell the boys? He'd been lying there alive from ten thirty last night to three o'clock in the morning."

I had to tell his grandsons that their favorite person in the whole wide world was gone. With unblinking eyes fixated on nothingness, they stood like statues. They cried, they fought, they crumbled. Life without their champion who bounced coins off his bulging biceps, did magic tricks, rode the waves, built sandcastles, and taught them how to throw and catch a ball didn't seem possible. At my wit's end, I was empty of ideas to help them deal with the loss of their hero. At thirty-five, I was an orphan, my mother having died when I was twenty-nine.

I think about the gift she gave me before she died, her warning not to let Eddie ruin my life. Maybe she did care, but not as much as Dad.

One night watching the very first election returns on TV, my dad railed against a military man in the Oval office. When it was clear that Eisenhower had won in a landslide, he smashed a marble-topped table to smithereens by pounding it with a clenched fist to emphasize his point, shouting, "Ike will be the best president we ever had!" That was my dad, who, at weekday morning breakfasts, read aloud Westbrook Pegler's columns against FDR and Fala, his dog. His temples pulsed, and the color red rose up from his neck to his cheeks.

I said, "Daddy, why do you read what upsets you?"

He pointed to his heart and said, "This is where our emotions come from, dear one." Then he touched his head to add, "This is where we hear the other side to get the whole story."

Politics for me was a home away from home, a place where I was one of many but on a uniting mission—a mission that started at the kitchen table. I lived with a recurring dream of my dad's ritual morning prayers laying tefillin every day but Saturday.

*A five-year-old girl traipses after her father. He's in his silk pajamas and soft camel-hair robe, handsome and tall, his arms bulging with muscles, his hair shiny and black. The early morning light creeps in around the window shades. Looking like a movie star, he walks from his bedroom carrying a velvet bag.*

*She follows him, skipping to keep up with his long stride. She watches as he wraps a long leather strap around and around his left arm, starting at the wrist. Her eyes follow every move. When the strap reaches his shoulder, he pulls out a small box and places it at his hairline above his forehead. She's fixated as he puts a yarmulke on his head and a fringed shawl called a Tallis around his shoulders. He picks up a book and begins to read aloud as he walks slowly toward the front of the apartment, reading and rocking as he passes an old faded green velvet sofa. She doesn't understand the musical Hebrew words but feels his deep voice in her whole body.*

*He walks reading aloud, stops at a window, rolls up its shade, stares out, and goes on reading and rocking. She steps up to the window and looks out too. He does the same in the parlor, then into the front room, where he reads, still rocking. She follows his rhythm. He moves forward, still rocking, and seems to be singing those strange words. She is behind him still, closer. He walks into an alcove and reads, facing the east window. She turns her head and stares through the same glass. They walk side-by-side into the bedroom the little girl shares with her sister. He reads facing south. She is close by, still staring.*

The girl in this dream is me in the mystery of my dad's private reverie. I felt safe almost every morning, even in the freezing winter in our underheated home with its drafty windows. I didn't want to miss a thing. He explained why he changed direction with his prayers, first to the north, then south, east, and west. It was to be sure that for at least one prayer, he'd be facing God—a kind of movable Jewish Mecca. There was solace in my dad's reverie, a sense of peace wrapped in that leather strap. Our private closeness became the core of my existence.

# My Darling Dad

Did I tell you I was mad as hell at that cop who woke me by calling late at night? Well, that was nothing compared to how I felt when he told me my daddy was dead. I wandered about the empty apartment, feeling lost in space. I'd never again be his "cheerful little earful." There would be no chance to gain serenity following his legs as he said his morning prayers.

My heart broken, I found a way to do what nobody else was available or willing to do¾take on the agonizing protocol of a funeral, the burial in the cemetery, and setting up the "sitting Shiva," a sort of Jewish wake. At the funeral parlor where my mother's passing was covered, I was shocked to see Columbia Pictures' big shots who'd just ended Dad's position there. Their arrogance to show up enraged me. But I contained my fury by attending to the huge crowd of friends, relatives, and neighbors. The funeral service was personal—our rabbi speaking of Dad's generosity of spirit, loyalty, devotion to family, and faith. At the crumbled cemetery, I stood in the rain for the morbid ritual. In the limousine drive home for the Jewish repast and followed by many cars, we arrived in sullen silence to sit Shiva in stocking feet on wooden crates as we'd done for Ma. The cacophony of attempted condolences was deafening until dear friend Leah said the right words in the right way. Zaybar's delicatessen delivered cold cuts, potato salad, bagels, Nova, cheese, and jelly doughnuts¾Daddy's Sunday morning banquets, now gone forever. Chita Rivera brought guacamole and chips from downstairs, and gay friends supplied a variety of tasty gourmet snacks. Daddy's sister came early to pay her respects.

My aunt Berdie was a rarity in those days—a lawyer with a vagina. Her husband, Charles Schwartz, was a lead attorney with clients like Charlie Chaplin, Columbia Pictures, BMI and ASCAP music companies—on and on. Uncle Charlie forced her to forego the profession, making her one more female trapped in a soundless scream. At least, Uncle Charlie helped Dad with Columbia.

Our home was crowding up. Sam's friend Bob barged in. "Your dad was the cat's pajamas, a nifty dude!" He got that right, and I remembered when Bobby got pinched for fixing a college basketball game and spent a year in jail.

He said, "Come on, Sam, spill your dad's story with the mob."

I shuddered and left the crate for my velvet sofa with Judy, our feet resting on Moroccan pillows with downy softness. Sam and Bob near the parquet coffee table and my boys at a distance but in view, Sam said, "Okay, here's the deal¾a golden globe teenage boxer, hung around with Lepke Buchalter and 'Bugsy' Goldstein."

Bobby's ears perked up like a rabbit in a carrot patch. Then came Sam's tales of my dad's "black sheep" period, some of which he'd shared with his son about hit men and gangsters hanging around. I felt better about the mob talk when he spilled the reason our dad became a strong-arm cash collector at prohibition's illegal "juice joints." It was to keep our relatives safe, and it worked.

The hours passed, and fine folks wished us well and said goodbye. An old unkempt man showed up. "I came to pay my respects to Mo, a good egg— always there for me. If I was down and he had ten bucks, he'd give me five."

Sam asked how he knew our dad. "Oh, we were pals. My name is Al. Your dad was a real 'darp' who never said no."

Sam asked Al what he did. He said, "I get no contracts anymore." When asked what kind of contract, he straightened his back, brushed lint off his jacket, and said, "Oh, I'm a hit man—top of the line."

Bob asked, "Hey, man, how'd you play the duck on a guy?"

With downcast eyes, he said, "When my legs carried five slugs all the way from Broadway to Brooklyn, it was over!"

Al then said goodbye and left. My brother collapsed onto the couch. What was wrong? He wrapped his powerful arms around me, clutching harder than made any sense. He rose and walked away without a word. I let him go. My brother must have been juggling contradictory emotions. I think they erupted in his consciousness all at once. There were parallels, and he was wrestling with them. I worried he'd heard too much—his misadventures shooting dice in the schoolyard and borrowing cash from vendors with debts he had no way to satisfy.

One day, I picked up calf's liver. The Kosher butcher asked me, "Where's your brother?"

I said, "Home."

He said, "If the brat doesn't return the five dollars before six o'clock, he'll be sorry." Sam had a hard time in a tough vicinity where his parents had to live, an area confronted by a scary population requiring scary ways to survive dangerous hardship. The good news is that it seems to have made my dad strong. His toughness and brave acts with the mob to make his family safe vanished in a puff of smoke when he moved to the mainstream as director of short subjects at Columbia.

He knew his strengths and weaknesses and acted accordingly. Then he fell on the sidewalk with a heart attack, and nobody cared. Linda's words in *Death of a Salesman* on Willy Loman spoke to me: "He's not to fall in his grave like a dog. Attention must be paid to this person." The core of my existence.

My boys' lives were so connected to their granddad, it troubled me that I'd failed to share with him a rather typical story about David when he was seven. All of us were in the car, with Ed driving, Paul in a car bed, and Richard in a car seat. David wanted to check the veracity of a friend's version of the "facts of life." He did his best to spell it out neatly and ask if it was true. Ed and I exchanged glances. David was too young, but we'd pledged to tell the truth when asked the question. We did so with decorous and deliberate precision. Our attempt felt like a burlesque comedy act about daddies and mommies kissing and touching, then planting a seed in mommy's egg that grows inside for nine months to become a baby.

David turned to watch Richard suck on a Tootsie Pop and cocked his head toward me, and from lips curled in disgust, he asked, "Are you telling me that you and Daddy did that, three times?"

At that hilarious moment, I was hit by the notion that it was my job to help them care about the truth and know how to distinguish it from false facts.

Growing up in an alternative universe buried by lies worries me more about its effect on their future than I can find words to describe. They've been well educated academically, morally, and experientially, and that surely helps. But in a country swamped by untruths, corruption, and greed, it's very hard to find a proud path to the future.

What comforts me is that they believe in fairness, justice, and equality, and do their share supporting those essentials for the endurance of the society we crave. And what moves me is that they're doing much of that out of worry about their own children's future. What aggravates me most at this stage of my life is the feeling that there's not much more I can do to make even a small difference. I think feeling powerless began when I was struck down and spent three years trying to matter again—to myself, to my family and friends, and to the future. Writing my memoir seemed the best option.

# PART 10

# A New Life Begins!

rticles on a new technology surfaced in the trade magazines. There was this budding industry called cable television, named for the coaxial cable that delivered the signal directly to home and business television sets. Rabbit-ear antennas no longer needed to stop snow and bouncing pictures on the screen. Broadcasters contrived to halt the competitive challenge. They lobbied the FCC (Federal Communications Commission) to invent rules severe and costly enough to slow down or even stop the new industry in its tracks. I thought their scheme would backfire. The regulations may have been costly, but the services mandated would be popular.

Eventually, cable's multiplicity of channels would bring art, Beethoven, botany, and freethinking into the homes of people hungry for these and other things. Could it be a brave new world that fitted my life's intention to matter where it counts? One article talked of an FCC rule that every cable system had to dedicate one channel to Public Access, programmed by anybody on a "first come, first served" nondiscriminatory basis—no editorial intrusion allowed. With the First Amendment serving as my bible, the idea of free speech on television was right up my wishful alley. I convinced myself that my acquired skills would work well with the new technology of cable television. A forum for the voiceless felt like a gift from the goddesses watching over me.

Word was out that the Kingpin of Cable was looking for a secretary. His name was Irving Kahn, founder and CEO of TelePrompTer, the largest cable television operator in the country. Based in New York, they owned seventy-eight systems coast-to-coast. I marched into his offices with no appointment and talked the personnel officer into letting me meet Kahn. I entered his throne room, my high heels sinking into the plush carpet. Electronic devices covered his mahogany desk that faced two Barcelona leather chairs. Remembering the bizarre Screen Gems interview with Lloyd Burns, I stayed standing. That I'd barged in seemed to intrigue him.

He said, "You're no secretary. What are you doing here?" I searched for a safe answer when he motioned me to a chair and insisted I explain.

"Mr. Kahn, I'm here because cable television itself drew me to your door." I emphasized that the FCC's regulations mandating that every cable system provide at least one channel to Public Access was a boon to free speech for everyone, especially those denied a voice. I admitted that free speech is my passion and that TelePromp Ter seemed the best place for me to use my new skills to bring access to those in the margins. I told him I saw it as a match made in my idea of heaven.

I studied his face. My goal was to impress him with my ideas on how his company's challenges could be met more effectively. It was hard to convince him that complying with complex and costly regulatory demands could be a win all around. He stayed silent for a while, fiddling with his gadgets. I waited. When he pressed a button under his desk, stood up, and walked toward the wall, I had a scary notion that a bed might come down. The Memory of the Screen Gems fiasco made me wonder how I'd sidestep this one. He walked back and sat down in the chair next to me. "I have an idea," he said. "How about consulting for a month or two. You'd test the viability of your strategies to generate profit by complying with FCC rules for local program origination and Public Access. Do it on your own time for a thousand bucks a month plus expenses. If you pass the test, we'll talk about a proper job."

I took a stroll in the park. Dark clouds smothered the sunshine. Then it rained, but not enough to disturb my mental search for a plan. The drops fell lightly on my face and in my hair. It felt wonderful. I surrendered to the elements and tasted the rain, still thinking and searching. Shadows skipped among the trees as I pondered roads I'd taken since the speed-writing ad in the subway. As the rain devolved to a drizzle, the sun peeked through the clouds, and wet leaves glistened. I envisioned weaving civil rights, female liberation, and open media seamlessly into my professional life. I could do this through Public Access and local program origination.

Kahn's compensation offer was a mere honorarium. Hard-earned insight and strategic thinking for a pittance? Should I or should I not take this risk? I decided I needed a massage.

Naked under a sheet, I listened to mellow Tibetan music. Nothing soothes me more profoundly than an expert's deep exertion on every muscle in my body. When the masseur dug into sore points, the pain shocked me back to decision mode. My mind warned me that when lightning strikes, the rain pours down like an avalanche. I believed the broadcasters' fear of cable was why they scorned it. It might also be why they persuaded the FCC to find ways to impede its growth. In my opinion, the so-called horrendous regulations presented a good side. The rule would open television to people out of the mainstream. Subscriber count would grow, and it would enhance, not crush, cable television's future. The high point for me was Public Access for one and all. The very idea that my acquired skills could be used to make life better was mind-blowing. That I might give voice to boys in the hood, to elites in a mansion, to workers on a farm, or anyone, anywhere for that matter, seemed too good to be true.

I had to convince Kahn that there'd be profit. Many diverse areas had little programming to watch that spoke specifically to them, and cable operators were not wiring neighborhoods populated by people they surmised would be unlikely to subscribe. But access to programs relevant to culture, language, or lifestyle that are unavailable anywhere else would change that. Subscriber count would grow as fast as barrios, ghettos, and Chinatowns all over the country could be wired. This was just the beginning. Cable could carry a menu of channels in specific categories with the new name, "narrowcasting," for particular interests, cultures, ethnicities. I felt it was my job to persuade Kahn that wiring areas out of the mainstream would feed the bottom line, sustain and add franchises, and provide serious social benefit. I was hot to trot as never before. Broadcasters saw cable television as a "dumping ground for losers." They said it would "die on the vine"—or so they hoped. Broadcasters' antagonism opened the door wide for smart women to join an industry coined by them as a "pig in a poke." I needed an inside track.

I devised a sneaky scheme to eke out key secrets from a guy famous for winning franchises all over the country for ATC, a large cable company in Denver. I knew the process was political, which was my turf. I invited him to lunch. His renowned egomania would be my trump card. He strutted in as if he owned the place and approached my table as if he owned me. Good- looking in a stylish suit with a pocket-handkerchief to match his tie, he bowed and kissed my hand as if I were a queen. I tuned into his braggadocio as he rattled on about beating the competition, boast-to-boast.

I posed a question about the art of winning franchises in case one landed on my plate, so I asked, "How do you almost always win?"

His chest inflated from a deep breath drawn from a wiseass smile. "I've got it down cold. When I hit town, I locate the best call girl outfit and deliver the goods to the councilmen who make the decision. That's all it takes." Smiling like a poker player who just won a huge pot by bluffing out a straight with a pair of tens, he asked in a seductive tone, "How can I get to know you better?"

For the umpteenth time I asked myself, *What is it with these guys?* My answer to turn him off was, "We'll surely run into each other at the cable convention," staring at him with steely eyes, just as I'd done in my first harassment sidestep. This one was easier to escape as I'd arranged for the check to be charged to my account. I said, "Have a nice day," and stepped into the sunlight not quite bright enough to match my winning mood. My lunch hotshot was too full of himself to be aware that bragging to an unfamiliar female about winning council votes by pimping prostitutes was a bad idea.

On the day I was to report to Mr. Kahn on my successful foray into cable systems in six cities, I painted my face and dressed to the nines, arriving at the TelePrompTer building on Forty-Fourth Street at the appointed time. My mission had been to convince cable operators that local program origination and Public Access would reap benefits. I explained the value it would have with franchise authorities, along with a lift in subscriber count. At TelePrompTer systems in Santa Maria, California; Walla Walla, Washington, Galveston and Palestine, Texas; and Tuscaloosa, Alabama, I taught managers how to operate video cameras for local programming and low-cost ads for local merchants. I did that and then emphasized that reaching out to underserved communities would expand their base of subscribers.

I pointed out that people from other cultures are more likely to subscribe if some programming focuses on their special interests and that on the Public- Access channel they'd be welcome to speak their mind, sing a song, or even create a program. I explained that we would support them with helpful strategies and tactics. Most of all, I laid out the rules of operation for the public channel and how to work them. I entered Kahn's office glowing with pride of performance and high hopes for the future. He gestured me to a chair and stood over me with his fists planted on huge Buddha hips.

He said, "Do you have any idea of the furor you've caused with my managers?"

My lips quivered. Disquiet buckled my knees. I turned my head to make sure he hadn't locked the door with one of his remote gadgets. I stuttered, "F- f-furor? What are you t-t-talking about?"

Kahn switched on the answering machine: "If you send that awful woman here again, I quit." Then another, "That crazy bitch was telling me to make programs for spics and darkies. Can you beat that?"

Thrown thoroughly off-balance and trembling like a child being scolded, I said, "Mr. Kahn, I did what you told me to do: teach them how to serve minorities."

He said, "Well, dear girl, you have much to learn about the country in which you live. You brought them New York liberal arrogance with little regard for the persons you were speaking to, how they live, or what belief systems they follow. Big mistake."

I was angry at myself. My first instinct was to run but feeling a failure fired me up. I'd not let this screw-up stop me! I said, "Mr. Kahn, how awful! Thank you for the hard lesson." I felt the chair under me, so I knew I was still there. "Mr. Kahn, tell me I have not blown being part of your company?"

He struck a gentler tone to say, "Not necessarily, but you'll need to know who you're dealing with and respect issues and feelings that aren't yours. If you can't do that, it won't work. They don't want a crazy bitch dictating to them." His words stilled me like a windup doll whose battery went dead.

I sucked in my stomach, jutted out my chin, and with determination and a phony smile, I said, "Mr. Kahn, it's in your best interest to give me another crack at this."

He eased into the leather chair near me and said in an even more tender voice, "I've been charged with a crime, Charlotte. I'm facing a trial for bribery. A lousy $1,500 check to a crooked mayor who extorted me a year after I'd spent a fortune building a cable system before franchises were required. When the rules changed, he opened the bidding. I had two options: submit to his petty blackmail or...at a capital cost of $45,000...risk losing to a competitor and bankrupting my company. I caved, and Constance Baker Motley will judge the case. I need her to see me as a man plugged into minority issues. You're in that scene. I need someone smart to deal with people who are not and make us look good. Can you do that?"

I had to get it right. He'd been indicted for bribery and perjury and hoped to influence the verdict of a black judge whom I knew would not be influenced. Judge Motley had clerked for Supreme Court Justice Thurgood Marshall and was known to throw the book at white "fat cats" and take it easy on first offenders of color in nonviolent cases. I made it clear to Kahn that even if that were true, her decisions were based strictly on the law. Her rulings were respected, and her integrity unimpeachable. She might be pleased with Kahn's apparent new appreciation for minority issues, but it would have no impact on the verdict? Her Honor Motley was a revered adjudicator.

It was an awkward irony that Irving's misbegotten personal agenda gave me a crooked leg up to make good things happen. Kahn would win or lose on the facts of the case and his lawyers' skills. Any notion that he'd gain judicial advantage this way was misguided, and I told him so. I was hired and quickly rose to director of Public Access and liaison for regulatory and legal issues. I was promoted later on as director of franchise acquisitions. Destiny dictated that I do my best on the minority front even though Kahn's fate would be determined by the facts. My focus turned to Public Access, and I paid close attention to the trial.

An opportunity developed that could raise national attention to Public Access. I'd eavesdropped on a groupthink Clarence Jones held at his apartment with Amiri Baraka, Andrew Young, Jesse Jackson, Walter Fauntroy, and Wyatt Walker. I listened and heard what sounded like a chorus of Martin Kings, his disciples talking about the National Black Political Convention to be held in Gary, Indiana.

I entered their sanctuary on a break and asked a question. "If I can persuade TelePrompTer to play the convention in seventy-eight cable systems across the country, will you guys let me produce it?"

Amiri glared at me. "A white bitch to record our historic event?" I'd gone from crazy bitch to white bitch.

Looking at him, I said, "If it's recorded fully and interwoven with interviews conducted by Clarence with everyone from Malcolm X to John Lewis, what do you say? How else will people of all colors see and hear this convocation? And with a national election coming up?"

Amiri softened. "Sorry for the crack. I'm open to it, but I will have demands."

The event began on Friday night, March 10, 1972, and ended Sunday. We transmitted the historic gathering of three thousand delegates and seven thousand observers to the entire TelePrompTer universe coast to coast. Clarence's interviews were brilliant.

Representatives from Chicago PBS station CTTW were present. They asked me to create a ninety-minute documentary for an even broader national audience. They insisted the documentary be delivered Wednesday no later than 3:00 p.m. for a 7:30 p.m. airing. And I'd pledged authenticity to Amiri, which was a fine idea until Sunday morning. That's when the collective mood darkened, energy waned and excitement dissipated. Jesse Jackson's keynote speech the night before had used the gestation and delivery of a baby as a metaphor for a brand-new start on the move for equality. As the roaring soared to deafening heights, he screamed, "And now our baby is born. A new life begins!" Thunder, lightning, and brass bands must have resounded in everyone's imagination in the room and in living rooms everywhere. Jesse at his best! How would I secure authenticity? Sunday's morning of low energy sullied Saturday's high.

It came to me the documentary's ending had to be Jesse's speech. But how? To turn twenty hours into a ninety-minute documentary in less than three days, I napped on a cot in CTTW's editing space, my sleep was filled with stress. An idea woke me. I made a predawn call to my friend, Ossie Davis. "You know the promise I made to Amiri, Ossie. And you were still here when the conference faded on Sunday. I have to save the doc and honor its integrity. An idea came to me that the close could be a repeat of Jesse's speech, but without his voice. Instead, the audio could be a muted roar of the crescendo with your voice narrating

Frederick Douglass's lines that end with 'and power concedes nothing without a demand.' Would you record it? I'll send a messenger to your place who'll get it back to me at CTTW in Chicago. It has to be here no later than 1:00 p.m. on Wednesday. Can you do that?"

He said, "I can if you get off the damn phone, Charlotte!"

It aired, and Amiri was pleased. When the Kahn scandal ebbed at TelePrompTer, it may have been because of the raised fees I was able to get from various franchise authorities.

I was promoted to franchise director. My ego and my bank account were up for a party as we'd soon be back to acquisitions. My tactic to research the principal issues and priorities in a few target cities and tailor each proposal and pitch accordingly had worked well. My main focus was to replace pimping hookers for council members with authentic benefits based on local research—like interconnecting university campuses or networking local clinics with hospitals for medical advice to the uninsured and even adding programs from Taiwan for subscribers in various Chinatowns across the country. It was fun to receive calls and emails from subscribers asking why the heck we had subtitles in Chinese? It was that the writing is the same for both dialects, but a Mandarin-speaking person can't understand spoken Cantonese.

Still obsessed with free speech, what troubled me most was that those who needed it did not show up to speak, showcase a talent, or even view it at home. To fix this, I had to strike while Irving's self-serving iron was still hot. He quickly approved the Public Access Storefront Studio in Harlem that I proposed. A good deed with a double purpose is still a good deed. People of color are accustomed to exclusion. The best way to get them on board was to create a studio in their neighborhood. We'd equip and staff it well for those wanting to create programs or appear on Public Access. Locals would be guided and taught at no charge. Those wanting to be on camera or produce a program simply had to apply on a "first come, first served" basis. The word was out for the opening via radio, leaflets, and newspapers.

On the fateful day, I peered out of the front window hoping for a decent turnout. Faces were pressed against the glass—a dark young man wearing a knit skull cap on a hot summer day, a spinsterish lady, a stunning young woman who would pass easily as a *Vogue* model. Most were frowning. I looked closer at the guy in the hat and spotted a designer leather jacket over designer jeans and boots. The spinster lady was dressed like my Bubbi, and there were teenage girls in short skirts and knee-highs holding school books. Almost all were people of color. They looked curious but skeptical. Notices and press were clear that the Public-Access studio was for everyone, but this dark-skinned crowd was used to "everyone" not including them. When they spotted mirror images of dark-skinned folks with cameras and microphones, their eyes opened wide, as did their smiles.

It was a pivotal moment in my mission to make a difference and prove that good works can be good business. In a few weeks, the demographic mix upended from 70 percent white and the rest a potpourri of "other," to the opposite, white now in the minority. Benjamin Hooks, a noted civil rights champion, executive director of NAACP, and the first black commissioner of the FCC, honored the Public Access Storefront Studio in Harlem at its official launch. When subscriber count lifted and feature stories popped up in the press, I hoped we'd be a template for cable systems across the country.

As anticipated, Her Honor Motley threw the book at Kahn—a five-year sentence. The scandal sucked the juice out of the TelePrompTer brand. A major shareholder and notorious bully, Jack Kent Cooke, took over. He fired people based on their jobs' impact on the bottom line. Warned in advance that he was checking and crossing out names on a list of executives and staff and that franchises would not be in play until the brand recovered, I had "rate increases" added to my job description. Winning them meant profit. Bad effects from the scandal ebbed further as I won increase after increase. My successes made it easy for me to stay, but I wondered if I would escape the bully who disdained my very female existence.

Under the radar, I focused on Public Access for people unaccustomed to being seen and heard. When digital compression expanded the bandwidth for a greater multiplicity of channels, narrowcasting—that is, special interest versus mass appeal—got serious. Channels appeared for golf, fly-fishing, fashion runways, cooking, bowling, books—on and on with cultures and language specific to viewers. We sparked the beginning of limitless changes destined to convert coaxial cable grids to other technologies for even wider and more diverse content: first the internet and smartphones, and now streaming and almost everything wireless.

Having a civil rights hero like Clarence on my side meant a lot. His respect for me brought a new and welcome change. The role he played in the civil rights struggle filled me with pride, a union of things that mattered to both of us. We were married by his great friend Bertram Harnett, a New York State Supreme Court Justice. My new husband took me to the Plaza Hotel for our wedding night. We entered the presidential suite with its master bed covered with a mink spread. I was ready for a night to remember. He turned to me and said, blowing a kiss, "I'm off to a brief meeting, be back in no time." I was fast asleep whenever he returned. Marriage trouble on my wedding night? A sign, an omen! It served me right. He'd been full of disturbing surprises since I met him, and I began to recognize that the attraction was largely to an admired hero.

When challenged, he could dissuade me, but suspicious scar tissue didn't go away. What the hell could I have been thinking? Years of regret and therapy have led me to forgive myself for fantasizing about love for someone attached to the struggle in which I devoted much of my life. I simply couldn't figure it out, this blind spot of mine. And the worst of it is that I took my boys out of the neighborhood and home they loved so Clarence could be near his kids in Riverdale. I've made many mistakes as a parent, but none measure up to that outlandish one. And the worst of it was not clearing it with my boys ahead of time.

On moving day, I said again and again, "You're going to love living in a huge house in a great neighborhood with gardens and parks near the Hudson River." David was at Cal Arts College, which left Richard and Paul without their big brother to lean on. As we left our gorgeous, perfectly located, rent-stabilized apartment, what I was doing to them hit me like a ton of bricks.

The movers were busy taking down drapes and filling wardrobe cartons, and it was too late for second thoughts. I hated myself for depriving my sons of favorite rituals, like walking Clyde, their beloved border collie, through our perfect West Side and wondrous Central Park. An event took place in the middle of the move.

Clarence was summoned to Attica Prison by both sides of an uprising that very day. The inmates' spokesman and Governor Rockefeller separately reached out for him to help calm the storm. Clarence's heroic and risky role is detailed in the book *Blood in the Water*.

Our move and the first five days in Riverdale were spent unpacking, with me listening nervously to radio accounts, step by step, including Clarence reading the warden's terms to the inmates in Cell Block D and facing threats. He'd pulled out all the stops to persuade Governor Rockefeller to come down to ease the tension. I saw images of the guards standing on the prison walls holding automatic rifles. My friend Tom Wicker, *New York Times* columnist, was taking turns with Clarence pleading with the Governor to prevent violence. Rockefeller refused, and the guards gassed some of the prisoners, killing and wounding more.

There were some proud moments with the hero I'd married. I'm afraid I'd allowed my political passion to capture me at the expense of my sons—a false move I'm still hounded by. The decision to marry and move to Riverdale had caused a major disruption. Although Clarence added dimension to my life, getting to know fascinating people like Muhammad Ali, yet Clarence's hurtful episodes and dalliances were deeply troubling. But he invited me to the Rumble in the Jungle. I swallowed bile and said yes.

# The Rumble

*October 30, 1974*

I held onto Clarence's hand on the flight to Zaire (now the Democratic Republic of the Congo). My insides churned as I neared a country infamous for abusing women. Fetid, oppressive air hit me on the tarmac the moment we deplaned. We drove to the hotel in a taxi. I stared at the lush, wild foliage between and around shanties and lean-tos. Every few yards, a decrepit food shop or stall poked its marred face out of the scramble of wild flowers mixed with broken Coca-Cola bottles. A foul odor of filth wafted into the car. I just couldn't understand why Zaire had been the choice for Muhammad Ali's shot to regain the World Heavyweight Boxing Championship. I thought it a shame that Ali's return to his profession from exile would be at a post-colonial hell of a place.

Yes, my marriage had been crumbling from too-familiar faults and unkept promises, yet closeness to Clarence had enriched my life in many ways. He made me this offer that I couldn't refuse. I shudder at my duplicitous decision, but he'd invited me to go with him to Zaire for the Rumble in the Jungle, and I couldn't say no. I wanted to witness this historic event, especially after having watched Ali's defeat in the Fight of the Century against Joe Frazier at Madison Square Garden. I'd grown up with boxing.

In 1948, my family was the proud owner of the first TV set on the block. I'd find my dad sitting in my chair, the one at the head of a line of chairs arranged in size places. We used a magnifier in front of the seven-inch screen to make the picture larger. When you sat off-center, the images were like the squirrelly figures in circus mirrors. Sitting very close to the set, Dad was in the ring—chin down, elbows in, clenched fists up, and shoulders hunched. His head jerked suddenly as if he'd taken one on the jaw. I don't think he heard or even saw me. He was in the fight—left jab, right cross, fists clenched. His body folded as if he'd taken a hard one in the ribs, and then he jabbed the air ferociously.

His amateur serial knockouts happened long before I was born, but the game stayed with him in a big way and with me. I wondered how my dad could have hit people. He never laid a hand on Sammy. Dad and Ali shared a love of boxing along with a love of humanity. My dad was a scrappy kid who became a true gentleman. And Ali captured hearts inside and outside the ring. With the Rumble, he hoped to recapture his championship after a forced hiatus.

Both boxers had changed their names. My dad, Maurice Grad, boxed as Willie Cole, and Cassius Clay became Muhammad Ali. For both, empathy was core. I was glad to know Ali, who risked prison rather than fight in what he believed was an immoral war. He was a gentle man, a kind man. One time we were watching the news at the Essex House Hotel on Central Park South, Ali's hangout when in New York. Joe Garagiola finished the sports section, and then the anchor reported a shutdown of a Jewish senior home due to an overdue balloon payment of $75,000. Seniors were in tears, not knowing where they'd go. Ali moved to the adjoining room with an aide, then came back and sat down. Garagiola showed up on the screen unexpectedly to announce, "An anonymous donor has pledged $75,000. The home is saved." Ali said nothing. But we knew.

And one evening, Clarence and I strolled with Ali in Soho. I lost sight of him and then found him sitting on the curb next to a homeless man who kept saying no to Ali's urgent pleas to let him help—to take him to dinner, to find him a place to live and get him a job. The man grew angrier at every attempt to break through. Ali finally stood up, tears running down his cheeks. And then there was the time we'd joined Ali on a chartered flight to the Bahamas for an exhibition bout. A boy of about seventeen in a T-shirt and torn jeans appeared to have lost his mind when he found himself a few feet from the champ. He eased over sheepishly to tell Ali he was a big fan. Ali said, "Okay, then, you want to see the fight?" He happily flew with us. The champ won the fight handily, and at the announcement, Ali called the kid to stand with him as he accepted victory.

Choosing Zaire for the Rumble in the Jungle grew more outlandish at every turn. The devilish Don King must have struck a deal with monster Mobuto Sese Seko, dictator of the murderously oppressive regime. Ugly scenes flash before me about Don King's self-serving ambition for self-promotion. Was he just greedy or simply sociopathic to choose Zaire? I shook my head free of these questions, and at the InterContinental Hotel suite, I showered, shampooed, and towel-dried my "Jewfro." I selected a halter-topped pale- yellow playsuit. With Clarence in his Armani khakis, tank top, and sandals, I walked down to the curved poolside bar.

Standing tall was George Plimpton, dressed in preppy pink and plaid. I'd been to brainy parties in his home on the East River, but he wasn't always there. Sizing up the bar, I eyed Norman Mailer at the far end, his thick, curly salt-and-pepper hair with his shoulders rolling like a boxer. I trekked over to the great writer I loved and hated and sat on the stool next to him. He went on a tear that Mobutu's thugs confiscated his passport and denied his credentials. Commissioned to write the story for *Playboy*, he was enraged. On impulse, I invited him to dine with Plimpton, Clarence, John Daley, and me.

In the early evening, I slithered down the outside winding stairway, one hand lightly tracing the brass banister, the other at my waist in a saucy pose. I wore a strapless red-and-white cotton dress with ivory earrings and bracelets I'd bartered for with Mickey Mouse hats when in Zambia. The men spotted me. Their discourse ended in silent attention. When voices returned, it felt like applause. Then quickly, they went back to boy talk as if I was a mirage. Norman, still on that stool, drink in hand, was sharing fight stories with Daley's dad. I watched as they punctuated every phrase with a mock left hook or right uppercut. In the restaurant, Mailer moved from tepid to fierce, with swallow-by-swallow of alcohol. I slid down to hide, not knowing why.

No one knew me in Kinshasa. But a smashed Mailer continually accosted waiters and guests with tirades about his press credentials. He yelled for us to party, to go to a "native joint," as he blasted "Jambo!" into everyone's ears and faces, which was more of an insult than a greeting. Clarence and George lifted him by his elbows and carried him to the car. I sat next to the driver with Norman still yelling, "I want to party."

When the engine engaged, he passed out. In bed that night, I wondered if I had a role in this situation. What was my story with Clarence? Moving my family and then getting married generated problems hard to rationalize or ignore—for me and for my kids. Perhaps my delusion was that this epic event might reignite my feelings for a beautiful, articulate, proud man, and we'd have to move back to Manhattan. But I was not sorry to be a witness to history. On fight day, we crowded into an airless room in a community center to wait for the bus to the arena. Everyone seemed sad except the children. A little girl wanted to touch my hair, my linen dress, my white necklace. Her head was graced artfully with cornrows and beads. She took my breath away. I wanted to lift her to my lap but didn't dare.

On the bus ride to the ring, crowds were shouting, "Ali! *Bumaye*! Ali! *Bumaye*!" (Ali! Kill him!) There were sights and sounds—barefoot hordes of kids, graffiti on stone walls, and drawings by children, photos of Ali from magazines. Women were wrapped in vibrant African cloth, all yelling the African cheer, "Ali, *bumaye*!" We reached the arena, which was actually a large open space with rows of wooden benches in a semicircle. Soldiers stood at attention toe-to-toe, M16s at the ready. I needed a restroom! A sergeant ordered the soldiers to part. Choking on my own breath and shaking all over, I ran the gauntlet between two lines of menace, surrounded by a people freed by their ancestors and now tyrannized by a tyrant descendant as in Haiti. Before the contenders were announced, a hush fell on the noisy crowd. I gulped for air and daydreamed of my dad in a robe emblazoned with a name given him after a string of knockouts—Killer Willie Cole. In my imagination, he climbed over the ropes into the ring. Muhammad Ali's name bellowed out, wreaking havoc. The Greatest danced down to the ring, head high, his eyes laughing. The crowd noise reached a fever pitch. I couldn't hear my own screaming as I jumped up and down like a child given a two-wheeler for her birthday.

The crescendo didn't die down until the boxers met to shake hands and hear the rules. Ali was all cocky banter and bounce. George Foreman looked hard to beat. Not one pundit gave Ali a chance, not even his devoted sports commentator, Howard Cosell. But the champ jumped around the ring like a tap dancer with not a worry in the world. The bell rang. Jabs back and forth. Ali up against the ropes. He stayed there. What's wrong with him? Foreman pounded his body. Ali's handler, Bundini, and his crew screamed, "Get off the ropes, get off the ropes!" And they were not alone. Ali had to win this fight! But having been on the ropes for seven rounds, he had to knock Foreman down and out to win. The crowd cheered the man who symbolized their every fantasy. They shouted, "Get off the ropes," as if he were personally fighting the ghosts of colonialism. An ache gripped my gut. More blows to his body. The end was near.

Suddenly, Ali stood tall and soared away from the ropes. He jabbed, punched, and slammed Foreman in the head. He knocked him down and out. The fight was over. Ali was once more Heavyweight Champion of the World. Ali let Foreman exhaust himself—by punching him for eight punishing rounds. Once "wasted," as richly expressed by Norman Mailer, "a big projectile exactly the size of a fist in a glove drove into the middle of Foreman's mind, the best punch of the startled night, the blow Ali saved for a career." Rope-a-dope was born, but all that head-smashing would have its deadly way one day. Norman wrote masterful portraits of Mobuto's brutal regime and the bout. He revealed Ali's secret game plan his trainer knew nothing about. His words in *Playboy* captured the entire experience exactly as I'd lived it, particularly his killer chronicle of the macabre regime.

On the night of the bout, my sleep was so sound it was as if I'd been in the ring myself.

The next morning, Clarence and I enjoyed a private breakfast with Ali in his compound. His new wife, wrapped head-to-toe as Muslim tradition dictates, entered with their baby. Ali picked him up with one hand. He was excited and proud of his infant son and excited to regain the title on African turf. When we stepped out, a rush of boys pushed forward and formed a circle around Ali, their eyes popping out of their heads, their grins threatening to crack their cheeks. He began mock bouts with them and allowed himself to be knocked down several times. Dad used to do that with my boys while his grandsons touched his biceps in awe. When Ali fell, the boys laughed so hard it made them cry, as if they sensed the magic would leave when Ali did. His act of love to dissolve into the third-world life dictated by a monster was the only life they knew.

This is the tale of a gladiator whose balletic presence in the ring led to Ali's stammering weakness. In 1979, he suffered tremors and dissociation attributed to Parkinson's disease.

Regardless, he agreed to be in the TV series on CBS I was producing. It was for a segment shot on the film set of *Freedom Road,* a drama based on Howard Fast's book. Ali's voice was quivering and low, his bearing was stooped, and his walk was slightly crippled. The segment never aired.

I wish I'd tried harder to get CBS heavies to cave. I believed Ali's reputation transcended physical disabilities, and there was tragic grandeur in his decline. A universal symbol of masculine reflective glory, Ali didn't need air brushing. He was on television, red carpets, and the Olympics, his life full of parallels with *Freedom Road.* He knew slavery. The recent *Underground Railroad,* by Colson Whitehead, convinced me that no African American is absent the genes of slave ancestors. In the book, a "semi-freed" slave says to others, "Its scars will never fade… Everything you ever knew told you that freedom was a trick—yet here you are."

He added, "Still we run, tracking by the good full moon to sanctuary." I was sad that Ali's segment never aired, but it was my chance to say goodbye to a man I'm grateful to have known.

# PART 11

# Power Move

Dr. Martin Luther King Jr. was shot and killed in Memphis, Tennessee, on April 4, 1968. Millions who adored his mind, his devotion to justice, and his person were left with broken hearts. Angry riots exploded. Were we safe? Would the violence reach school playgrounds? We'd lived through JFK's murder, but Lyndon Johnson was there—the burly, vulgar, ruthless politician morphed instantly into a leader who pushed through civil rights legislation originated by JFK. With Tip O'Neill's master legislative help, LBJ achieved so much.

The civil rights struggle and the women's movement were important to me, to David, to Richard, and even to nine-year-old Paul. They knew I fought for higher teacher salaries and upward mobility and justice. And they marched with me against racism, the Vietnam War, and the awful treatment of women and people of color. We went to the be-ins in Central Park to be with hippies and flower people to feel their love, kindness, and devotion to peace. And it was time to include support for those ostracized for their sexual identity.

At dinner one night, twelve-year-old Richard didn't come home, Ed still with us then. The sky turned dark, and our son still hadn't shown up. I was on the verge of dialing 911, when the door opened. A tattered, tired boy shuffled in.

I screamed, "Where the hell were you?"

He answered, "Flo took me to the riots at Columbia University, Mom. Haven't you heard on the radio? It was about Vietnam and gyms only available to white kids."

Torn between anger and relief, I channeled my fury on a phone call to Flo. I scolded my brilliant African American lawyer/activist friend for taking him without asking me first.

She said, "My dear, Charlotte, I knew you would say 'no way.' Loosen up." Flo was so far left she teased me like she was talking to a hard conservative.

In truth, I was in the mix with her most of the time, with my older boys pretty much in it with me. I had also taken David to a Black Panther meeting at Flo's home and law office on Forty-Eighth Street. She was a fierce, proud woman. A priority among the myriad of her advocacies was to help the Black Panthers redeem themselves by feeding poor school kids.

My son said, "I'm so jealous," as we walked down her front steps to the street.

I asked, "Jealous of what?"

He said," Jealous of those guys. I wish I cared that much about something."

It took time for him to be aware of his character and skills that led to a deep sense of fairness and empathy that is loved by everyone who knows him, which has much to do with building an exceptional reputation, which is not so easy in Hollywood. I took the boys with me for marches, be-ins, and other events that opened their eyes and spirit. And Richard was taken by Flo to Columbia University to experience a riot. He loved it!

# A Better World?

Working on Bobby Kennedy's campaign, I shared a lot with my sons. I wanted them to see the candidate in Harlem surrounded by children looking up to him with adoring eyes. I wanted them to know that this man of privilege faced a moment of truth with poverty and racism that transformed him. I wanted them to know that he'd sent troops to protect Dr. King and his backers from a raging white mob and that he made it possible for James Meredith to be the first black student at Mississippi University. My boys went to public schools where whites were not a majority. In my mind, that was a way to grow up comfortable in the real world. It was the reason I'd chosen the West Side of New York to escape from the sterile suburbs.

Helping Robert Kennedy become president was a mission that meant the world to me. His belief system had evolved from elitist to humanitarian. Clarence Jones was still the stranger who'd flirted with me at Eddie's birthday party, the man I'd been running into from time to time, who was cochairman of Eugene McCarthy's New York campaign for president. One of my RFK tasks was to monitor his star-studded Madison Square Garden rally. Speeches, comedy riffs, and songs raised thunderous roars of approval. The crowd was thrilled by Peter, Paul, and Mary, Elaine May and Mike Nichols, Dustin Hoffman, Paul Newman, and Joanne Woodward. Then Clarence stepped up to the podium. He was handsome, tall, and exquisitely dressed. In a cadence influenced by Dr. King, he introduced the man of the moment to deafening applause. McCarthy strode onto center stage. Thousands rose to their feet, cheering with almost riotous ferocity. The candidate opened with "you people," then talked about "those people." People of color are familiar with white folks referring to them in that generalized, stale appellation. The roar from a stadium filled with "those people" and "you people" answered with a sigh. Many thousands of people must have felt the insult. The crowd silenced like an unwinding clock and departed silently at the end of his remarks. On my way out, I collided with Clarence. I couldn't resist.

"Why have you championed a candidate who says 'you people' to thousands of your brothers and sisters?"

He replied, "Let's have a drink and talk about it."

At Jimmy's, a political haunt, he told me he'd grown up in foster homes, studied on a scholarship at Columbia University, spent hours at Paul Robeson's knee, and was dishonorably discharged from the Army for questioning the Korean War. The decision was reversed in court with William Kunstler's help. Clarence was able to earn a law degree in Boston. I was awed. Then our mutual friend, Don Elliot, the man who'd brought Clarence to Ed's birthday party, was seeking marketing help. Jazz was underwater from the rock and roll tsunami.

Don retained me as a marketing consultant, which raised the flurry of contacts with him and Clarence. We became friends. On June 6, I stayed late at Kennedy campaign headquarters to be part of what we hoped would be the pivotal California primary victory. Our candidate won and made a heart- stirring speech. Reveling in his triumph, we slapped one another's backs, chanting, "Bobby's our next president!" All of us shouted wildly ecstatic cheers, and we hugged anyone near enough.

And then came a shriek so loud it broke through the noise. "Bobby was shot!" My eyes spun to the screen. At the sight of him on the Ambassador Hotel's pantry floor, my heart stopped. We all left in a slow, sullen walk out the door after copious weeping, the lucky ones clinging to their partners. Robert Francis Kennedy died the next night, twenty-six hours after he'd been shot. My family still included Ed on occasion, so we watched TV every minute of the terrible days and nights. I hugged my boys tight and had trouble finding the right words of comfort or reason. Ed reminded me we held tickets for that night at the Village Gate to see *Jacques Brel Is Alive and Well and Living in Paris*. I felt it impossible to go anywhere while mourning the hero meant to save the world and was shot to death at the vortex of his presidential victory. Ed pressed the issue, and with an entirely spent heart and mind and no desire to be at Ed's side, I swallowed a large glass of wine in a gulp and dragged my feet out of the house.

Waiting mindlessly in my seat, feeling crazy and ashamed, my eyes red and swollen, the first song was a relief. It told me this would not be a musical comedy. It was more a musical poem on how overwhelmingly sad life can be. The lyrics were about surviving deep anguish about family, death, drugs, war, love, hate, and the willfulness of time. I stopped waiting for a plot. The words connected to the grief I felt for the hero murdered. The show ended with "Carousel" and "If We Have Love." My sobbing was out of control. I felt weird to be in a theater on that night. But it was in Greenwich Village, the tiny city within a city that houses and honors its rebels and poets.

As Jacque Brel's heartfelt genius took over, the anger and tension that were smothering me were lifted a bit. There could have been no greater eulogy for the man set to be one of our greatest presidents. Still in a zone of desolation and wonder, finding some sanity helped. My sadness turned to fury when Democratic National Convention nominated Hubert Humphrey for President of the United States, and the Chicago police provoked a violent riot at the convention. Humphrey said nothing.

I'd not vote for a coward, and I wasn't alone. Our act resulted in the Nixon horror story. My regret never ends, and neither does the power of the lesson learned. I fill out and mail my ballot well before Election Day. The Nixon nightmare pales in comparison to days with a President Trump who neither knows nor cares about the country he was elected to run and protect. I keep wanting that human nightmare and his minions to be gone with the wind.

I hadn't understood Clarence's choice for president, but through business, political, and social ties and our respective roles in the civil rights struggle, we'd spent a lot of time together way before the Rumble. The idea of a weekend in Puerto Rico had come up on our first real date. Romance hadn't happened for over a year of a growing friendship. Old

San Juan was beautiful, but dining outdoors and looking at famished and scrawny dogs made it hard to chew, feeling like an animal abuser. They glared hungrily at my every move, their ratty tails wagging with hope. The next day at the rain forest, mosquitoes as hungry as the dogs satisfied their appetites mostly at my expense.

Dancing in a nightclub to "my music" became a romantic odyssey. The idea of making love with this brave, beautiful civil rights champion awakened my erotic self from a deep sleep. We loved the same music, and Clarence was a champion of issues I believed in. And he believed in me. It is said that love affairs that grow out of friendship enjoy sublime providence, and this friend was a respected attorney for Lorraine Hansberry and Martin Luther King, for whom he'd cowritten the Dream speech. Well integrated into white society, he was as comfortable in my world as I hoped to be in his. In my West Side apartment, I ran backers' auditions for *Raisin*, the musical version of Hansberry's great play, *Raisin in the Sun*. I did that for Clarence's dear friend, Bob Nemerof, her widower, who was destined to keep her great work alive.

Clarence was a partner in a major finance company, Carter, Berlind, and Weill—CBW. The move to Wall Street interfered with allegiance closer to his roots. In spite of his success at CBW, he devised a plan to revitalize Black media and entertainment in Harlem. *The Amsterdam News*, Apollo Theater, and radio stations WLIB and WBLS were his targets. With partners, he bought the paper first and became editor in chief and publisher. The fit for me felt profound.

I was in the Student Nonviolent Coordinating Committee, SNCC, and the Congress of Racial Equality, CORE, and on the board of the Negro Ensemble Company, run by Douglas Turner Ward. My activist life was spent as much with the Women's National Political Caucus, working on Bella Abzug's 1976 Senate race and being a Shirley Chisholm delegate when she ran for president in 1972. I was very proud of spiriting the right report on the National Women's Political

Conference in *Time* magazine. My old Professor Mordecai's counsel had heightened my drive to make a difference.

With my bushy black hair and eternally tanned skin, my relationship with Clarence created a "What is she?" storm on both sides of the racial aisle. One fine day, Edward Lewis, editor/publisher of *Essence* magazine, invited me to lunch at 21 Club. I sat with him and two female editors, wondering why they had invited me. Edward announced the purpose, "We'd like to do a cover story on you." I knew I had to maneuver my way out of an awkward moment, but correcting their mistake would be humiliating for all of us. When I started by thanking them for such an honor, they stepped on each other's lines saying the honor was theirs. My response was an apology for appearing to be but not being black. I heard a chorus say, "Oh, that doesn't matter." And then Edward said, "We are so impressed with all you've done for social justice, we want to do the story, anyway." They never did.

# The Oldest Crime

On a March day in 1975, I was at the top of the grand steps to the Manhattan Municipal Building on Center Street. A crowd spread out on the wide, steep steps eyeballing me, waiting for me to speak. My goose bumps were not from March's chilly wind; it was my nervous system on overdrive. With a microphone in my shaking hand, I said, "Today begins the first Women Against Rape Month in New York City. I beg you to understand that post-rape cruelty can be worse than rape itself. We must feel the victim's trauma. It starts with the assault, then it can get worse—with more assaults from police, hospital, spouse, father, boyfriend, and mother. Every one of them asking the worst questions: 'What did you do to provoke him?' 'What were you wearing?' Or a father saying, 'I can't look at you.'" I shouted to the growing crowd, "What are we going to do about this horror? First, the rape law must be changed. Second, we need to work to sensitize police, nurses, doctors, judges, family, and friends. Victims are in danger of never recovering if empathy and understanding are missing in the aftermath."

I kept at it, took a sip of water, and buttoned my jacket, ready to move on what females fear more than anything. A short break was called to fix a glitch in the audio system. I stood at the podium wondering what had happened to me that made rape an obsession? Nothing ever kept me from saying no, except cleverly sidestepping my first harassment. I searched my soul to find out what fixated me on the subject of rape. Suddenly, a buried memory came alive—a movie I'd seen in the fifties.

Rain poured down in sheets as I schlepped my pregnant self to a movie theater on Flatbush Avenue on a weekday afternoon. Ed was overseas, and I was living with my folks. I didn't know what was playing, but I needed a distraction. Then there was a happy surprise. On the marquis, it said the film was *Two Women* starring Sophia Loren, about a mother and daughter. About to be a mother myself, I was happy to see this movie.

The film began with the beautiful young widow and her thirteen-year-old daughter wending their long way home on foot from the safe countryside. World War II had ended. I loved the characters and looked forward to getting to Rome with them. Exhausted from climbing hills and walking great distances carrying their belongings on their backs, they stopped for the night at an abandoned church to sleep outside on some benches. Suddenly a horde of Moroccan French colonial troops filled the screen. I watched them capture and brutally rape the two women, forcing each of them to see the other's horror. Every cell in my body was on fire. My heart felt ripped open. The monsters left them bloody and unconscious. When they came to, they ran to a stream, frantically lifting their long skirts, wildly trying to splash clean their ravaged flesh.

The pain of knowing that no amount of water could cleanse them of this brutal violation was unbearable. It completely changed my view of the world and my role in it.

It was Betty Friedan and Gloria Steinem who had asked me to host the Women Against Rape launch. I asked, "Why me?" They said that as a noncelebrity, I would not engender the hostile press coverage they suffered. I was known as a cable television pioneer mostly by the industry, so the media was less likely to bury real news with sexist-driven female trivia. The great champions for women were right as we were given full, straight coverage.

When the failed audio was fixed, I cleared my throat and asked the first question: "What don't you like about the rape law?" There was no answer. In a calm tone, I helped them out: "In the current law, there can be no conviction unless someone has watched the rape. I ask you, do you think a witness who has done nothing to stop a sexual assault on a woman would be willing to show up in court to testify?" I added, "And what's beyond absurd is that the suspect's semen must be found in the vagina as well. Think about an innocent woman's life threatened, her body assaulted, her psyche traumatized, but by law, it isn't rape even if he wore a condom or didn't ejaculate." I explained that under the existing law, a conviction almost never happens. If New York State's rape law is changed, convictions would still be hard to get but at least possible.

The crowd stirred and started asking questions all at once. I did my best to keep order so that passion would stay focused on reform. The inauguration of Women Against Rape Month was meant to change the legal landscape and also to bring sensitivity to those who were part of the aftermath. Judy and I read Susan Brownmiller's *Against Our Will: Men, Women and Rape* a while back. I urged everyone in the crowd to read the book for its cold, hard truths. On rape, the book speaks for itself.

Judy was a feminist before it had a name. Having taken different life paths, our sisterly love was enlivened with awesome power when we met at a Women's Political Caucus meeting, thrilled to find ourselves on the same page. Judy earned a master's degree in clinical psychology in 1955 but couldn't stomach the absence of empathy among the mindless bureaucrats. She resigned and chose a nine-to-five job as a legal secretary for more money and less aggravation. She rewrote briefs, passed notes to her boss about points of law he'd overlooked at pretrial meetings, and rose to a paralegal on high speed.

At his office window one day, her boss pointed to the NYU School of Law building across the street. He said, "Judy, if you're not at the front door tomorrow morning at 8:00 a.m. to take the admissions test, you're fired." It's hard to imagine a male attorney in 1959 saying that to a female, especially an obese female, no matter how smart she is. But at the risk of losing an exceptional paralegal, he did exactly that.

She scored 800 out of a possible 800 and was given a full scholarship, plus a significant stipend to take her through law school. She attended classes at night to keep her day job. At her graduation in 1962, Judith Grad, editor of *Law Review*, was named again as number one in every category but one, social service. The irony of that struck me. She was heralded on top of both her day and night classes. And when we changed the New York State rape law, she was chief of opinions and legislation for NYC Corporation Council. She also wrote and passed the first gay rights act.

I asked her help in revising the existing rape law with amendments to exclude the need for an eyewitness or semen residue. My brilliant big sister and I flew to Albany. We proceeded to the legislative building to lobby for votes on the amendments to the rape statute. I talked to the legislators and their staff and kept the pitch humming. Some were my friends in the Democrat Reform Movement, but I also crossed the infamous aisle. The new law passed by a generous, bipartisan margin. Judy and I were honored with plaques from Governor Hugh Carey.

Felix Rohatyn, who'd saved New York from bankruptcy, nominated me to serve on New York City's Employment Council. And I worked with groups to encourage enlightened rape victim protocols and treatments. Nurses and doctors were sensitized in how to treat victims, and I begged them that they do the same for friends and families. It mattered a lot to make it at least possible for a rapist to be convicted. Unfortunately, so many women and girls still are controlled, brutalized, shamed, or threatened into submission and silence. We, as a society, have continued to improve rules and treatment, and it thrills me to the core that women are rising up and speaking out now and with #Me Too on their side. It brings a real chance for abusers to be punished appropriately for all kinds of brutal and hurtful misconduct.

The hope is that greater awareness will push such men into decency. If and when harassment happens, women need to report it or shut it down early by saying, "Do not talk to or touch me that way. If you don't stop, I will have to report you and resign." All women need to be able to speak up without fear of retribution. I have no idea what had moved me to fake out my Screen Gems/Columbia Pictures boss so brazenly, but his apologies led me to stand my ground on subsequent insults by men in other companies, and most of the time, successfully. Sexual misconduct has been a constant in Corporate America and most male-empowered settings.

On my next job, three desperate telephone operators came to me sobbing about their boss's ugly harassment. He'd frightened the married twenty-year- old into submitting, and she was terrified to tell her husband for fear he might kill the brute. The other two young women fought hard to keep him away, but their anxiety and abject fear were affecting their lives dramatically. Using my persuasive skills at the top, the brass would not allow charges to be brought against the disgusting offender. At least I got him fired with no references. And with the amended rape law, there's hope some sex offenders will be charged and even convicted when guilty.

In *The New York Times*, columnist Nicholas Kristof wrote, "Ever since Eve bit an apple in the Garden of Eden, God's been rough on women."

Not a shocking notion to me. I've always seen Eve as the victim and Adam the villain.

# PART 12

# Get Outta My Way!

I'd returned very late one night from the Cannes Film Festival and was dead asleep when the phone rang. It was Dick Galkin, the boss at Sterling, the other cable system. Exhausted and angry, I asked why he called so early. He said, "We need to talk. How soon can you be in my office?" I'd barged into his office months before to tell him then to get out of my way! His pulsing temples told me I'd hit a nerve when I laid out why he and his associates needed to stay out of sight until I finished a presentation to the New York Board of Estimate and Franchise Commission to raise subscriber fees. If that demand bothered him, I wondered why he waited so long to complain about it. I told him then that if I won a rate increase for TelePrompTer, it would benefit Sterling automatically. I reminded him of Sterling's bad karma with the city and subscribers and that they needed to stay out of my way or we'd both lose.

My final words at the time were, "Do you or don't you want a rate increase? If you do, it won't happen unless you're neither seen nor heard. The franchise rules are clear: rate increase awarded to TelePrompTer automatically applies to Sterling and vice versa." You're in trouble and wisely didn't seek a rate increase. I'd done for TPT what hadn't been done for Sterling. The process for acquiring franchises or rate increases is basically the same. To the Board of Estimate, I presented a success story, a two-day procession of constituents brimming with anecdotes that glorified cable's contribution to their lives and businesses. They praised the service, the programming, and their time with Public Access. It had to be an increase for both companies or neither. I was shocked when Galkin admitted that after having been warned to stay away, he and Dick Munro, the head of Time's growing video division, had taken the risk of watching the spectacle hiding on the sidelines. *Time Inc.* was about to take full ownership of Sterling and change its name to Manhattan Cable Television, MCTV. His eyes brightened, and his cheeks flushed as he expressed gratitude for what I had achieved. And why not? It was an unprecedented 50 percent increase.

I finally figured out what was behind the dawn phone call. If I had it right, the timing was fortuitous. I'd been seeking a way out of TelePrompTer since the misogynist bully had taken over the company. And there were other options now. I'd just returned from Cannes, where I was the guest of chairman Steve Ross, founder of Warner Communications, for its fiftieth- anniversary celebration. When asked to lunch with him at the Majestic, he interrogated me intensely on cable television. It felt like an audition. He revealed that his company's toe was in the cable water, and he was hoping I'd help him learn how to swim in it.

With that on my mind while talking to Galkin, I asked, "What makes you think I'd leave a company with seventy-eight cable systems across the country to be vice president of a single system with only fifty thousand subscribers?"

# Time Inc.

Galkin called Dick Munro. "I'm talking to Charlotte. I think you should join us." Munro entered, shook my hand, and said in a soft voice, "Charlotte dear, it's *Time Inc.* that wants you. We have big plans for cable television, and you will be an integral part of that."

*Time Inc.*, that's a different story. When wholly owned by *Time Inc.*, MCTV was to be its flagship for a national cable television expansion. I liked the prospect of being part of an institution I revered. They were the publishers of *Time, Life, Fortune, Money, Sports Illustrated,* and *People.* If I would have reported directly to Steve Ross, I might have hesitated, but I'd met with the man who would be my boss at Warner. He was a sexist. No contest! I made a deal and was to start on the same day as MCTV's new president, Nicholas J. Nicholas Jr., who for eight years had been *Time Inc.*'s finance guy, reporting directly to President James Shepley. I phoned him and made a date. I stood at his closed office door in the Time-Life Building for a long time before opening it. He was the chosen one, not me. He didn't even know me. Shepley picked his right-hand financial genius to run the cable company, and I was being forced down the genius's throat. I'd seen that movie more than once and never liked it. I needed to do something before our first day in a new job. I needed to meet him and talk things over.

He was sitting at a desk covered in family pictures, his feet on its top, straddling a monitor with stock prices rolling down the screen. He lifted his glance from financial news with a twinkle in his blue eyes and a gentle smile. When he stood up, I felt like an aging giant, struck by how much younger and shorter he was. A pleased expression on his good-looking face put me at ease. He gestured for me to take a seat and sat down again. He was warm, likable, and a bit baffled. I thought of how little, if anything, he knew about cable television. A financial genius for a magazine company, he seemed as nervous about this move as I was.

I said, "I know Sterling will soon be MCTV, and I'm familiar with the cable television industry at large, Nick. We have work to do. We need to trust each other, and that's why I'm here."

He leaped to his feet again, this time startling me. He took my hand and said, "Good idea. You want what I want. Let's talk." We enjoyed a chummy chat for nearly an hour.

In the elevator, I spoke to myself in the mirror. "Hey, Nick knows the numbers. I know cable television. He's a money man, and I'm a strategist. I'll give him the inside scoop on cable. He'll make me smart about *Time Inc.*" The mirror smiled back.

I wrote a private and confidential memo to Nick, laying out the hard truth of MCTV's lousy reputation with its customers and the City Franchise Bureau. I outlined the false moves and missed opportunities and spelled out the key vulnerability: the license to build and operate cable systems, with the franchise always at stake. Sterling had not fulfilled the FCC regulatory mandates so far. There were cardinal blunders with the city, and poor customer service that put the franchise in jeopardy. My memo was addressed only to Nick. Home Box Office had been launched by MCTV in New York in 1974 before I came on board. I learned that it had sold like pancakes but was facing a rush of disconnects. I wondered why. To find out, I asked Nick to authorize some focus groups. What I learned from them was that the cause and effect of the turnaround was not the product. It was the sales pitch. I decided to create a strategy for a remarketing plan along with an agenda to uplift our standing with the city's authorities. Nick set up my first meeting with President James Shepley, the man who ran the most significant magazine company in America, a man without a college degree who rose from reporter to editor of *Sports Illustrated* and ultimately the corporation's highest-ranking executive, second only to Andrew Heiskell, the Chairman of the Board. Nick and I shared a taxi to the Time-Life Building and waited with several other big wigs in Dick Munro's office for a call from President Shepley's secretary.

She announced precisely at what moment to begin a "leisurely stroll" to his conference room to arrive at a specified time. I didn't know whether to laugh or run away. I felt like I was in a Woody Allen movie. We followed the dictate and arrived at his conference room at precisely

10:25 a.m. as ordered. I saw him at the far end of a long table, head bowed over some papers, spectacles on the tip of his nose. I walked in and sat down next to him. No one followed. Something was wrong with this picture. Shepley never raised his head to acknowledge my existence. I must have broken rules that Nick never shared with me. I'd entered the room before signaled to do so by "The Man." There probably was a pecking order, and even worse, I'd not been beckoned to come in or sit down at all. A bolt of lightning hit my brain! I was guilty of what felt worse than treason. I had strolled in and sat down next to the head guy. My eyes fixed on my highly critical private and confidential memo sitting at Shepley's fingertips, the margins scribbled with notes in red ink.

The men crowded at the conference door filed in, clearly taking predesignated seats at the table glaring at me with disdain from every pair of eyes but Nick's. Hedley Donovan, successor to founder Henry Luce, looked really angry. Munro instructed my boss to begin. Nick broadly outlined the purpose of the meeting. Shepley was yet to raise his head or look at me.

With his reading glasses still balanced precariously on his nose, he spoke to the group as he stared at the memo, his fingers folding its corners: "So, Nick, you want me to have dinner with Morris Tarshis. Is that what this is about? I can do that." He spoke as if he was ending the meeting, his hands on the edge of the table as he was about to rise.

I got up before he did to exclaim, "No, no, Mr. Shepley, you are not to have dinner with Morris! Not until you get up to speed about cable television," I added emphatically. "Morris Tarshis carries our fate in his hands. He has made the cable universe his life's work. To win his favor, you must be on top of the issues when you dine with him."

The president's chin rose. He swept the reading glasses off his nose as if a hornet had landed on it, looked straight at me with shimmering greenish eyes, and said, "Hello, Charlotte. How do we go about this?"

Like Little Orphan Annie, feeling glad all over, I said, "You should start by reading the cable trades. I'll get back issues to you along with comprehensive archived articles. And if you like, I'll highlight the most relevant sections. And I would be honored if you'd ask me any questions you may have along the way."

We began a beautiful business friendship. Allies up high are always welcome. My behavior stunned everyone in the room but Nick.

Later in his office, his feet, as always, were up on the desk and now revealing a hole in the sole of a shoe. He asked, "What can I do for you?"

I entreated him to please explain why he credited me with so much at the meeting and explained, "I'm used to my work being hidden from the big bosses, and never before experienced such recognition inside a big company."

With a smile and glimmering eyes, he replied, "Charlotte, it is in my best interest for you to shine. As I'm MCTV's president now, anything my vice president does credits me. Don't you get that?"

I got it all right. A lesson in management I employed for the rest of my career. And Shepley took on the study of cable television the way a college freshman crams for a final exam. He read the trades and the archival selections I sent him, called me with questions, challenged my answers, and set up private lunches for talks, and after nearly two months, he knew enough for me to say, "You're ready. It's time to dine with Morris. Both of you will enjoy this long overdue rendezvous. I'll send you the relevant talking points and sensibilities." The honey-blond Anglo-Saxon sail-racing champion and the obese sedentary man with the *Yiddishe kop* had dinner. They clicked. MCTV was now on the right track with the authorities.

I'd been learning about Home Box Office, cable's first premium network for which subscribers had to pay an added monthly fee. HBO was an experiment fighting for its life in a magazine company. Nick sent me to represent him at a meeting of Time's division chiefs. The top magazine gurus were not used to competing for resources with what they called "a pig in a poke." I listened intently to HBO's champion, Jerry Levin, as he made his case. I learned from his Olympic fight for the life of HBO and had won my own shot at launching it again in New York.

# Do or Die

Had they made a costly mistake? I'd learned enough from the focus groups Nick had approved, followed by expensive quantified analysis to explain the cause and effect of the downturn. I'd learned enough. I knew what went wrong without spending another $50,000 to generate a hypothesis. As I mentioned before, the cause was not bad product. It was the sales pitch. I presented my analysis and a proposed game plan to Nick. He liked the premise and instructed me to put my ideas into a presentation for the top brass. He wanted me to explain why so many HBO subscribers canceled the service and to provide a corrective strategy to remarket. I had not made such a presentation for top management anywhere, ever, so I enlisted help to create a presentation I hoped would include visuals to support my words.

On D-Day, I arrived at the senior executive conference room with my words on paper and graphic displays from the art department. My heart was pounding. The first thing I saw when I stepped in was a wall-sized window on one side and a line of eight men who looked like Boston Brahmins sitting still as statues on the opposite side. And there was Nick, my Greek boss. He gave me a "don't be scared" squeeze and escorted me to a seat.

President Shepley nodded agreeably to me. The other men rolled their eyes, tightened their ties, and glared at me in a way that told me they wished to be somewhere else. They saw me and the medium I represented as the enemy of print, which was actually a prescient concern. I wondered if they understood that *Time Inc.* would have to reinvent itself to fit into the future. I needed to persuade them to adopt my plan for healing HBO's wounds incurred by a misguided New York launch. Jim Shepley, master of the *Time Inc.* universe, extended his arm toward me as if asking me to dance. I shuddered forward in a cream-colored silk blouse over a brown suede skirt. My armpits were drenched, the blouse sticking to my bra. I tugged to separate it from my body. Shepley smiled. I sighed, hoping for a fair fight. He broke the silence to announce that I was about to present a plan to turn things around. He pointed out that the HBO flagship launch in Manhattan had started strong but that tons of subscribers were jumping ship. The chiefs were obliged to listen to the big-mouthed Jewish radical feminist married to a Black civil rights champion. Not only was I way out of their league, they perceived me, a female cable television pioneer, as a threat to their supremacy.

The stakes seemed higher than I'd expected when I met their stares. Primal fear was in the room, a fear exacerbated by a threat that, if not stopped, cable television could be the death knell for print. My bones were chilled by their barefaced hostility. I clenched my manicured hands into fists as if about to smash their heads together. Was there a way to beat some sense into stratified, sanctified, status quo consciousness? They surely wanted to nullify me, the pesky pain in the butt who just wouldn't go away. I thought cable television was the young horse I could ride. I didn't know it would take me to an institution and industry deeply invested in the past. I was glad that Time's Brass Knuckles Shepley was the heavyweight. So far, he hadn't used his brass knuckles on me. I could tell from our first encounter that this man who'd risen from the ranks was not afraid of the future. But my proposal was missing a critical piece—validation. I did not have the skill to support my projections empirically. I was not favored with financial wisdom or the skill to reliably research relevant data. How would I overcome the absence of proof positive? Shepley's reputation was for zeroing in on fatal flaws, however well hidden. I sucked in a breath. I was afraid it would stay down. Then my chest relaxed with resolve to hide what was absent with "smoke and mirrors." It was do-or-die time.

Shepley's voice broke my head trip. "Charlotte, let's get this show on the road." I rose and held onto the stand to stay upright, my notes patiently awaiting my attention, my anxiety palpitating, my verbal swirling and weaving began. I was talking them through each step. It was important to let them know that focus group participants who'd canceled HBO did not complain about the programming. It was the salesmen's false promises they resented. They had been sold on the idea that, with HBO, they'd save money normally spent for movie theater tickets, popcorn, parking, and babysitters. The focus groups were filled with former subscribers who canceled because the promise was false.

I spelled out what the sales strategy should be: First, forget the saved money promise. Second, fill their minds with HBO's exclusive, true benefits and the ability to choose movies, comedy, documentaries, and specials that appeal and can be viewed at a time of their choice, in their own home, in bed or while cooking supper. Third, employ an entirely different sales commission policy that ties commissions to customer longevity. Subscribers need to be enticed and reminded not to miss exclusive specials by the salesperson that signed them up. When my presentation ended, Shepley hunched over, head in hands, distractedly fiddling with the ends of his hair in some kind of trance. Was he searching for a way to fire me without hurting my feelings? Maybe it was hard to fire someone he'd admired. I summoned the last iota of energy to keep calm or at least to look calm.

He butted into my thoughts: "That's an impressive churn reduction you're projecting, Charlotte. Very ambitious. Trouble is, I neither saw nor heard anything that supports your estimate for such a high turnaround. Please elaborate on your assumptions."

*Brass Knuckles* lived up to his reputation. He'd listened attentively to a thirty-five-minute presentation without interrupting, and his penetrating mind radiated right through the smoke to the key flaw. I had promised a 25 percent churn reduction. He wanted to know how the hell I was going to reach that ambitious goal. What does one say when one has nothing to say but has to say something? The silence challenged me. In a calm, strong voice, my first words were, "Because I can! Let me explain." Attention was paid. I paused to let my cocky claim sink in. Then I continued, "The focus groups told me what I needed to know. My gut did the rest. (Disconnects hadn't come from dissatisfaction with the program fare. It came from a promise not actuated. We need to replace that promise with HBO's greatest asset, which is convenience. The wherewithal to watch chosen programs from a couch, a bed, or a favorite club chair at whatever day or time that suits the subscriber. And to ensure the subscriber satisfaction quotient to stay high, the revised commission structure would encourage the salespeople to stay in touch with their subscribers using promotional material we would supply, like a giant picturesque postcard about an exclusive one-night-only special." In a stronger voice, I said, "My projections are actually conservative, not ambitious."

"Okay, Charlotte, proceed with your plan, and next year at this time, you will report the results. We'll see how close you've come to your estimates and where we go from there."

Shepley strode over to thank me for my hard work with a firm handshake. He wished me a pleasant weekend smiling broadly. He'd given me a whole year to prove myself and hadn't gone for my jugular. I'd won the toss, but what was on the other side of the coin. I looked on the bright side. At our very first meeting, Shepley hadn't acknowledged that I was even there until I drummed up the gall to do the right thing: tell it like it is. I'd missed a bullet but was not in the mood to celebrate. Maybe it was the absurdity of a test year as a win that kept me at bay from feeling a victor. The naysayers might use the year to find a way to get rid of the pushy broad. I needed fresh air. Getting out of the lobby against heavy human lunch traffic was a challenge.

Free at last, I decided on a long stroll. I walked up and down the streets of Manhattan, where I belonged. This city was a good place to hunt for answers clouded by uncertainty. I turned toward Fifth Avenue for a browse in my favorite bookstore.

The midday sun was so brutal, my light-sensitive eyes shut down. I couldn't find my sunglasses in my bag, which was big enough to carry horse feed. I proceeded with hand over eyes to shield against the glare. At last, inside the darkly paneled Rizzoli Bookstore, my haven, I flipped through a new communications magazine and found an article by Leonard Cohen of *The New York Times* about the interactive capabilities of tomorrow's television. Wow! I felt certain my dreams of the future would come true. I thought, *I can do this.*

Although I exceeded my projections before the year was up, the do-or-die episode did teach me to never storm the battlements without the right weapons. Shooting from the hip brought me far, but I wouldn't go against them again until I'd learned their vocabulary. It made me think of the failure of my first marriage to a man who talked too much, drank too much, messed around too much, and was mean on Mondays.

The boys and I lived on our own in the Langham on Central Park West. From our terrace, I watched rust-colored leaves tumble to the ground in a drizzle, the sidewalk shimmering in a golden glow. We were back in the neighborhood we loved. I'd transferred Paul to Walden High School, chosen for its artistic emphasis that suited his creative spirit. Richard was at the City College Davis Center for the Arts, where I watched plays he directed. His artistry was a thrill to witness. I visited David at the California Institute for the Arts, where he was studying world music and loving it. My young men were doing well. I was ready to take on the business of business school.

But still feeling the strain of making my case to corporate masters, I asked my boss, "Nick, do you have a minute? I want to talk about taking an Executive MBA Program."

He sat up straight. "You do? Marvelous! We'll send you to Columbia if you pass the test."

The video division became *Time Inc.*'s highest earner. The magazine group had reason to be worried. Public access was the free speech magnet that drew me to cable television. It was a surprise that Red Burns, widow of Lloyd Burns, was codirector of the Alternate Media Center affiliated with NYU and heavily engaged in Public Access. She was dean of a graduate division on telecommunications. We'd been at odds when I worked for Lloyd at Screen Gems but were now on the same mission to help New Yorkers perform, do a talk show, televise a ballgame in a schoolyard, read their own poetry, and all on the Public-Access channel.

At MCTV, I devised an internship program for college students. My son Paul still, in high school, begged to be included. I said, "Sorry, darling, it's for college kids."

On his knees, he pleaded, "Mom, please. You won't be sorry, I promise."

I caved, and he did so well he was hired part-time at NYU by a grateful Red Burns, who later hired me as adjunct professor.

Since including my boys in my work felt very good, I arranged a summer job with the cable installers for Richard. Offended by the rude verbal epithets the crew hurled from the truck at innocent women (I must have done a good job on that score), he switched to the stock room. He didn't like it there either and wanted to quit. I begged him not to. He bravely made it to the end and rewarded himself with a trip to visit his best friend in Colorado.

I wrangled corporate funding for Public Access, but no one knew how users would find the cash to keep at it when resources ran out. An idea surfaced. Why not add a leased access channel, allowing commercials to cover producers' expenses while giving an advertising path to local shops? Commissioner Morris Tarshis approved the plan, but I needed verbal jujitsu to sell it to magazine magnates seething at "indiscriminate babel." They hated Public Access, and who could blame them? What they viewed as "amateur drivel" was not on their polished menu. We needed to know if a noodle shop in Chinatown or a record store on Broadway would buy cheap entry to visibility on television. Of course, *Time Inc.* feared a free for all kidnapping of space for random fare as ordered by the FCC. I must admit that it should have occurred to me that censor-free leased access would attract a sleazy side that might put us in a pickle. And it did.

# Porno Political Pickle

*Screw* magazine sullied the landscape with its very first program, *The Underground Tonight Show*, a titillating, offending, and shocking spoof of a late night popular program on broadcast TV. *Screw* magazine had a show on a cable system owned by *Time Inc.*? Yes, it was first come, first served, wasn't it? And yes, it is nondiscriminatory, and free, too.

Publisher Al Goldstein had ripped the lid off Pandora's box. Very quickly, a new offender called Ugly George surfaced. He was a weirdo traveling New York with a half-inch Porta-Pak (newfangled video camera) on his shoulder, stopping vulnerable young women and enticing them on a false pretext of social science to be interviewed half-naked. A feminist mom of three boys, I felt like a hypocrite to be, protecting First Amendment rights for two peddlers of female objectification. Goldstein offered a freewheeling series of salacious exploitation. Ugly George posed as a college professor to persuade innocents to expose their low self-esteem and their breasts. The FCC forbade editorial intrusion on Public Access. Free speech being my gut issue, to quiet corporate nerves, I struck a deal with Goldstein. My leverage was a fake threat to turn him off if he didn't go along with some discretion. We agreed to edit what was beyond the pale and to play it after midnight. *Time Inc.* might face FCC wrath if we didn't find a way to abide by the rules.

*Screw* magazine's publisher dropped the other shoe with a new series, *Midnight Blue*. Escort services and erotic toys were advertised, and near-naked women sold sex ambiguously enough to be legal. Goldstein put out press releases with ribald boasts. I had to protect the decent Public-Access users—homeless street philosophers, teenage film critics, a Frank Sinatra idolater singing his songs, civil rights advocates pleading for fair housing, rape victims brave enough to go public with their stories to help others. Today the #MeToo movement makes speaking up easier, but it still takes courage to come forward. Too often in the work world, the victim is fired, not the villain.

And then Goldstein sent me a tape I thought too hot to handle. I begged Nick to look at it and tell me what to do. He stiffened his shoulders like the marine he once was and said, "No, this is your baby." There was no other option. I fast-forwarded to the troubling segment, a female sexuality panel hosted by sex therapist Betty Dodson and followed by four naked women on mats, with another directing sex exercises. The tape ended with closeups of the climactic consequences.

On obscenity, judges disagree—different strokes for different judicial folks. Supreme Court decisions call for the following test to define obscenity: "(a) whether the average person, applying contemporary community standards, would find that the work, taken as a whole, appeals to the prurient interest; (b) whether the work depicts or describes, in a patently offensive way, sexual conduct specifically defined by the applicable state law; and (c) whether the work, taken as a whole, lacks serious literary, artistic, political or scientific value."

With New York my hometown, I would challenge anyone to chart community standards, the issue considered core to the Supreme Court's decision.

I said, "Nick, tell me what to do."

He said, "Take it to the top."

Nick must have briefed them before I entered Munro's office with VHS in hand. When I opened the door to a group of men with heads bowed, they sneaked side glances at one another but never looked at me. I forked over the tape and excused myself. "Some urgent calls I must make. Look at it. I'll be back." A half-hour later, I reentered. They looked away, their bodies squirming as if the springs in their chairs were breaking through.

Hedley Donavan, Time's chief editor, standing with arms across his chest, asked harshly, "What got us to even consider unredeemable filth?"

My eyes stared at my shoe buckles when I told him that Public-Access channels belonged to the public and that the issue was free speech. I thought it shouldn't be hard for the chieftains of a publishing company to understand that FCC rules made us a kind of uncommon common carrier.

My voice gained strength as my words flowed. Tension ebbed a bit, but Donovan transformed into Darth Vader. I warned him that if we violated the FCC rules, our cable franchise would be in jeopardy. I warned him, too, that the success we'd achieved improving our bad reputation with subscribers and the city would be undone. Donovan didn't budge. I resorted to a Hail Mary pass.

"Humor me, sir. Please sit down, lean back, and close your eyes. Imagine this: the FCC orders ten pages of every *Time* magazine to be yielded to the public, no holds barred, no edits." Color drained from his face. I snapped him back by describing our disclaimer—mandated by FCC: Public-Access content is for and created by the public with no interference allowed.

Donovan interrupted with an urgent plea: "How do we keep this mess quiet?"

I assured him we'd do our best to obscure the connection between the cable system and *Time Inc.,* for now. What's more, I promised we'd play this episode when no one would be watching television, on July 4. I added that doing so would buy time for me to conjure a better deal with Goldstein. The men squinted in unison as if to shut out a blinding sun. Then Donovan said, "Okay, do it if you have to. And be damn sure to keep us out of it." I hurried the hell out of there

It got harder to keep *Time Inc.* out of it when ABC's *Good Morning America* invited Goldstein and me to be on their program. The subject, obscenity. Time's heavy hitters protested. They couldn't abide the idea of *Screw*'s publisher and me talking about smut on television. "She'll be crowned porno queen, humiliating herself and us," was the common refrain. Shepley and Chairman Heiskell insisted that I handle it. They trusted me.

In the ABC studio, my poor eyes winced against the bright lights. Red camera lights on, the segment was introduced. Al Goldstein immediately threw me a curve ball. He read aloud the FCC rule against interfering with content and then asked cynically, "Charlotte, are you or are you not going to comply?"

I did what I do when stumped. I switched gears to throw him off-balance. With contempt in my tone and on my face, I said, "That you chose to publish a pornographic magazine makes me suspect you suffer some sexual dysfunction." I said this looking straight at his eyes, then turned to the camera, victory on my face.

Silence lingered. Dead air is television's black hole. The lights generated heat, and I felt sweat drenching my armpits. I worried that I'd put him in an unfairly tough spot. Finally, with aplomb and a smile, Al looked at me, then at the host, the audience, and back to me. He said, "Of course," then nothing. I felt naked as a jaybird in an empty nest but steeled myself against being drawn a diatribe.

In the end, I asked, "Why in the world would an intelligent man like you make obscenity your life's work?"

This time he answered quickly, again with aplomb. He said, "One person's obscenity is another person's marriage."

This unnervingly formidable man reduced me to a pile of putty. That I'd used feminist outrage to win against a public relations master made me mad at myself. I raised my voice against his twisted assumptions of entitled access to women's bodies. The audience applauded.

But I'd been so bent on getting him out of my way. I was worried Time management would be disappointed and angry at my poor performance. I walked back to the Time-Life Building slowly to gather my wits, afraid they'd fire me as a crazy bitch for sure! A rising star at

*Time Inc.*, I must have embarrassed them on national television. When I stepped out of the elevator on our floor, there was no mean spirit in the air, not the antagonistic atmosphere I'd feared. Surprisingly, people popped up like buds blossoming on high speed in a Disney movie. They assembled around me in a group hug. Wariness about a prurient embarrassment was gone. Even naysayers told me my performance was more endearing than upsetting.

This was not an end to the titillating travails of the Public-Access saga. It remained a controversial challenge. Al's provocative press releases created small storms. I was called to testify before the United States Congress. They wanted me to argue the awkward subject that aroused the Old Guard's battle cries once again. The common refrain was something like, "A woman defending racy material to Congress is a terrible idea."

But my man Shepley arranged for me to fly to DC on the corporate jet. I sunk into the plush upholstery in a black-and-white herringbone suit over a white silk blouse. I sipped champagne and nibbled on jumbo shrimp and caviar. There was a limousine to take me to the Hill and a man to escort me to the hearing room. High double doors opened to a huge, half-moon-shaped room that was wood-paneled from floor to elevated ceiling. A panel of white men sat in high-backed chairs behind the dais. Their grimaces made them look ready to accuse me of degeneracy. A gastronomic tornado in the pit of my stomach threatened to go public. The sergeant-at-arms ushered me to my seat at the table.

Committee Chairman Peter Russo, his gray hair begging a trim, talked like a tough guy from a Brooklyn crime family. He carried on about "horrendous improprieties" on Public Access, like cats mating cats and dogs mating dogs. I was thinking, *He finds animals doing what they do obscene?* Relieved that my rumbling tummy was squashed by a giggle as incredulity turned to farce. I was surprised he didn't bring up the masturbation video. I thought maybe he'd missed it altogether or had chosen to ignore it. I was armed with rationale to defend it. The tape had redeeming value that the Supreme Court would have had trouble overruling. I felt redeemed by all it had taught me about female sexuality.

What followed was Russo's rant on so-called past offenses. He said, "Mrs. Schiff, can you defend such trash playing on a *Time Inc.* cable system?"

About to answer, I heard a rumpus from the press and turned my head. The next witness had arrived. He was a spooky-looking man wearing a silver vest with a Porta-Pak camera on his shoulder. It was *Ugly George*. I took a breath and proceeded with my testimony to make my point clear: "The Public- Access channels belong to the public, and we are 'uncommon common carriers' of messages. The FCC prohibits censorship of any kind."

The legislators' conspiratorial stopped when Russo, as if scolding his daughter for coming home after curfew, challenged me. "How can a grown woman—a mother, I'm told—defend such obscene programming?"

In a calm voice, I proffered, "I do not defend what I find atrocious. Your next witness infuriates me for what he does to innocent young women. He lures them into closed spaces and then coaxes them to disrobe on camera. If the FCC and/or Congress want such fare eliminated, they should change the rules and establish a scrutiny panel. We'd abide by that with pleasure. But if you're suggesting that I be the official arbiter of taste and decency, the first show I would take off the air is *Let's Make a Deal*—a truly obscene program!"

The press laughed and then barraged me with questions. I became the story. Their oft-repeated query was, "What's obscene about *Let's Make a Deal?*" I answered as best I could in the commotion to explain the obvious. Russo thanked me and sent me on my way. The story ran in Charles Krauthammer's column in the *Washington Post* and was picked up by Liz Smith and other major columnists across the country. Fighting for the First Amendment made me famous for fifteen minutes. I was having fun. Andy Warhol was right.

I felt my dreams of the future would come true. And as it happened, I had exceeded my projections before the year was up. The do-or-die episode taught me to never again storm the battlements without the right weapons. Shooting from the hip brought me far, but I wouldn't present to the gods again until I'd learned more. A similar lesson should have been learned from the failure of my first marriage to a man who talked too much, drank too much, messed around too much, and was mean on Mondays. And on the Clarence home front, my uneasy premonitions had proven accurate. I'd married another serial womanizer whose uneasiness with telling the truth was too familiar.

A terror hit me. I hadn't thought this through before opening my mouth. Could I spend two years at school, virtually run MCTV, attend to the ambitions and wellbeing of my sons, and maybe have a private life? The questions stayed unanswered, but what kept me going was that I needed to do this to feel at home in the future. My dreams were full of digital video magazines in the sky. Yet I wondered how my ambitions could thrive in a bastion of powerful men. I wanted to be like them. But not too much! I wanted a piece of their power, but for a purpose, they were not likely to share or even understand. It had been more than two decades since I'd seen the inside of a classroom. There was the fear of what might be a poor performance in an Ivy League university. *Time Inc.* might see me stripped to the bone. And maybe I'd not even pass the qualifying entrance exam.

The blue booklet of multiple-choice questions did not have room for persuasive narrative, and that's my "forte." Correct answers had to check D when the answer was D. The rub in the math section was that in 1949, girls at Brooklyn College were denied advanced math and forced to study "survey math" (deductive and inductive reasoning) instead. Judy's advice was to skip the questions with unfamiliar formulae and equations and to answer the narrative questions logically. I followed her instructions and felt I'd climbed a tall and icy mountain when I finally handed in the blue book. A week later, there was an envelope in my mailbox. I paced the floor, crushing what looked like a letter in my sweaty hand. I took a breath as if it were my last, then flattened out the wrinkles. Primed for the worst, I looked at the thing.

There was one word in caps at the top: Congratulations. My body shook. I felt a rush of relief. Then pumped with pride, I sized up what might have brought me to this moment. After all, I'd been anointed "Pioneer" by the Cable Association, had breezed past the fearsome barriers of entry at Time, testified before the United States Congress on obscenity, and now won a ticket to an Ivy League university for a graduate degree in business, an MBA. *Time Inc.* was not only footing the tuition fee; it was freeing me for the intense full week at the start of each of four semesters for the next two years—should I last that long. I was ready to drive to Woodbury for the first week - long session at Arden House, the Averell Harriman estate bequeathed to Columbia University. My two boys still at home sent me off, filled with love and pride. I thought the situation served my most prominent and persistent purpose as a mom, focused on an obsession to instill in my boys' respect and appreciation for the females in their lives.

# Ivory Tower

The drive was long, the setting magnificent—a multiacre swath of prime land surrounded by rolling hills, rocky outcroppings, and huge old oak, pine, and spruce trees. We would study, eat, and sleep for a week in a French-style stone mansion. As I wandered through the pathways and gardens, treetops oscillating in a cool breeze seemed to be telling me I was meant to be there. Classes began. My first assignment required the formula for a straight line. I mulled over the first unknown entity. Was there a formula for a straight line?

Then came, "Do the matrices in the normal fashion." In the remedial math guidebook I'd brought just in case, I found the formula, and I learned that "matrices" is the plural for "matrix." As an honor

Latin scholar in high school, how did I not know that? It's the word for womb, that from which everything comes. It's the source, the origin. Being reminded of that truth brought me to the troubling reality that females leave the womb to enter a deeply patriarchal culture.

Earning an MBA wasn't going to change that. It had taken two hours for me to understand the assignment for one course. It was midnight. In a week of lectures and hard work, I listened, took notes, and contemplated calamity when awake or asleep. To be one of only three females in a class of fifty students bugged me too. On the drive back, fear of the massive body of work ahead refused to go away. At home, a fresh look at my notes hit me even harder. I stared at four walls. The beauty of our paneled library metamorphosed into a crib too small.

Even the park view became a black hole, like my brain. No ideas. No solutions. No sign of life. I felt *Time* watching me. I paced in smaller and smaller circles and then grabbed the phone to beg Judy for help. She said, "Shut up and listen to me, darling Charlotte. They do this to teach you the big lesson that you can't do it all, so you prioritize. First, tackle what you can handle. Then take on unfamiliar but bedrock essentials and use logic. You must learn how to discern what's foremost and what is of lesser weight. Also, know what needs outsourcing and consult with experts. Most vital, make sound choices." Judy confessed that at the start of law school at age thirty- seven, she'd panicked. My genius sister panicked? I felt much better.

The BMT subway took me to 120th Street. I walked through a gut- wrenching blighted area to a shining oasis on a hill. I stared at the gorgeous stone-faced buildings dating back to the nineteenth century. Uris Hall, the newer business school building, was nowhere in sight. I hunted for it while pondering what I was facing. There would be full Saturdays in class, twenty to thirty hours of homework a week, a troubled company to run, and a household and family to manage. My heart pounded. With a lump in my throat, I climbed the stone steps, grabbed the door's brass knob, and went inside. I'd spent a week as one of three women and forty-seven men at Arden House.

They were an odd mix: a nuclear physicist, two lawyers, the heir to a newspaper delivery company, and other people with singular profiles. Each student was on board for his or her own reason. It bothered me that on skin color, there was no mix. And Tom Ference, dean of the executive MBA Program, was also the professor for the Behavior in Management course. The few women mentioned in the course textbook were either typists or file clerks. The year 1975 was still early, but for pity's sake, Columbia's mandate was to enlighten future business leaders! I would not stay silent on the book's failure to respect working women for what threads they bring to the fabric of management and leadership. Then the professor paired his students for a social awareness exercise. We were to identify primary drives: achievement, power, excellence, affiliation. Mine came out to be power and affiliation.

The dean said, "Not possible!" He insisted we do it again. We did. Same result. Certain that we'd done it wrong, he conducted my test himself. It was the same.

"This cannot be, Charlotte. Power and affiliation never combine in the same person."

"With respect, sir, your definition of power may be what for me is the abuse of power."

"So how do you define power, Charlotte?"

"Power is the ability to affect events and people toward a positive end. And since affiliation means caring, those intentions work perfectly well together."

He shifted to the term-paper assignment, which was to create a *Harvard Business Review* type of case study of a company in trouble, which was good news for me. I was vice president and director of MCTV, a perfect company for the study: a $45 million investment, now wholly owned by *Time Inc.* losing $3.5 million a year and rightly given bad marks by the city franchise authority and consumers. I showed my review to Nick, who lauded the analysis. He said it "informed the present and divined the future." I received an A for my paper and for the course.

Then came summer break. The Public-Access obscenity furor was not on vacation. I'd muscled *Time Inc.* into underwriting a Public-Access video group experiment to cover the protests outside both parties' presidential conventions in Miami. The candidate on my side was George McGovern, and on the other, Richard Nixon. It was hard to persuade *Time* to finance a bunch of "hippies," but they were glad to have done so when their work gained critical respect and awards. I was at the Democratic Convention in Miami with the group, and I was excited when Jessie Jackson's delegation managed to oust Chicago Mayor Richard Daley's Illinois group, ensuring McGovern's nomination. Unfortunately, Jackson's win occurred at 5:00 a.m. when the TV audience was fast asleep. And McGovern's campaign was a huge disappointment. C'est la vie! The Democratic Party had allowed the high point of the convention to take place in the middle of the night, and Republican highlights always happen in prime time. I smelled trouble. What made it worse is that McGovern's campaign became a huge disappointment. But it was a hot summer, and weekends were spent in South Hampton or Fire Island.

On my first day back after summer break, the professor with whom I'd argued about the dismissive treatment of women in the text and in class ran to me shouting, "There's a new edition of our textbook! You're going to love it." He placed the magnum opus in my hands, smiling broadly. The table of contents looked the same. I kept looking and finally noticed that there were two new chapters listed at the bottom: "Women" was one, and "Minorities" the other. Apparently, the new edition still considered females and minorities unworthy of integration into the text. I asked in annoyance if any real changes were made other than in the isolated chapters. He clutched his middle as if punched. "But that's what you wanted," he said. I felt bad. He meant well and had gone as far as he could. I thanked him and excused myself to get to my Accounting class on time. The unpleasant exchange taught me that to make a difference in a deeply patriarchal culture, one must employ thoughtful diplomacy or change the subject.

In our large apartment, you could hear a pin drop. The TV was as silent as I'd been lately. Most of the time we'd be studying—all eyes on the prize with my younger boys still in school. Dinners were a catch-as-catch-can affair: pizza, Kentucky Fried Chicken, meatballs and spaghetti, takeout Chinese food. I agonized over cutting domestic corners. Now I wonder how my sons are dealing with time as husbands, fathers, and professionals. Are they suffering from not enough hours in the day? Are they so stretched now that anxieties are hammering their brains with what's still undone? I found enough energy to function effectively at work. At home, I collapsed right after dinner. A second wind came later to carry me through homework until midnight. One hard truth is that my schoolwork tipped a delicate balance and not in my sons' favor. I suffer big-league regrets for that and for the ephemeral marriage to Clarence that had caused added hardships.

In the second semester of Ference's class, I created a business plan for MCTV, the same troubled company I'd addressed in the *Harvard Review* format. I was in charge of nearly everything: marketing, sales, programming, Public Access, public relations, government and civic affairs, and liaison with Legal. Data was at my fingertips and inside my brain. Nick was now in charge of HBO. Thayer Bigelow, former executive vice president of MCTV, replaced him as president, and I was promoted to his job. I was living with two kids still at home, in the messy endgame of another broken marriage and endless study hours with no dog to blame for eating my homework. Well, I'd asked for it. But Thayer liked the business plan and wanted it implemented.

By year's end, we were operating in the black. Close to running the company, I'd spent a couple of years breaking ground with office personnel and structure on many fronts. To see how the physical guts of the system worked, I went to the garage to speak to Shorty, the main man in operations and top dog in the union. I asked him for a day with a crew in the field. Even though he and I enjoyed a good working relationship, he balked.

"The guys won't like taking a lady vice president around the city wiring buildings, installing cable, and fixing amplifiers. We can explain it all to you here in the garage, ma'am."

I said, "No deal, Shorty."

He gave instructions to foreman and crew and warned me that they were not happy.

Then, out in front of Saks Fifth Avenue, wearing a hard hat, I felt great. But the crew cringed, with embarrassment to be seen working with a broad. One of them lifted a heavy lid at the roadside, under which were metal steps to the sewer. I moved close.

"Stop. You can't go down there. It stinks of rats and bugs."

I said, "Hey, this isn't easy for me, but I need to know what you guys are up against."

Yes, the odor and creatures were daunting. When I came up, their mood did too. They let me do an installation in the parlor of a nice lady in a housedress. I stapled cable along the carpet and connected it to the TV. She gave me a tip.

I said, "Thanks, ma'am. Most honest dollar I ever made."

The guys chuckled. I'd broken my own rule against accepting tips.

This episode sparked a bond that spread through the ranks. It moved me to take a shot at changing a union contract midterm. It's very rare, but it worked. Five eight-hour days were replaced by four ten-hour days. An extra day at home for them, a higher productivity ratio for us—a win-win. With my business plan in effect, I created incremental revenue by selling time on our exclusive coverage of Madison Square Garden sports, the first mainstream commercials on cable. With no ratings and no precedent, I sorted out advertisers whose targets were wealthy sports lovers.

I'd say, "Hey, man, this is a romantic buy. Put your calculator away. Your brand will be seen on Knicks games the way Mobile sponsored Masterpiece Theater."

That approach hit the mark with American Express first, then Mercedes and American Airlines. What became Time-Warner Cable, after a merger with Warner Communications, was an even more powerful and profitable piece of *Time*'s portfolio. Subscriber counts lifted exponentially, telephone and internet services were added. MCTV became the flagship for a stream of awards for original content from HBO. On basic channels, industry-wide cable advertising was on its way. In a few years, it would grow to a multibillion-dollar industry.

I often asked myself how I rate years of my life splintered—work, family, school, and always politics and purpose. The answer is still a work in progress. It helped that my boys were on track toward their goals, and I was zeroing in on an MBA with still one more final exam to the finish line. There was just enough time to fly to Chicago to oversee MCTV's presence at a cable convention. On the exhibit floor, an attendant rushed toward me with an urgent message. My brother had suffered a massive heart attack! I flew to Los Angeles, fearing the worst.

When I found his hospital room, Sammy was negotiating with a young doctor. With abject sincerity, he pleaded, "I'll change…eat right, work out, eliminate stress. My wife will take care of everything. All that will fix this, Doc, won't it?"

The young doctor's cruel, honest response was, "Mr. Grad, I don't believe you will leave this hospital alive." My brother's face lost all color. Tears welled as the doctor said, "I'm sorry," and left the room. I threw my arms around Sammy's neck, my sobs stopping his. His wife, Connie, came in. He told her the news. I left to give them privacy.

David raced to be with the uncle he dearly loved, and Judy arrived. We did our best to comfort and support Connie, her four children, and my devastated David. Sam's crusade to be readmitted to the California Bar Association had been long years driven by a futile obsession. He was a man who'd made and lost millions with a reckless disregard for consequence. I had witnessed examples of how unbalanced my big brother's mind had become, like the auction notice posted on the garage door of his fine house in Palm Springs. The house would be lost because of way overdue mortgage payments. In the garage was a Rolls Royce. Judy and I did all we could to comfort and support Connie and the kids. Dennis was only sixteen years old. We were horrified but not surprised to learn that Sam had failed to keep up on all insurance policies and car payments. And then he died.

The family was left without wheels, home, or money. Connie's reaction was to tell them, "You're on your own now. I have to take care of myself." Judy and I gave them all the resources possible, along with advice and counsel on necessary next steps. My sister had to get back to work, and I had just enough time to take the final exam at Columbia.

At age forty-five, I was awarded my master's degree in business. Judy, David, Paul, Richard, and his girlfriend, Aili, witnessed the event on the terrace of Uris Hall. I felt awful and was very sad that Sammy wasn't there. He would have been so proud of his baby sister. He would have asked, "So, little one, what have you learned?" I'd have told him about the decision tree and its meticulous steps toward projecting each course of action to its probable outcome, and use that wisdom to choose the best option. "How has this changed your way of thinking, smarty-pants?" would likely have been his next question.

Sammy being Sammy, I surely would have said, "It helped a lot, but innate female intuition was still my mainstay." What I thought but did not say was, "Sammy dear, the use of such a tree might have saved you from yourself."

At that moment, the forces that moved my brilliant brother's modus operandi and warped moral compass were impossible to justify.

# PART 13

# Quantum Leap Forward

T*ime Inc.* appointed Charlotte Schiff-Jones to assistant publisher and general manager of *People* magazine. Their vice president and legal counsel, also Jewish, called me in disbelief that I'd been raised to such a prominent position. He interrupted his own doubtful discourse with these words: "It must have been the Jones that did it" His call came just as I was reading Liz Smith's column, and this is how she wrote on my new job. "Dorothy Schiff's daughter has been appointed associate publisher of *People* magazine."

I was so infuriated by the assumption that my promotion was achieved through nepotism, I called Liz to say, "Unless I'm in that super-rich bitch's will, do correct your mistake." She didn't laugh. I'd been in the same room with Dorothy Schiff so many times, and she never even said hello.

In my new office on the thirtieth floor of the Time-Life Building, a life-sized Wonder Woman doll was stretched out on an Art Deco chaise. It amused me that her eyes seemed focused on my framed Columbia University certificate. The plaque was mounted alongside a farewell note from my colleagues at Manhattan Cable, the ones who sent the doll. Their words: "Who says a woman can't have it all? They don't know our Charlotte!"

My appointment to *People* was to be a training ground toward publishing *Time Inc.'s* first woman's magazine. Doubting such a magazine created in an atmosphere of male primacy would work, I sought advice from Gloria Steinem, founder and editor of *MS*, a powerful feminist magazine. She encouraged me but emphasized that separation of church and state was a time-honored credo at *Time-Life*. My editorial input would be disallowed as "never the twain shall meet." Yet they did accept my suggested name for the magazine: *WOMAN*.

The dice were loaded. Seventeen men went on a retreat to devise the prospectus for a magazine dedicated to women, a subject that for them was at best a mystery. I had a craving for a conversation with Gloria one more time. I needed to ask her how I might guide the prospectus toward a feminist base, if not all the way. Of course, I nearly cried telling her about the retreat. A note: mixed in with all that testosterone was a soupçon of estrogen, one woman, an editor deeply embedded in the institution. I was afraid the long shot would be a whole lot longer.

But Gloria urged me to grab the chance to be part of history: "Just get in there and take it one step at a time to slowly and subtly steer the magazine toward at least a feminist base." I was confident that if Gloria thought it a hopeless cause, she would have said, "Don't do it."

It was a marvel to find myself a female executive on a high floor in the *Time-Life* Building. I stood at my office door to soak in what seemed unreal. And then I spotted the male crew just returned from the retreat. They passed by as they walked from the elevator. I wondered how they'd ready me to be a publisher without involving me at least in the prospectus. To be honest, I feared that the machinery for female failure might have been written into the architectural specifications of the Time-Life Building. It appeared there might be no real chance for me in this enterprise.

I was called to a meeting by Arthur Keylor, head of the magazine division. I tiptoed into his office with no confidence, real or imagined. After all, his boss had chosen me for the job, a woman from the video division no less. I stepped into his office on schedule. He stood planted in a wide-legged stance at the far end of the room. He was just another tall silver-haired white Anglo- Saxon male in Brooks Brothers best. He stood staring with an adamantine scowl. He stiff-armed himself from the wall as if to commence a yoga move, but I read it as letting me know he intended to keep his distance. Without so much as a fake smile, he pointed me to a chair as he settled into his high- backed throne.

The short meeting was mean. I wondered if his animosity came from fear of his colleagues, or just of me, the pushy broad inserted by those of whom he really was afraid? I wondered if terror might be the secret that binds men together, a warning system for male rituals driven by dread. I thought I'd better tell *People*'s managing editor, Dick Stolley, and my boss, publisher Dick Durell, the truth about my concerns, come what may. Stolley was a sexy, confident, irresistible straight arrow. He was *People* magazine's Steve McQueen. His office was a mass of papers, photos, books, magazines, and Post-its. His high-wired aura pumped my blood.

He invited me to sit in the chair beside him, then leaned forward with interest, his elbows on his knees, his chin in cupped hands, eyes beaming with curiosity. I said, "Dick, you guys didn't ask to be saddled with a magazine greenhorn. What can I do to win your support?"

The smile in his eyes preceded the one on his lips as he said, "Clever girl... so cool to come to me with sincere concerns. Durell and I have been wondering what to do with you. You'll be fine. Talk to him. He's your boss. You'll like each other." He was touched by my confession and quick to empathize with my jitters. He offered a foothold into his world of codes and Kabuki dances. "This is how we do things here..." I liked that Stolley appreciated my femaleness, and I was glad his welcoming embrace was absent of any semblance of harassment. I told him of my fearful encounters with sexual misconduct. Somehow he sensed I'd pulled it toward myself and would not run away from it. I had hoped both Dicks would appreciate my angst, and they did. You can imagine how much it helps a lone female to have agreeable male colleagues in the corporate drama.

Weeks later, another Dick showed up and was one who might not cool down so easily. Last name Thomas, this Dick had served as ad sales director since *People*'s inception four years before. He'd managed to attract advertisers to an untried magazine. *People*'s standard for accuracy and editorial integrity distinguished it from the usual tabloid gossip genre. Yet all new publications start at the bottom of media buyers lists, so it must have taken great skill to make it a success so fast. I was eager to meet him, but the feeling wasn't mutual.

Stolley explained, "I think he's pissed that some dame from the video division has been given what he believed was rightfully his job."

I thought there must be a way to bring dark Dick around. After all, finding holes happens to be my thing. It didn't take long for me to find a big one. Clairol was the only female product ad in *People*. It made no sense. Males might read the magazine, but it was women who'd buy it. If Thomas had been one of the happy Dicks, I'd have rushed right in with this lightning bolt. But dark Dick lived in a negative universe where I was concerned, and I didn't know how to navigate in that space.

I decided research might earn his respect and appreciation. It took no time to find out that ad sales events tended to be Super Bowl parties or golf outings and the like. Articles in the trades reported that women media buyers' ranks were growing. A few, if any, females showed up at those events. To raise the attendance quotient of women media buyers, I added spa outings, theater parties, and weekends in Tanglewood with ballets and concerts. Women buyers came, and female-oriented ad pages grew. They'd multiply even further if *People* hired a few saleswomen. Durell told me to "go for it."

To earn dark Dick's respect, I interviewed candidates for him to consider. His mood got darker. An attempt at civility led only to more tension. Internecine rivalry called for strategy and grace, but I'd gone full speed ahead like a submarine firing torpedoes without a periscope. I stared at my Wonder Woman doll and felt an unsettling measure of shame.

In any case, my interaction with the promotion and circulation departments proceeded swimmingly. My *People* learning curve began to level out. As a feminist and civil rights activist, my political agenda grew strong and controversial, both in and outside the workplace. For example, I was appointed to represent the magazine division in collective bargaining. A Writers Guild strike was threatened.

The main issue was upward mobility gender discrimination. As I was chosen to represent management, my social conscience made me the outlier. I argued against the traditionalists on the corporate committee. I'd spent my life on the workers' side where gender or minority issues were involved. We battled behind closed doors, but on that subject, I took a risk. I turned fierce on the issue. I insisted that female and minority researchers who could write be raised to writers. I was tickled pink that some good changes were made for both, and there was no strike. The experience empowered me to enlighten my boss's somewhat benign misogyny. It was fun.

When I pointed out his sexist flaws, he pled innocent. "I'm not a bad guy. My wife's a state legislator in Connecticut, and my daughter drives a tractor. I take a lot from them, and now you. Help me out, won't you?"

Music to my ears, I convinced him to replace "chairman" with "chairperson" or "chair," a counter to the knee-jerk reaction to a word that conjures an arrogant man in a pin-striped suit and a cigar jutting out of his mouth. I urged him also to give up setting the main theme of Monday staff meetings with football analogies. "You're not offending anyone, Dick. But at least three or four people in the room aren't getting your point." He shelved football references for months. Then one Monday, a fabulous Sunday game on his mind, he was about to use a bad play as analogy for a misstep in circulation.

I knew what was coming because I'd watched the game. His eye caught my scowl. About to say "lineman," he switched to "line person." We all laughed with affection. The wonderful moment became an inside joke. But it wasn't a joke when I raised the issue of the internet as a serious challenge to the future of print. It made me think of my mother's eternal answer: "No, it's not necessary."

To gain balance in a male world, there was Bill Wilson from Screen Gems. Our long friendship had shifted to romance whenever we were simultaneously unattached. He was great at making me feel better about myself. As I look back at our multi-decade amity, I see a moveable feast indifferent to time or place. Our romantic interludes were a steadying thread in my busy, often stressful life. He saved me from being alone with only ice cream for comfort and proudly escorted me to my first *People* party. He fit in beautifully, looking like them, talking like them, dressed like them, and a product of the finest schools like them. He'd been the only man I desired to be with for years. And when our romance reached no-next-time, our friendship stayed strong. I met the love of my life, and Bill fell in love with Melody, Ted Kennedy's former chief aide. Bill, a politico in the sixties, produced the fateful Nixon/Kennedy debate. I was happy that now he was back inside a world he missed and with a woman he loved. I saw it as a gift of life for my dear friend. My new man and I were happy to be at their wedding. So many of the legends were there, including Senator Ted himself.

Many years later and not that long ago, a poignant message came to me from Bill's wife, Melody, telling me that he had died. It was no surprise as he'd been ill, but I was and still am sad. Bill was my gift of another kind for so many years and remains a powerful memory of a beautiful and loving friendship with a very special person.

At *People*, I enjoyed producing promotion events. One was a Halloween party for ad agencies. I set it up in a Studio 54-type nightclub in Chicago. Tents were placed in a mezzanine for fortunetellers, card readers, psychics, and the like, to ply their mystic trades as party favors.

New Age powers were not in my cup of tea leaves, but the characters and atmosphere made for a fun-filled Halloween. The music hot and lively, the food and decor a perfect mix. Feedback was positive, and media buyers waited hours to get through over-burdened telephone circuits.

# *woman* Magazine

It surprised me to be invited to the brainstorming sessions about *WOMAN*. It breached sacrosanct church-and-state separation by including the potential publisher in editorial meetings. It freed me to speak my mind, and they responded positively, maybe because I did pretty much stay inside the publishing sphere. I suggested an editorial baseline that would attract untapped advertiser segments, for example. Their praise for my suggestions triggered a delicious dream from which I awoke with a plan for *WOMAN* to be a friend to female doubts, yearnings, and aspirations.

Then came what I thought was a prank: Time's first woman's magazine was to be the size of *TV Guide*. It was not a prank. It was a decision justified by the availability of an attractive rack position in supermarkets next to the popular *TV Guide*. I'd learned the importance of rack position by touring Piggly Wiggly supermarkets in Alabama as part of my training. Few women could resist buying a *People* magazine with sizzled covers staring at them as they moved down the checkout line, the secret to a successful "newsstand" circulation. Editorial decisions remained on the other side of the divide, but its size was publisher territory. Marketing and promotion were on my turf. I was convinced that if marketing priorities dictated a small size, *Time Inc.*'s *WOMAN* had to be a gem, a Time Tiffany box. I stressed that if the number one magazine magnate in the country was to present its first woman's magazine in miniature, it had to be big in every other way: Perfectly bound in high-grade bond with cutting-edge graphics to magnify and legitimate its petite posture, and with content that honored the rising consciousness of women.

Tall, dignified chairman Andrew Heiskell charged into my office gleaming with happiness. He put the tiny *woman* dummy in my hands, hovering over me as I flipped through. He couldn't help asking right away, "So what do you think?"

I replied, "Not ready yet."

"What do you think, Andrew?"

He chuckled. "What does it matter what I think? I'll bring it home to Marion. She'll know."

My brief browse revealed a dumb dummy with no idea of what it was or who or what it was for. With my wish-fulfillment dream denied, the chairman of *Time Inc.* gave me thirty minutes to look it over. Heiskell had joined Shepley as my champion, but what would I say to him when he returned for my assessment? He came back to my office enthusiastic about a planned twelve-city market test. He asked me to start thinking about it. In my mind, the market test could be done by passing the dummy around to all the secretaries in the building. They would have the answer. The inevitable bad result could be kept private and not cost a dime. Andrew expected me to "tell it like it is." He trusted me. It could trigger a pink slip, but I laid out my ideas that were critical and pretty fierce. Instead of the gem the model needed to be, it was about teenage mothers, girl gangs, and how to arrange dry flowers.

I felt as if I'd fallen off a cliff. How would my broken self be whole again? To create *woman* out of the Time-Life rib was as cockeyed as it gets. Shattering masculine mystique's eternal power over women was at least declining, but in 1977, it was gut-wrenching still. In the end, not one of my inputs that were praised at brainstorming sessions was taken seriously. I spoke my mind. They liked my ideas. I'd been led to believe that being an exception-to-the-rule might be good enough. It wasn't. What Einstein is arguably reputed to have said: "There are only two ways to live your life. One is as though nothing is a miracle. The other is as though everything is a miracle."

I came to believe it would take more than a miracle for a woman's magazine birthed by men in a stratified institution to make any sense. I wrote a gutsy autopsy of the dead dummy. My first words were, "*woman*'s trial dummy was not only not the gem it needed to be, it wasn't even a shard of beach glass." Surely the kill order would come down on me, and when it did, I would not let it take me with it or define me as a failure for what was not my doing. Judy helped me tone down my lengthy critique from diatribe to what I hoped was merely pensive putdown. I'm afraid it was still fierce even with Judy's judicious edits.

Letting go was not in my playbook. I'd held on too long on Harry's water- ski rope and hit my head on the floating hardwood ski. And I'd stayed glued to two marriages long after they were over. Yet I walked away briskly from ABC Screen Gems and Drew Lawrence Productions. It's just too hard to walk away from the company that lifted me to record heights. I decided to stay at *People* a few more months until I figured out my next move. I knew the twelve-city test for *woman* would kill it. Truth is, if, by some weird stretch of the imagination, it didn't, I wouldn't want anything to do with it anyway. I kept my eyes open to get to a place where I might make both a living and a difference that matters.

Now a single mother whose professional life had reached a scary impasse, I had to make some changes. Only one son still living with me, it was time to move out of a too grand and too expensive apartment. My friend Lewis Rudin, head of the powerful Rudin family's real estate empire, kindly and swiftly responded to my request for a modest-sized and modest-priced living space. I arranged for the move without even seeing the apartment. I had no time to be picky. Paul and I moved to the East Side.

Surrounded by cartons still waiting to be unpacked, I was crushed by a heavy sense of loss that was triggered by thoughts of Zabar's, the best-ever deli on Broadway, where I'd see Isaac Bashevis Singer sitting on a bench feeding the pigeons. In chilly weather, he wore a hat like my dad's felt fedora. On hot days, I'd see his bald head with wisps of gray at the temples. I liked being a quiet witness to a storyteller who helped me imagine the smoke from the chimneys of Auschwitz, his tales an excavation of hidden history. On the busy boulevard, I'd stand on the median loving the sight of him, thinking about what he knew—the history of the Jews.

I loved his rationale for writing in Yiddish. He'd said, "I like to write ghost stories and nothing fits a ghost better than a dying language…ghosts love Yiddish, and they all speak it."

His wit survived his Holocaust obsession. I felt bad that my folks did not read Singer in any language. I wish I could have talked to them about *In My Father's Court,* his eighteenth-century tale of a Jewish boy in Poland who hides under the kitchen table to hear the scandals, trials, and tribulations of townspeople seeking advice and rulings from his dad, the village *shames.* My dad was our neighborhood's arbiter of fairness and decency. He would have loved that book. I wish I had stepped up to Mr. Singer to say hello and thank him for informing me of my ancestral history.

# *People* Prime-Time Series

It pleased me that the plan to create a TV series based on *People* was still alive. I giddily enmeshed myself further in magazine pages to create *Time Inc.'s* first nonfiction prime time TV entertainment series. What kept me fretting through the nights was that a TV series based on gossip was not likely to make life better for anyone. It didn't fit into my mission to make a positive difference. I had no option but to live with reality and keep searching for gravitas. It helped that *People* magazine's policy was to triangulate, to demand three valid sources for every segment to ensure accuracy. That's what separates *People* from standard tabloids. My series would do the same. I hunted for the public pulse through dozens of *People* magazines spread out on my living room carpet. Segments in the series needed sizzle to excite and substance to uplift, as in the magazine.

Just as I came close to a viable concept, something happened! An interruption I welcomed unequivocally. It was the first National Women's Political Conference in 129 years that was on its way to

Houston, Texas. I had to be straight with the boss. He had to know I needed to be at this conference with press credentials for full access even with no journalist role to play. Durell barely took a breath before saying, "Of course, Charlotte."

My missions had always been strong for women's and minorities' rights. Shirley Chisholm was the first black woman elected to the US Congress. Her words when running for office were, "If they don't give you a seat at the table, bring a folding chair." I was joined by New York Mayor Paul O'Dwyer and Betty Friedan as delegates in her presidential primary campaign. It was a gift from the goddesses to work with the brilliant, brave Shirley. She ran not to win but to set the stage for the future. Both Shirley's and Jesse Jackson's purpose in running for president was for us Americans to at least start thinking about the position being filled one day by a dark male or female. As to color, we've now been gifted by Obama's superb two-term presidency. A female president of any color would be another step in the right direction, and we have made it to the vice presidency.

There was one person in Congress who seemed always speaking to me before we'd ever met. She was Bella Abzug, the lady with the hat, shaking fist and loud mouth. Her commitment to women's issues made me cry with grateful happiness. I worked passionately in her Senate campaign. After she lost to the great Daniel Patrick Moynihan by one percent, President Carter appointed her to head the National Commission for International Women's Year. Bella, being Bella, quickly brushed the Senate loss off her tough self to journey across America, teaching women of all stripes the architecture of the political process: how to elect delegates, how to caucus, how to define principles and purpose and how to compromise and deal. It was her bill in Congress that sanctioned and funded the conference. That's one of the many things I loved and still love about the late, yet never forgotten, Bella Abzug.

# National Women's Conference

The flight to Houston was crowded with women on a mission, the energy strong enough to power a rocket. That's what we were aiming to do. The rocket we were firing was aimed for gender parity. The Houston locals at the airport were taken aback by women pouring out of so many flights from all over the country. Voices from every corner asked, "What's going on?" Texas wasn't ready for thousands of women on the march, and the tense atmosphere was far from welcoming. Resolved to stay cool, I went to the hotel. I knew there'd be various points of view among democratically elected women. There were divisive issues—abortion, the Equal Rights Amendment, sexual identity, and equal pay. I prayed we'd all stay cool.

The next morning in a shared cab that got jammed in a traffic bottleneck, we finally reached the Colosseum. My cab mates entered the great hall. I stayed outside waiting for the Olympic torch being relayed on foot from Seneca Falls, 2,612 miles away. It was the place where the first and only Women's Political Conference had been held in 1848. I felt the goosebumps I'd felt in Gary, Indiana, at the ground-shaking Black Political Conference I produced in 1972 for TelePrompTer, and the documentary for PBS created in Chicago's CTTW.

In a sudden downpour, a huffing and puffing Bella and tennis star Billy Jean King carried the bronze torch for the final few yards. They arrived at a band's blaring rendition of "Yellow Rose of Texas" alongside hundreds of women shouting, "ERA! ERA!" which in my mind was an oxymoron—equal rights for women heralded by a Texas anthem in a state with an infamous history against so many women's rights. There were two thousand delegates from coast to coast, all colors, ages, professions, lifestyles, and attitudes. They were women elected by women and ready to address our most crucial issues. There would eventually be nearly twenty thousand observers. Delegates elected at fifty-six meetings around the country were there to endorse the National Plan of Action.

What caught my attention was an enormous banner across the room. It said woman in huge block letters, the name of the defunct magazine at *Time Inc.* the name I'd lobbied for and won. Here it was, thirty feet high and one hundred feet wide, the sad irony breaking my heart. The delegates were seated in the center of the great room with observers and press around them and guests largely in the mezzanine. My designated spot happened to be with radical, feminist, lesbian journalists. I was cool with that. They were not. My inner voice said, *Hey, not belonging is where I come from. How can that happen here? Do they think I'm some kind of homophobe or spy?* The atmosphere was tense and suspicious. I wanted to say out loud, "C'mon, gals. We're on the same side!" I stared at the woman banner to catch my breath. Then I let them know that I was eager to know them and their platform. I was not going to let them bring me down.

On November 18, 1977, the conference chair, Bella, welcomed us with stirring words. Coretta Scott King, Betty Ford, Lady Bird Johnson, and Roslyn Carter stood behind her. Maya Angelou read the 1848 Declaration of Sentiments and Rights. When the roar subsided, Bella explained that each of the twenty-six resolution summaries and the positions voted on by delegates from each state would be presented over the audio system. Each one would be followed by debate and then a measure of yeas and nays for each of the twenty-six planks. The goal was to hammer out a plan of action to present to Congress.

In my childhood bedroom shared with Judy, walls were covered with photos of Eleanor Roosevelt, a bust of the great lady residing on our desk has been prominently displayed wherever I've lived since. We would not be there were it not for Eleanor's devotion to issues women care most about. Her struggle lived on in the great hall, and one way or another, we all wanted to honor her words: "A woman is like a tea bag, you can't tell how strong she is until you put her in hot water." Thousands of women wearing yellow armbands signifying the lesbian cause were streaming into the mezzanine. Heads were tilted up to watch; elbows poked ribs and fingers were pointed to make sure others saw what was happening. My seatmates produced boxes of yellow bands. They put them on their arms, and I asked for one. As their leader handed it to me, I looked up to see yellow bands and new banners saying, "We are Everywhere" and "Lesbian Rights." My seatmates grumbled in fear of a scam and their plank failing.

I said, "Let me tell you a story."

"A story? Now? Are you crazy?"

"You'll be glad, I promise. Legend has it that in Nazi-occupied Copenhagen, King Christian X of Denmark spoke from his balcony to a huge crowd pronouncing the order given him by the Nazis for all Jews to wear yellow Stars of David. As he said that, he placed one on his chest. The entire population donned yellow stars that had been passed to them surreptitiously. It stymied the SS that planned the shipment of Danish Jews to their deaths! It's believed that the King and the Danish people saved nearly all their Jews from Nazi persecution."

"What does that have to do with us?"

I said, "Get me boxes of yellow bands, and I'll show you. I'll start with Carole Belamy, head of the New York delegation. She'll put one on, and the rest will follow."

In fifteen minutes, the Colosseum became Yellow Roses of Texas. When Plank 25 on fair play for lesbians finally hit the airways, there was not a sound in the room. After a few hard words, we heard a nay, then a yea, then a pause. The next and decisive speaker's voice silenced the room.

She said, "I'm a grandmother from Kansas City, and I'm not a feminist..." There was a group gasp, and then, "But I'm glad my daughter is raising her daughter differently than I raised her. I vote yea."

The plank passed and then screaming, jumping, hugging, being hugged, kissing, being kissed, laughing with all of us crying so hard, you'd think hunger and cancer had been obliterated. My seatmates had no idea their cause had lived long in my heart. The words "unity" and "bonding" were redefined that day but what really mattered most was that we were all proud females.

Before that climactic moment, I'd nosed around to find out who from *Time* magazine was covering the story. A *People* photographer told me that a male reporter was across town at the Phyllis Schlafly anti-conference. I grabbed onto a railing for balance. And in a deliberate frame of mind determined to stop *Time* magazine's steamship from continuing to head in the wrong direction. With the photographer's help, I gathered up other colleagues attending the conference without portfolio and persuaded them to write the truth. I called to warn *Time* magazine's managing editor that they were covering the wrong story.

I played back the quote from an anti-conference remark in the blurb printed in the prior *Time* magazine issue: "Affording rights to women is not a question of how but whether it should be done." I challenged him. "Whether it should be done, not how? Is that how women's history in the making should be reported in the most widely read news magazine in the country?" The call ended, and a terrible truth hit me. Trying to convince the man who would eventually run the entire *Time Inc.* print empire to do what was right would be like trying to pivot a huge freighter in a storm.

Yet for some reason, when I was at Henry Grunwald's desk in the Time- Life Building with the ad hoc copy in my sweaty hands, not a cell in my body wanted to flee. My ribs tightened as I handed him the story created by *Time Inc.* writers, researchers, and photographers, all at this conference for personal reasons like mine. I watched and finally heard, "Yes, this is excellent! How did it happen?" I told him how and by whom. He asked if I understood that I was asking for a 180-degree turn in direction from the story that had run the week before.

I said, "Of course, that's the point. You covered the anti-conference."

After a mind-numbing pause, he said, "It needs work, but we'll run some of it in this week's issue."

*Time* magazine, first of its kind in America, ran an important part of the article with a headline that read: "Women March to Houston." It started with "Feminists and their foes squared off around the big national meeting. Nothing like it has been seen in the U.S. in at least 129 years—or ever."

Bella Abzug, who had trotted the last stretch with Billie Jean, said, "We are here running for equality. We'll never run for cover on this journey.'"

*Time* was the first national magazine to print the true story on the National Women's Political Conference, spreading the word women had learned the art of politics to achieve change. We'd scratched the surface, but much remained and still needs to be done against abiding resistance—to be done by me and every other woman and man who cares. #MeToo resistance has grown like a tidal wave getting higher and wider. I'm proud that I had something to do with *Time*'s truth-telling in 1977.

But centuries of abusive wounds have a lasting effect, as Maya Angelou knew when she quoted the African proverb "The ax forgets, the tree remembers."

## *People* Television Series

The tendency toward short attention spans had me consider brief segments for the series, the way the magazine is browsed. There'd be segments with ordinary characters doing extraordinary things, and we'd feature the famous and infamous to feed the celebrity craze. There'd be no sense of urgency in this concept. No "Who shot JR?" suspense to draw audiences from week to week. What was urgent for us was to make sure that viewers always knew when and where to find this new, unusual series. It would take time to accumulate a loyal fan base with nothing urgent ongoing.

My biggest worry was that Susskind, a drama guy with no sense of humor, seemed lost. His anxiety about pleasing *Time Inc.* stirred up his cranky side. His eyes would go skyward as if fearing something heavy was about to fall on his head. Maybe he knew buyers' regret was seeping into Time's corporate conscience about buying Susskind's company. He needed this series more than I did, but if we did well, we'd both be on top.

Magazine division chief Arthur Keylor remained convinced that a television spinoff would tarnish the magazine's integrity and hurt its circulation. However, his bosses believed in me and embraced the prospect of reaping reward from acquiring Susskind's Talent Associates.

On the day of the big pitch, I towered over David in my spiky-heeled black pumps and high coiffure. But the skyscraper called Black Rock towered over me in more than the obvious way. It unsettled me to be entering the palace built for the Columbia Broadcasting System in 1961.

Susskind tried to ease my tension. "They will adore you, be pawns in your hands." In a cavernous conference room with head guys Bob Daly, Harvey Shepherd, and Alan Wagner, I hoped they'd like the treatment and be keen on the *People* franchise. Daly OK'd my plan for handheld cameras to be close and personal with our subjects. The meeting was fruitful: $375,000 for the half-hour pilot and, if picked up, the same for each subsequent episode. We could deliver the series for less, leaving a nice profit on top of a boost in circulation.

In expansive offices, I set up base camp. A carefully chosen staff of forty young talents met weekly for brainstorming sessions. Everyone participated—segment producers, operations managers, writers, researchers, production assistants, secretaries, and receptionists. A huge cork bulletin board on which to post idea cards covered a wall. There were Americana stories for nobodies, like senior sex in the Catskills, a popular, whacky fitness professional, a convention of identical twins and, of course, celebrities with stories to tell that were hot by definition.

I established offices on both coasts for locations across the country. Alan Wagner of CBS asked a favor. "I'd like my son, a Yale sophomore, to work on the series for the summer."

I cleared my throat to say, "I… I can't do that, Alan."

He said, "What do you mean you can't?"

Gulping, I sputtered, "I've given both summer jobs to my sons Richard and Paul."

He said, "What a shame, but I like that you're a great mom."

What working mom would pass up a chance to hire her sons to work on a television series teeming with creative people and opportunity? It felt great to let my boys know how much I trusted and respected them. And I knew they'd do their jobs superbly. On a choice of host, I wanted a savvy woman of style, sexy beauty, and a touch of edgy wit—an acerbic chronicler of the times. I wanted her to be a cross between Doris Day and Lily Tomlin. Daly declared that not using Phyllis George was a deal breaker. Phyllis George? Was he teasing me? A former Miss America on a three-year contract with CBS Sports that didn't work out?

Standing with my hands fiercely planted on my hips, I said, "Her patina is gorgeous, but what's inside?"

Susskind scowled and asked for a break. Outside he whispered, "If you want this to happen, we must live with Phyllis. Let me close the deal. We'll make it work." He was the Emmy Award-winning master. I acquiesced and slumped back onto my chair, very unhappy. The pilot script was approved, and talent and staff were lined up. Susskind was billed as executive producer with me as the producer. With the pilot crew still in place, I added a few segment producers, writers, and researchers, and the brainstorming began. Susskind would show up, play big shot, and rail against whatever struck a chord on his negative keyboard, often barging in unannounced and spewing inane attacks. He'd offer nothing constructive and then stride out of the room, leaving the staffers and me upset. He was overanxious in bizarre ways and for insipid reasons. I finally got it. He was a humorless master of fictional drama and felt alien in the real world.

His seduction attempts included ploys to inveigle me to join him at a sex club called Plato's Retreat. His despicable intentions annoyed me, but I had control and kept him out of my way and out of my pants. I knew from experience that resisting harassment from a boss or colleague must be firm and artful. Before #MeToo, the powers were not on our side. In this case, though, David befriended me because I was the one with power in the corporation that had acquired his company, and he hadn't yet delivered. That was my ace in the hole, and he knew it.

I didn't need a big stick to beat off his offensive agenda. Of course, it was necessary that I deal with his insults cleverly as he had the power at CBS to make or break the deal. I hated to have to live with Phyllis George as host, a really bad idea. I'd seen her photo as Miss America and on TV sports events. She was very beautiful but didn't have the spontaneity or wit to give the series a winning personality. There was no there, there.

A few weeks earlier, surrounded by thousands of women making plans for the future of women in my country, Miss America contests had no place on the agenda. The series was my baby. The aim was to create a genre with an unexpected edge. I thought there must be a way to rid ourselves of the Phyllis thorn. I felt I'd made a mistake to accept David's insistence that not using Phyllis would be a deal breaker. Nick Nicholas had asked me to join him when he took over HBO, and I'd chosen *People* instead to learn the ropes and be ready to publish *Time Inc.'s* first women's magazine.

I couldn't say no to that, no matter how risky. CBS green-lit the series I created and would produce. A hit would take me further on my private marathon, but I hadn't produced a prime-time broadcast television series ever—my only Emmy was for a local daytime show. There were three obstacles blocking the series's success: the wrong host; a snarly, humorless womanizer as executive producer; and the magazine division chief Keylor, constantly spewing fire.

But the picture brightened when my two older sons were on the job.

Paul chose to work in the LA office to feed his appetite for cinema. His college choice was Wesleyan University. Having carried a video camera on his shoulder to capture the architecture and the basic culture of Manhattan, he didn't want to get stuck in a rut.

His choice reflected a desire to study Russian literature and other academic pursuits. Yet it took no time for renowned Hollywood professor, Jeanine Basinger, to spot Paul's advanced understanding and skills in film and television. She persuaded him to shift his intention. In his senior year, he served as assistant director for an independent film on weekends.

At his graduation, Jeanine raved to me about his exceptional talent. He rapidly moved on as producer/director of music videos and promotions in the fledging years of MTV. He surprised us all when he left what had become the hottest ticket in town to try his hand at feature films. I like to imagine that doing well working on my series might have taken him a step toward a successful film-making career. His productions of films like *My Cousin Vinny* and *Rushmore* demonstrate a particular talent for intelligent, romantic comedies. He followed them with *Maid in Manhattan* and *Mona Lisa Smile* and also his dark movies like *Solitary Man* with Michael Douglas and *Vanishing* with Jeff Bridges, David's decades-long special client. Paul once said in a published interview, "In negotiating with UTA, the talent agency where my brother is a partner, when we're in deadlock, one of us usually threatens to call Mom."

Richard chose the New York office. I sensed that working for his mother might be awkward for him so I kept a diplomatic distance. I learned from his girlfriend, Ailie, that he'd been in deep depression when living in a small apartment on his own. I'm eternally grateful that she loved him through the worst of it. And I'm furious with myself for thinking his moods were the result of his seriously ill infancy and near death. That surely factored in, but I should have gone deeper. Yet at every play he directed at college, I saw greatness. The actors in his plays did too. And at our offices, he earned solid, positive feedback from the staff, established firm friendships, and was an asset at every turn. A few months later, he directed plays Off-Broadway, like *Antigone* with

Angela Basset. Then he decided to perfect his directing skills by studying acting at Neighborhood Playhouse. I attended the final showcase in which Richard starred. In his role as a madman in an asylum, he was so convincing I shuddered in a panic.

My talented son ultimately moved on from directing plays to a successful career as an actor, winning that Emmy for his role on the hugely praised and awarded *West Wing* series. Now a star, he acts in many TV shows, Broadway and West End plays and a ton of feature films. At this writing, he's been starring in the *Good Doctor* series for several years, filming in Canada due to the pandemic. While there, he was attacked by his second death-defying illness, a life-threatening COVID-19 episode that had him in the hospital fighting for his life. I knew nothing of the crisis until it was over. Watching *The Last Word* on MSNBC, Laurence O'Donnell introduced Richard to tell his story, which he did with powerful effect. It brought me back to the fear for his survival when he was three months old.

Their older brother David already had his foot in the door of what would be a brilliant career as a talent impresario and producer. And he was nominated for a Gotham Award as executive producer for of the limited series, *The Good Lord Bird*. His client, Ethan Hawke, won a Gotham for his performance. My sons were gaining ground on their futures.

David began by delivering the mail at William Morris talent agency. Then he beat the standard wait time to agent status by signing John Malkovich for his first feature film. I'd taken him to see *True West* at the Cherry Lane Theater. David, with a history of spotting high talent, went backstage, signed him, and placed him in his first film. David became an agent way ahead of the official calendar. He moved on to partner in three major agencies before founding the MGMT talent management company. Managers are allowed development, production, and independent entrepreneurial ventures, which was a welcome change. He develops and produces TV series and feature films. All in all, I'm a very proud mom.

Phyllis George arrived at the studio, a Texas beauty with no clue to what had happened in Houston. She hated working for a woman, especially an attractive one. At the first sight of me, she shouted at her manager to have me fired and wouldn't look me in the eye. On a trial shoot in Central Park, my cameramen shared horny winks and thumbs up. A bit later, their thumbs went down. I asked why. They said in unison, "She's a lox." When the camera light turned red, Phyllis smiled and fluttered her eyelids flirtatiously. When the red light turned off, her theatrical comedy mask turned into the tragedy version. I'd hoped she'd surprise me, but it became painfully clear that she had neither acerbic wit nor the ability to be chronical about anything. I searched my feminist soul to find a way to enlighten her, to win her over with kindness.

I tried hard but couldn't unveil the woman behind the pretty face. I enticed Lee Strasberg to let us do a segment at the Actors Studio. He was the man who'd taken Stanislavsky's acting method a step further. His quote on how to act was, "Becoming the characters they're portraying." I believed he might be the one to touch a nerve in Phyllis. We entered the revered method acting temple. Students were on a drill to stretch their emotional range and depth. From the gallery, we looked for the next Brando, Pacino, Bancroft, Hopper, or Fonda. The students were searching their souls and memories for deep emotion—to be a tree, birth a baby, ache with grief. Some just grimaced, slumped, leaped, or fell. One had me believing she was afraid of being swept away by something.

Sitting in the gallery apart from us, Phyllis muffled sobs. Lee noticed, and he kneeled down at her side to talk her through what she was feeling. It turned out she'd grown up being demeaned by her mom. I felt her pain and signaled the crew to start filming. Lee invited her to study with him privately. She reacted with enthusiasm. What a story! Our star would be seen as a person with blood running through her veins and tears in her heart. I saw the classic female victim in her and took her to Elaine's for dinner. In female confession mode, she told me sad stories about her former marriage to the late, pugnacious producer Robert Evans and the wild parties that pained her. She complained of drugs everywhere but never consumed by her. Celebs were omnipresent in ways she found unnerving. She was an innocent in the lion's den. I begged her to care about herself, to know her right to be whatever and whomever she chose to be.

I went on to share what Houston was about. What I was about. We smiled a smile neither of us had seen on the other. At home, my last thoughts before slipping off to dreamland were of Stanislavski's concept of acting as "creative inspiration." I wondered if our former Miss America could be a contender? The next day we were enjoying the footage from Actors Studio, and Phyllis arrived.

She shouted, "Oh my God, mascara all over my face. Stop the tape! You can't use this. I'm not going to the Actors Studio. That awful man gave me the creeps. I'm calling my manager."

Her invective sickened me. High hopes hammered, it was critical that I be professional with my bruised star, a woman bereft of wit or enlightened self- awareness. I pushed buttons hoping to ease her out of her cage. I hoped for another real smile and treated her gently, but it was never returned. Every week, *People* TV told its stories and won the highest ratings out of the eight new CBS series.

Our challenge was to pick provocative, poignant, or funny ideas. Willie Nelson's Cajun country western concert near Fayetteville, Kentucky, took top position. We landed at the airport and drove a rented van to the site. I was surprised by a large muddy field covered in broken glass, beer bottles, rocks, gravel, and a stage for the concert. Willie's aide-de-camp—or better still, sergeant-at-arms stopped me cold as I approached his boss's Winnebago parked in the grass. His frown telegraphed, "No access." I told him my name and that I was the producer and needed to speak to Nelson. He cleared his throat and turned his back on me.

No stranger to male hostility, I knew he was protecting his *god* from the nervy broad from New York. I was there to produce an important episode. I walked away distraught and saw saddled horses nibbling weeds freely. I thought maybe I'd win points with these guys if I got on the back of a horse, a regular pastime of mine that began in Brooklyn's Prospect Park stables. I climbed onto a toast-colored mare, feeling lucky to be wearing jeans. I kept trying to wiggle my feet into the stirrups when an ear-splitting noise from the amplifiers erupted, and the horse reared up. I held on with all my might, not knowing her next move, and she took off in a gallop over bottles, boulders, and broken fenders—a terrifying obstacle course. My feet out of the stirrups, I had to grip tightly with my thighs and knees and hang onto the horse's mane, the reins, and the horn of the saddle. If I fell off, I'd break my neck. I'd learned how to talk to a horse's wild spirit, but this mare wasn't listening. I pulled the reins hard with one hand and stroked her with the other, shouting, "Whoa!" Finally, bored with it all, she slowed to a trot and then halted.

I dismounted and walked toward home base holding the reins. I was too damn scared to get back on the saddle. As the mare and I made our way back, it occurred to me that Nelson's crew might have enjoyed seeing me scared silly. Not so. I was greeted by an ovation and lots of back-slapping. It wasn't the first time that being "one of the boys" was the only way for a bossy female New Yorker to break through. It made me think of the time I hit seven strikes in a row in a bowling alley at a TelePrompTer retreat in Sun Valley. None of the cable systems guys from all over the country had ever seen a female do that. Likely they'd never seen a female executive do anything. I gained their grudging respect for my bowling phenomenon by saying, "Hey, I don't know how that happened—must have been a miracle!"

While I continued to deal with Nelson's crew, Willie fell hard for Phyllis George. No surprise. I wondered how long it would take for his thumbs up to go thumbs down like my cameramen. Then concert music filled the space. The pain in my thighs eased off when the combination of music rocked. Cajun drums, accordions, rub-boards, and harmonicas with the Nelson band's guitars, banjo, and fiddle created a sound most of us had never heard before, along with the full support of vocal harmony from Willie and the marvelous Cajun fellow whose name I've forgotten. As we started to wrap the smashing shoot, a savory, pungent scent overwhelmed my senses. I traced its source to the other side of the stage where a crowd had gathered. When I got close, I saw a gigantic kettle on a fire. The locals were celebrating the pairing of their own Cajun star with the great Willie Nelson for a TV show on a major network. It was clear that the Cajun party was for all of us. Up close to the kettle, my appetite was whetted by a spicy aroma from the sausages, chicken wings, black-eyed peas, and crabs in a peppery sauce.

It was jambalaya! And a smaller kettle alongside was brimming with shrimp gumbo. I slept like a baby that night but woke with a dark premonition about the *People* series. Our television canvas was painted with human comedy and drama, but to be freer and funnier, we spun what might offend to get a hearty laugh. To be on the safe side, I screened the edited spitting contest for CBS boss Bob Daly. He laughed and approved the edited segment. Susskind later showed up in the editing room and deleted every stroke that pivoted foul to funny. Susskind was never amused, not even by hilarity that was spontaneous. My executive producer's maddeningly witless bad taste was dangerous. He was intractable and bull-headed but had broadcast rank.

On a shoot in Beverly Hills with Carroll O'Connor, the Archie Bunker character in *All in the Family,* my tale of a silly event brought giggles to everyone but Susskind. Not knowing where the Ginger Man Restaurant was located, I'd waited at the Beverly Wilshire Hotel for a cab. Finally, one reached me. I stepped in, sat down, and asked the driver to take me to the Ginger Man restaurant.

He screamed, "Ya mean, I've been on line for a half-hour to take some crazy bitch two blocks?"

He sped out of the driveway and onto a sidewalk near the back entrance of the famous Brown Derby restaurant. He yelled for me to pay him and get the hell out of his cab! I was so nonplussed with his bulging eyes and oversized overalls, I jumped out without remembering to give him any money. He leaped out, came straight at me, and started pulling away my shoulder bag. I was in a physical fight with a lunatic who looked like a Halloween monster.

Out of the corner of my eye, I saw a gray man in a gray suit, shirt, and tie. He was headed my way. When he got closer, he asked, "Madam, are you in distress? Can I be of assistance?" The guy in the gray suit turned out to be George Raft, the film gangster of old. He gave the angry driver a fiver and escorted me on the short walk to the Ginger Man. At the coffee bar, we laughed, telling the story together. Press was there, and next day, the anecdote hit the columns coast-to-coast. My dream that night took me back to George Raft flipping coins on his knuckles in some noir gangster movie I'd seen as a child with my brother and sister.

Back in the editing room, I pressed Susskind to look at the spitting contest segment we'd edited and the unedited original one. I argued that Daly loved the version we'd screened. I fought hard and warned Susskind that Daly would be upset and angry to see a segment different than the one he'd approved. He shrugged his contrary shoulders and walked away saying, "Don't you dare touch it again."

Executive producers call the shots. I crossed my fingers, toes, and eyes and moved on to the post-production studio, Elliot, Unger, and Elliot. I chose EUE because Mike Elliot was a Fire Island friend I trusted. I was there to create the first three-minute montage opening, a template for how we'd start every episode. That the editing console was capable of repositioning images digitally was new, but even with an expert running the machine, I needed to stay awake all night to get the job done right. Our friendship survived Mike's efforts and my refusal to be seduced. The impasse was short and its resolution sincere. I took short naps in his upstairs studio flat, enjoyed his fabulous foot massages, and accepted the gold bracelet he made for me that I've worn ever since. It was no big hassle.

On the next day's shoot, Paul Newman would be demonstrating his speed skills on the Bridgehampton Race Circuit. At dawn, a limo picked me up at EUE for a long ride after the all-nighter. There was no way to change out of my sweater and jeans. When I arrived, the temperature was eighty-five, and morning shots of Paul racing around the track were done. The heat then hit ninety. The caterers didn't show up and couldn't be reached. I sent Paul and crew to a diner for lunch.

Then I pleaded to the guard at Paul's air-conditioned Winnebago. "I'm boiling hot and haven't slept for days. Can I please cool off in there?"

Later, a hand gently nudged my shoulder, and then someone whispered in my ear, "Are you okay?"

Still on my back, I opened one sleepy eye to see a bronzed body. When the other one opened, I saw a pair of eyes so blue, I thought I must be dreaming. But they were real. "Just give me a few minutes," I muttered, then apparently went out like a light. I woke with a memory. There he was, Paul Newman, inches away, half-naked, tanned, and gorgeous. And I'd gone back to sleep!

*People*'s ratings were happy news, but not for long. Getting the highest ratings of CBS's eight new series, master programmer Harvey Shepard used us as a band-aid to stop the bleeding from its failing series. He scheduled us on Monday nights against the blockbuster hit *Mork and Mindy*, with Robin Williams, a fast-rising superstar. And if that unbeatable competition wasn't bad enough, we were on against *Monday Night Football* on the West Coast. I was amazed that we scored as high as we did. It was why Harvey moved us to Wednesday, then Saturday, on-and-on positioning our highly rated series in front of their losers to raise their ratings. The last-minute schedule changes never showed up in time, not even in *TV Guide*. How could we be found when no one knew when or where. The ratings started to slide.

One morning months later, the phone rang. The clock's little hand was on the 7. Harvey said in a raspy voice, "Charlotte dear, sorry to call so early. The *People* show is over." I stopped breathing. He said, "It's not your fault. Just one of those things. Susskind scratched your edits, like the mud spitting one that Bob loved when he'd screened it." Harvey then quoted Bob as having said, "It's revolting."

I put the phone in its cradle, switched on the lamp, and sat staring blankly. Then rage threw me into a mindless rant, shouting every foul word I knew. I think I may have even made some up. To the empty room, I screamed, "When we were on top, you moved us around to save your losers. What were you thinking, damn it? You had a winner!"

I paced the floor, smashed my favorite down pillow against the headboard, and yelled, "Take that!" Susskind had edited out exactly what turned the spitting contest from horrendous to hilarious. Soon I was in a feather storm. I slammed the bedroom door and tore up photos of Phyllis George, me, and Willie Nelson. A thrown pillow knocked framed photos of my boys off the wall, shattering the glass. I tried to take the pieces to the trash, but the bedroom door was stuck. Dad must have felt like this in the ring. I wanted to pick myself up like he must have done.

Suddenly my bladder called. When I flushed the toilet, I felt my life going down with the rush of water. I tried the bedroom door again. This time the door opened with a mere turn of the knob.

My series was over. A failure is a failure. I thought of my devastated staff. Yet when we gathered for the bad news, they refashioned the death knell into a wake and thanked me for a "Woodstock experience." They said they'd never forget it. My own boys were sad for me and tried to cheer me up. Then I thought of Phyllis George and wondered what her next gig might be. It was not a shock to learn that without Strasberg, she found the perfect part. She married the governor of Kentucky.

What would be my next move? *Time Inc.'s* word to me was "We can't lose you." Options were offered that didn't fit my fantasy. Jerry Levin came up with a mandate I liked: find HBO's second network. He asked that I assess the news and children network options and then consider other genres. After thinking about it, neither of the first two made sense. Ted Turner's heavily financed CNN was close to launching on a budget more than twice the size of *Time Inc.'s* intended one. On the children's idea, Geraldine Laybourne's *Nickelodeon* had already reached the pot of gold. I saw no point in chasing those two rainbows, especially if on fixed on lower budgets.

Jerry asked, "Any other ideas, Charlotte?"

There had been a big one on my mind. I said, "Jerry, I've been exploring a performing arts channel, a three-hour block of programs daily. Three fresh hours repeated eight times a day so viewers can watch anytime. I see it as a premium channel patterned after HBO with a monthly fee from subscribers. No ads." I fleshed it out for him.

My pulse throbbed in my neck when I heard, "I love it."

With a lump in my throat, I said, "Jerry, Jerry, I'm so—"

He cut me off with a big "but." I choked up. He explained that he was looking for an incrementally modest and safe way to expand HBO's success, not another costly start-up in an entirely new genre. Money talks, and I'd seen him keep HBO alive in its early phase. He encouraged me to conjure something better suited to his business plan. I tried but was haunted by the idea of a high-quality performing arts network at a modest monthly cost for anyone and everyone. I had to find a way to make it happen.

For five-star advice on how to get past Jerry's rejection, I had a friend whose genius rose above even sister Judy's transcendent intellect. It was the same Felix Rohatyn, the financial wizard who'd saved New York from bankruptcy and later served as ambassador to France. Earlier, we enjoyed a romance and remained friends after his second marriage. We made a date for lunch in the Oak Room at the Plaza. I sipped my favorite Montrachet as his agile brain shifted from current global economic and political crises to my culture channel concept. The idea tested well with him. I was touched that it reminded him of the time I'd brought Public-Access camera equipment and training crew to the halfway house for ex-convicts he secretly supported. Felix suggested I take my idea to Bill Paley, founder and CEO of the Columbia Broadcasting System.

He added, "My dear friend Bill thinks you're terrific." I assumed that must have come from the times Paley and I had met regarding the *People* series, along with the fun he had at our launch party. I put Paley's name in my mind, but I'd need Jerry's help to protect my standing at Time. He'd rejected my idea for HBO but shared my belief that great art should be available to anyone who craved it.

At a private meeting in his office, I floated a self-serving scheme to bring the concept to the one man likely to take it on. I added that it needed to be without endangering my future at *Time Inc.* Jerry agreed that Paley would favor his return to excellence, okayed my scheme, and promised that if it didn't work, my situation at Time would be protected by an eyes-only mission. "Yes, do it, Charlotte. It'll be our secret." I thought again of Einstein's clever take on miracles. For years I'd wanted to actualize ideas that appealed to me culturally and politically.

If there was anyone who could bring this channel idea to fruition, it was William S. Paley.

# PART 14

# Labor of Love

Smack-dab in the middle of all this, David and Lucinda decided to take the plunge. My son getting married was a very big deal for me. David enjoyed a superb reputation for integrity and high taste. I loved that he asked me to produce their wedding. Lucinda's dad had abandoned her, three sisters and their Irish mother in his country, Puerto Rico. Lucinda's mom died in her fifteen-year-old arms. It was written in the stars that I be mom to the bride, which stayed true for thirty-five years—starting when we were three thousand miles apart. My bi-coastal career made for frequent visits.

I chose the Harkness Pavilion on Fifth Avenue for the ceremony and reception. Formerly the home of a ballet company, the space was a gorgeous mansion with elegant, large, yet homey rooms and a winding staircase to the lobby where we held the ceremony. I stood with David's proud brothers, their dad, and the guests at our version of the traditional *chuppah*, the bridal canopy. The young, smashing rabbi's limpid eyes were rapturously focused on Lucinda's exquisiteness. She told him she wanted to be Jewish. He told her that would take a complex, time-consuming conversion process. Her pleading eyes were fixed on his as she begged him to "do it now." The smitten rabbi said a few Hebrew words and, with his hand on her brow, declared, "You're Jewish." As I looked at my stunning son and his bijou bride, my life flashed before me as an affirmation. I knew that as frivolous as Lucinda's unexpected request to the rabbi appeared, she was dead serious. The years that followed proved me right. And there'd been a grand reception. The caterer's parting words were, "This is the best-divorced wedding I've ever done." The compliment made me laugh proudly that we'd pulled off a bi-partisan wedding party harmoniously. I went to bed that night feeling fine and woke in the morning with a different production on my mind.

I was about to take my brainstorm to the King of CBS. His passion for excellence had earned the nickname "Tiffany Network." When he'd withdrawn from making award-winning program decisions, *Beverly Hillbillies* and the like tarnished the image of the once resplendent network. I hoped to persuade him that a fine cultural cable channel could be his legacy-restoring swan song. Dared I approach him after he'd canceled my *People* TV series? Would he even talk to me? I took a shot with a letter:

*Dear Mr. Paley,*

*Last year I created and produced the* People *series. You may have been too hasty canceling a show with a name and a concept as good as* People, *the first prime-time nonfiction entertainment series on television. The quick success of NBC's* Real People *thrown together as soon as we were canceled is testimony to that mistake. Reality television is a trend I'd anticipated not knowing it could include a horror story of horror stories. On the frontier of cable and pay television for nine years, I felt it inevitable that broadcast television would need to do more of what it does best, i.e., news, documentaries, live events, sports, and new generic forms arising out of those specialties.*

*R-rated uncut movies, Vegas shows, the Richard Pryors and George Carlins in their raw honesty of language and style, and so on will cut into primetime audiences more and more as the cable universe grows, requiring innovative and less costly competitive fare from the broadcast networks. There are two ways that I can help: I am knowledgeable and experienced in the alternate technologies of television, their programming, marketing strategies, and needs, and I can assist CBS's entry into that world, and quite good at producing, as you know. Can we talk?*

*Sincerely,*
*Charlotte Schiff-Jones*

"Mr. Paley's on the phone," whispered my secretary in a shaky voice. Her eyebrows high in disbelief, she handed me the receiver.

A sonorous, commanding but gentle voice asked, "How soon can you be in my office?"

Three hours later, still in the jogging shoes I'd forgotten to exchange with proper ones I kept in a desk drawer, I watched the stunning man stride toward me. His outstretched hand gripped mine. On our way to his inner office, we walked through a panoply of great art, exquisite Rodin sculptures resting on the Persian carpet as if they'd never been anywhere else. Then, sitting behind his horseshoe desk, he motioned me to a chair I'd seen at the Museum of Modern Art, which he'd cofounded with Nelson Rockefeller. I prayed he'd notice neither my sneakers nor my trembling. I managed to say boldly, "I'm sure you regret canceling my series, Mr. Paley. I'm here to steer you away from a bigger mistake…letting cable television pass you by." He nodded. I took my time to spell out the cultural concept as I'd done with Jerry and Felix. I segued to compliment his genius in making mass entertainment award-winning and profitable. Then I enlightened him on the uniqueness of narrowcasting that made possible multiple venues for quality programs, not just the few Emmy Award shows squeezed here and there into the mass appeal schedule. He heard me, his smile wider, his back straighter. He was as green about cable as Time's Jim Shepley was when we met.

# Big Art in a Small Box

I talked with William Paley and explained how a multiplicity of channels made it possible for a three-hour block of programs to be repeated daily, the monthly subscriber fee replacing ad revenue. That the content would be all the arts led to a rich dialogue filled with positive energy. An hour later, I tried to rise from my seat as Paley, still smiling, pushed back his giant chair and stood up taller than before. But I was stuck, I lifted my butt to pull the bottom half of my sweat-dampened Armani pants suit from the chair, so I could stand. He escorted me to the side door of his outer office. I was struck again to see those paintings by Rothko, Matisse, Sargent, and the original CBS microphone on a pedestal beneath them.

I stopped to say, "Mr. Paley, may I take a moment to enjoy the masterpieces I sped by on the way in?"

He sat down on a Knoll sofa, legs stretched out, arms resting on his chest, and with a broad grin, he said, "My pleasure. Take your time."

I met with the head of the Broadcast group at CBS Television City in Hollywood, as arranged by Mr. Paley. In a room flooded with omnipresent sunshine, a striking figure stood well-lit at center stage. Gene Jankowsky's restless moves and shifty glances told me he wished the meeting were over before we'd even said hello. He muttered, "Cable's a pig in a poke. It'll never make a dent in the power and reach of broadcast television." Then he remarked snidely that his leader's frequent "spasms were humored until they faded away…as this one will…the old man should have passed the baton to his successor long ago."

It was hard to believe. The top executive of network operations was trashing the King of broadcasting. He was committing outright sedition by revealing it to a stranger. Had Paley become King Lear? Was I expected to go through the motions until the Paley spasm sputters out? The traitor opened his office door and stood waiting for me to leave. His last words were, "Your scheme will not make it to the light of day if I have anything to do with it, which I do. Have a good flight."

His troops might have been restless, but the King would prevail, and I'd try to be a smarter Cordelia. Or, like Lear, would Paley become a dead king walking, past adoration, loyalty, and respect? Were fear and imagination making me paranoid? I was ordered to conduct an evaluation process to assess the broadcast executives' cable channel ideas along with mine. I was expected to report my analysis at a retreat upstate. When I presented all the options, including my culture cable channel concept, to nearly a dozen white male broadcasters, I recommended culture as the clearest way to enter the changing television universe with a winning package.

They preferred their idea, which was to emulate local stations by using reruns of soap operas, *60 Minutes*, and other programs that broadcast networks were now allowed to own. They chose a sneaky way to tread water until Paley's spasm ended. My savior chose the culture channel. And having failed in its ploy for a cheap way out, the broadcast group fought me like a den of rabid dogs, especially on the issue of ads versus pay. In that fight, Paley agreed with them as it was what he knew. I told him that having commercials was a bad plan for a narrow audience without ratings, but they closed in on him. I wondered if they knew that once you strike at a King, you cannot go back. But I was sure they'd fight like hell to keep the crazy broad from getting in the way of their palace revolt. I had to convince the man who raised his network to great heights that a premium channel would attract modest-sized but loyal audiences willing to pay monthly fees for programs not available in this volume anywhere else and that his plan would put CBS on the competitive edge of the future. I stressed that HBO's format was the way to go. He appeared persuaded.

At a hotel in Montauk with ocean on three sides, we held a retreat to choose performing arts experts. On the first night, I sat on the sand listening to the ebb and flow of the ocean, feeling familiar damp sand between my toes. I thought, please let this be the place to carve out direction amid crass cross-purposes. Premium versus ad sales was not the only rift still unresolved. I was dealing with broadcasters who loved *Hee Haw* and had never heard of Balanchine. They lived in a universe of soap operas and reality shows, a very different sphere than the one with Paley's classic, award-winning *Omnibus*. We assembled the best and the brightest for high- quality content: For the head of programming, Jack Williams, creator of *The Great American Dream Machine*; for dance, Merrill Brockway of *Dance in America*; for specials, Stephanie Sills, television and Broadway producer; for music, Roger Englander of Leonard Bernstein's *Young People's Concerts*; for acquisitions, multilingual Brazilian with global connections and a great track record, Regina Dantas. They were a stellar group with more to follow.

I created a stunning pictorial brochure with graphic help from the CBS art department.

In the narrative, "CBS Cable for poetry in motion, a symphony of the ages, a festival of drama, a celebration of the arts." For me, it would be a labor of love to bring high art to everyone, a dream that had moved me to walk away from *Time Inc*. But if the King was fading, I worried I might be a casualty of his declining power. I needed to create a campaign against the conspirators, lose a battle here and there, but win the war. The first fight was waged and won by them unilaterally.

Jankowski brought in Dick Cox, his out-of-work local station's former manager buddy, to run CBS Cable—or to kill it. He met not one requisite for the job. I'd departed *Time Inc*. on Paley's word. And I'd always worked without a contract. Even with an MBA, it hadn't occurred to me to ask for one, another common female mistake in those days. That excuse doesn't free me from an egregious error with reckless disregard for consequences. Time's door was now closed.

Fueled by enthusiasm from the mogul who ruled, my job was to survive the enemy.

Hoping to win yet another Dick over to my side, I entered his office every day to sweetly say, "Good morning."

Without fail, he clutched his head in his hands and growled, "You're driving me crazy!"

But the top boss had my back, and the channel would move forward. For our first cable convention in Anaheim, California, I engaged a multimedia genius. Together we created a show for a custom-made mini-theater on the exhibit floor. It was a four-wall montage of splendiferous video clips exemplifying what CBS Cable would be, a fifteen-minute taste of what was to come. The lines of eager viewers getting longer and longer, the goal was to excite them with fabulous clips of superior entertainment by known stars.

The mainstay of cable channel success was signing up systems to carry their fare. For CBS Cable at this convention, I hosted a posh party on the Queen Mary to win over as many major cable companies as possible, fully aware that everything had to excite them whether or not they had any history with high-quality culture. I persuaded Sarah Vaughn to be our show's star by giving her something she craved. I'd learned from Susskind the trick of digging deep to find a superstar's secret wish. My research uncovered Sarah's yearning to be backed by a symphony orchestra, so I arranged a seventy-five- piece Los Angeles philharmonic orchestra. Sarah reacted as if heaven had come down just for her, and the musicians were ecstatic to accompany her, and they did so at minimum cost.

We'd gained access to two million subscribers before we'd even launched. I was confident we'd earn critical raves and awards across the board with programs like Joseph Papp's *Taming of the Shrew* with Meryl Streep, Twyla Tharp's first televised ballet, and an interview series suggested by Paley we named *Signature,* modeled after one in the UK.

The cameras studied the subject's face. The unseen interviewer was to let silent pauses instigate richer answers. It did move subjects to dig deeper and be personal to fill the disconcerting black hole.

High quality was a nightmare to the fearful little men who surrounded the King. Their bad dream made them think they'd lose it all. If they'd been blessed with foresight, they would have ended up owning the future. In any case, Paley was still smiling, the saving grace that kept me moving forward. I knew he had to keep his crown long enough to outplay the forces against him—and me. I counted on it.

It's hard for me to explain the multilayered complexity of creating a network in the early stages of a brand-new industry. Ambience speaks volumes, so I held parties in places that naturally reflected the channel's profile. The black-tie Queen Mary affair carried an Elizabethan theme, counterpointed by featuring Sarah Vaughn living out her dream of being backed by a classical orchestra. Son David and his lovely Lucinda were my gorgeous guests in exquisite formal attire. Cable operators surprised the cynical CBS brass who had warned that "operators will not comply with the dress code." In fact, formal rental shops were sold out in a fifty-mile radius.

Months later, at the Natural History Museum in Los Angeles, guests danced around the dinosaurs. I'd known for some time that the official launch should take place at the New York Public Library. Marion Heiskell, wife of *Time Inc.*'s chairman and a member of the library's board of directors, graciously afforded access when I asked, and she expanded it to include historic private spaces yet unseen by the public. The next cable convention would be in Las Vegas. Fake Roman statues at Caesar's Palace, neon lights, and gaming tables did not cut it for our theme. On my first drive on the strip, I felt like I was inside a pinball machine. I found no right setting in Vegas. We needed suitable aura to persuade operators who'd never seen a ballet to sign up for culture. There wasn't a right setting. And so, I created a Pahlavi in the distant desert, replete with wild chickens, Persian rugs, and barrels of pomegranates. A curtain would open at dinner time to reveal a dance floor and tables.

Our eventful parties had cable systems across the country signing up for our network. The subscriber potential each one generated was proof in the posh pudding that we had sparked an appetite. Our parties were the talk of the cable universe, and our programs were winning awards. The broadcaster insurgents claimed we would go broke spending all that money on parties. They must have gotten their information from alternate facts, as our events were produced way below budget, mostly due to smart tradeoffs and clever planning.

Back at Black Rock, it remained a war of the worlds—the old and the new. I kept pressing what I envisioned was the only way to proceed: a premium channel for which subscribers make a monthly payment. Persuaded by me again, Paley called for another re-run of the numbers. When I marched with the men to his grand conference room, I was told, "Do not speak on the subject, not a word. If you do, there will be consequences."

Once inside, my King moved right to the point, and Jankowski's troops argued for commercials. Paley raised questions and listened to the answers. As commanded, I stayed silent. Then the whole room went silent. The founder of the top broadcast network turned to me. "So, Charlotte, I need to hear from you. Be straight with me. How do you feel about this?" I thought if I uttered a single word, they'd take out a contract on my life or smash my kneecaps. Orders are orders. Threats are threats. An inner voice told me to say nothing. My mind answered the inner voice. It warned me that the founder, chairman, and CEO of this giant organization was still the King who'd commanded me to answer his question. If I was Cordelia in this play, look at what staying silent had done for her. She said nothing. To her silence, Lear said, "Nothing will come of nothing," and he disinherited her. I stated strongly that it should be a premium channel.

The boss demanded they take yet another look at the numbers. Returning with the cortege to the elevators, I felt like I was walking the last mile. I held my breath as if under water. As we dispersed, farewells were monosyllabic with no eye contact. We had access to millions more subscribers after the Vegas party. Weeks passed before Paley called me to a private meeting. He rambled on as he picked up scraps of paper and napkins scattered on his desk, which were scribbled with ideas: "How about parades—the Chinese New Year?" Paley had become King Lear in the fullest sense. Lear's words toward his tragic end came back to me:

> *I am a very foolish fond old man,*
> *Fourscore and upward, not an hour more or less,*
> *And, to deal plainly,*
> *I fear I am not in my perfect mind.*

Paley asked, "Charlotte, why were you not at the last meeting on ads versus pay?"

"What meeting?" I asked.

He frowned at the exclusion. To watch the revered master of network television as he reacted to an insult was heart-rending. The man who was still my King stood still, staring at nothing.

I leaned toward him to hear his whisper but couldn't make out what he was saying. I needed to press the case that my secret master plan was making headway. But his wretched embarrassment from the mutiny of his troops made me think of him as a dead King walking. His infected court was committing slow regicide, and I could do nothing. Unlike Cordelia, I had not been banished and was still breathing. I worked overtime, continuing to persuade major cable companies to assume payment of ten cents per subscriber each month to save a network they didn't want to lose. A look at the numbers told me we'd be operating in the black in less than a year. My offer was what no one with any sense would refuse, surely not the man who ordained me to go for it in the first place.

Working on my last chance to save my prime venture, I was hit by a bolt that rocked me so hard I nearly fainted. William S. Paley retired.

The pirates were now free to sink the ship with me in it. The board refused even to hear about the deals I'd made or the financial benefits guaranteed. The "broadcast mafia" allowed fear and resentment to get in the way of what was right for CBS's future. I had given all to a labor of love beyond anything I'd ever known. My heart broken, tears slid down my cheeks. I'll never forget the pain. The self-serving falseness of their narrow-minded refusal to even look at the truth brought me down with a hurt not likely to ever heal entirely.

Writing a eulogy in *The New York Times* entitled, "Who Killed CBS Cable?" critic Les Brown's answer to the question was "Senior CBS management did." And thirty-five years later, he agreed that CBS Cable would now be worth at least $5 billion and might have transformed the relationship between true art and the medium of television.

Actually, this is the story of a love affair and a murder. The hit men had fulfilled their secret pact. But let it be known that if Paley had not been driven off the stage, his love affair with quality, combined with CBS's deep pockets would now be seen daily on our huge, flat, around-sound television screens. Shakespeare had King Lear say at his end, "As flies to wanton boys are we to the gods. They kill us for their sport." The metaphor stayed true right up to the end.

All of the above is true, but sadly there's more. CBS Cable was dead also because I tried and failed to get the mutineers out of my way. I'd failed against their hate. I'd failed to push back harder. I'd failed to protect William S. Paley, the man at the top of the television world. The gravest failure of all was allowing myself to believe that since he was on my side, we'd make this thing come to life in spite of the insurgents plotting to topple the King who was no longer theirs.

In dim light and alone, I poured Saint-Émillion red wine into a crystal glass normally saved for special company. This night, I was the special company, torn by the insurrectionists' hard-edged bitterness and my wounded pride. For a journey into my soul, I played Billie Holiday laments, lit candles in the empty bedroom, and lay down to hear her throaty, pained voice sing to my heart, "Don't Know If I'm a Comin' or a Goin'." I listened, thinking of her struggle in a fight she couldn't win. A crushing blow hit me—my madness for having left

*Time Inc.*, a better situation than I'd ever dreamed possible. I'd been a woman who was held high by a revered institution. It was a serious mistake to look down at colleagues whose work was focused largely on future financial security. I'd already been awarded hundreds of stock options with promises of more, but with raw arrogance, I refused to narrow my ambitions to ensure my own staple future. How foolish it was for me to see those who passed up creative challenges in favor of job security—corridor zombies who benefitted by playing it safe.

When CBS Cable was assassinated, the realization of my former *Time Inc.* colleagues' far-sighted clarity of purpose made me jealous and full of regrets. My worst failure of all was failing to codify my CBS deal with a signed contract. I believed the handshake with the revered magnate was my contract. The idea to bring culture to everyone was ahead of its time, and it bedeviled me. And did so just as the notion of ending his career with a new round of high-quality programs certain to win Emmy Awards galore bedeviled Paley. That was enough for me. It should not have been. It was absurd to think I could beat insurmountable odds apparent at the start. The mutineers won. I lost. And so had the cable subscribers who could no longer enjoy a wealth of superb, top-of-the-line television.

Somehow even after it all, nothing kills my cockeyed optimism. My answer to what's next was to get corporate cheating hearts outta my way. An urge returned to do what I'd done once before after not succeeding to get a bad situation out of my way. I opened the same window that faced the park, felt the breeze, and sucked in its freshness. It was vital I find a way to pay the rent since my divorce provided miniscule financial support.

# PART 15

# On My Own

Corporate job offers proliferated. I hopped, skipped, and jumped around them like a kid playing hide-and-seek, not wanting to be found. I emptied the mailbox out of robotic habit, expecting only marketing garbage and unwelcome bills. I was surprised to find a personal letter. It was from Dick Leghorn, a good-natured fellow cable pioneer from Cape Cod. He wrote that he needed me. I could feel something else in the envelope. It was a contract for a one-year $12,000 monthly retainer. He wanted me to create a market strategy and campaign for a new technical invention by his partner, the man who'd created the chyron crawl that electronically presents messages on the bottom of TV screens. This looked like a possible way to escape the corporate cauldron, but the complex invention was over my head.

I phoned him to ask, "Why me, Dick?"

He said, "I've watched you interact at conventions, conferences, panels. They adore you. You can do this."

He whetted my atrophied appetite, but since I could only notionally grasp the technology, I declined.

Dick pressed on with, "No, Charlotte, we'll give you talking points. You could sell brassieres to the Maasai."

Since there were no other noncorporate options open at that moment, I said yes and took it on. I finagled a free desk in a friend's law firm as a workspace.

# Schiff-Jones Ltd.

With an eye toward using that spot for the start of a consulting company, I incorporated Schiff-Jones Ltd. and wrote my own press release. Clients started knocking at the door before I had one. They must have been inspired by the strong feature articles in the trade papers about me and my new company. Client volume was growing. It was time to move my headquarters. A friend offered space in his suite of offices in the Hotel Delmonico on Park Avenue. I walked through the glorious high end of the East Side to check it out. I tiptoed through an arc-shaped doorway into a lobby with museum- worthy art on its walls. At his suite, there was enough space for me and two staff people. I negotiated a reduced rent in a barter exchange for my services. I was helped by former associates to find and hire a secretary and a savvy alter ego named Mikey. She eased into a role that would prove to be more critical than we could possibly have imagined.

I walked to work, taking different routes every day. With fresh turns on the side streets and avenues, I soaked up faces, traffic, and store windows as if I were in some foreign city for the first time. Each pathway felt like a river that narrows and bends. I liked where it would take me. There was no way to escape giant corporations entirely, but they paid me to tell them what to do. One new client was RKO Pictures. I dug into the archives for its long history: the first talkie, with Al Jolson; the masterstroke of coupling Hepburn and Tracy; Fred Astaire and Ginger Rogers. Most notable among their successful films was *Citizen Kane*, considered by many to be the greatest movie ever made. Bob Manbe, as chairman and president, was on a hunt to bring

RKO Pictures back to life. Was my connection serendipity, or was dark destiny on its way again?

I was given a handsome retainer to find producers who were "wholesome and positive" and open to a deal with RKO to finance their overhead. In exchange, RKO would reap half ownership of all their TV and film projects. I engaged a well-connected friend's friend, Frank McKevitt, to set up meetings in LA with Jon Peters, Peter Guber, Robert Evans, and others.

They were not interested in the deal, but luck struck a match with Ron Howard and Brian Grazer, who worked together. Howard started in 1959 as a child actor in *The Journey*, then *The Music Man*, and an episode of *The Twilight Zone*. Still very young, he directed the film *Grand Auto Theft* in 1978. Grazer started producing and developing TV pilots in 1975. These young men were start-up, multitalented makers of family-friendly fare, as evidenced by their separate work even before 1980, the year they met. Both were directors and producers whose tastes and ambitions were a good match. Their first joint feature film was in production. Frank and I worked out a contract with them that honored RKO's specifications. I came back from LA with RKO's future (and mine) in hand. Bob told me to expect an answer after they'd examined other options—other options?

He was slow to decide. I warned him that Howard & Grazer's first major film would be released fairly soon, and if a hit, RKO would have missed the boat to partner on all their projects for a $2 million annual overhead. The partners were getting more than antsy. I pressed hard for a decision. Finally, Bob confessed that he'd chosen a David Hare film to produce in New Zealand, "a tax-saving money decision." He passed on the coup of the century. It so happens that in 1984, their first film was released by their new company, Imagine Entertainment. *Splash* was a blockbuster, as nearly all their films that followed. What a blow! I'd hit the jackpot and lost a life- changing deal yet again. A curse? I'd been pretty good at getting obstacles out of my way, and those damn forces butted in and messed things up again. First, it was the mutineers at CBS Cable, and a month later, waiting for a golden green light for a once-in-a-lifetime opportunity, Bob went for a loser to save a dime. If I believed in astrology, I'd think some planets were lining up against me. Or was it just another notch in my belt of smart moves that went up in smoke? For some reason, RKO remained a client. Maybe Bob looked in the mirror and saw the guy who'd said no to a mine that would have produced diamond after diamond. Instead, he made a myopic choice that bombed.

Wallowing in a blue funk, I received a message from Sir Denis Forman, Chairman of Granada Television, with whom I'd worked when at CBS Cable. It read, "We think we should enter the cable television business, Charlotte. You're the expert who can tell us if, when, and how we should do that." Saved by the bell! They flew me to London on the Concord. I arrived in time to change clothes for cocktails at Sir Denis's lovely home. A bit late, I entered to hear a ferocious battle about the recent British invasion of the Falkland Islands. Lady Helen, Sir Denis's wife, was battling with their guests, the maharaja and maharani of an Indian province where Granada had filmed *Jewel in the Crown*, the latest among a stream of highly acclaimed, epic series. At the end of their highly charged political dispute, we were driven to Covent Garden Theater and ushered up to the King's Royal Box. I sat struggling to keep my jet-lagged eyes open in order to watch a Kenneth MacMillan ballet. To be served a King's dinner at our seats at intermission was like living in Downton Abby. Sir Denis hired me to put together the American cable story from all its aspects relevant to the UK. I stayed in London for a week, spent time at BBC headquarters asking questions, met with President David Jones of Century Television, and learned a lot about the tele-viewing habits of the British people.

In the US, there used to be only three commercial broadcast networks and one public channel. The signal was broadcast through the air as an electromagnetic wave that traveled fast but not far, so transmitters were needed. Coaxial cable took care of that by adding more bands through, adding many more channels were possible.

However, my recommendation to Granada was to refrain from entering the capital-intensive business of building system hardware and wiring neighborhoods and buildings. My rationale was based first on the fact that tele-watching in the UK was nowhere near the American addiction, and the independent network, Channel Four, was about to cater to minorities, and Rupert Murdoch's Sky Network was up and running.

The high costs to build each cable system might bear fruit in the short term, but I knew cable's lifespan had to be measured against the growth rate of competitive technologies. And although I gave Forman a step-by-step history of the successful American cable television evolution, I ended my report with this: "Don't do it. Cable will be replaced by more efficient and less costly technologies." I added a main point peculiar to his company: "The steady flow of superb series like *Brideshead Revisited, The Jewel in the Crown, I, Claudius,* and on and on, your content was and always will be evergreen. As creators of honored and prized television, you do what you do magnificently. Keep building your superb library of universally acclaimed programs to feed a demand headed for expansion with venues and devices multiplying exponentially." I felt strongly that Granada should respect the fact that cable television was destined to be replaced by myriad alternatives, eventually reducing it. I recommended that Granada continue to do what it does best, feed a demand that would keep growing. Sir Denis Forman took my advice, and when what I'd predicted started to happen pretty fast, he must have been pleased that he hadn't poured millions into hardware when software was Granada's strength. And that year, Granada and RKO were my clients at the TV version of the Cannes Film Festival. Bob out of his comfort zone, I became his seeing-eye dog through the boisterous, bustling buyers, sellers, and sycophants. I produced events for both him and Granada's Leila Maw for their targeted buyers and sellers that were successful.

Mikey's first words on my return were "Hugh Heffner had a heart attack."

I asked what that had to do with me. She said, "Christie Heffner wants to talk to you about Playboy Enterprises."

What in the world would they want from a raging feminist? Maybe a prank! In the end, curiosity won the day. I flew to Chicago. A harsh lake wind hit me on the short walk from the Drake Hotel to the Playboy Building. Inside, the plethora of Playboy bunnies and playmates gave me the creeps. Hefner's philosophy was always anathema to me. This was a strange turn of events. Christie confirmed that her dad's heart attack put him out of commission. She wanted me to assess what resistance she'd face modifying the company's image. Ah, I liked that! She was looking to know in advance who'd be receptive to change, who would not, and why. The mandate intrigued me. Christie turned out to be smart, straight, and of all things, a true feminist. This could be fun!

My first interview was with the editor in chief. What's with these guys with heads down and spectacles fighting to stay on their noses? He kept checking his watch as I spoke. I couldn't get a conversation started.

I tried, "Who chooses the fiction? Often quite good, by the way." No answer. "Who's your brilliant cartoon editor?" Nothing. "Why do you still use the Playmate of the Month centerfold? Photos of near-naked women in *Vogue* are more beautiful and sexier."

In a nasty tone, still looking down, he said, "That's why men buy the magazine."

In spite of his temples pulsating, I persisted. "Then I must ask you…with *Penthouse* and *Hustler* crossing the gynecological line, and you don't…how many one-handed readers do you still have?"

He whipped off his eyeglasses, covered his watch, and leaned back in his chair, suddenly alert and more than willing to engage in an honest exchange. It turned out he was open to change. We connected. Then he made a pass, but in a decent way, so I declined gracefully. Then I interviewed the cartoon editor, the cable channel manager, the head of the Playboy Clubs, and several others in management positions. The degree of resistance was marginal. An early suggestion I proffered was to terminate the Playboy Clubs and follow Disney's lead in protecting their powerful brand. Corporate cultures can change, but brand names known globally like Disney and Playboy must be protected. I submitted a final report.

Christie planned to incorporate several suggested changes, but her father recovered and ordered everything "back to normal at once." Moving on is easy for consultants because clients come and go like good meals—but not always. That was not the case when RKO chose a loser over the big winners who had bought into the deal. I didn't lose RKO as a client, but by Bob making a very poor decision, we all lost.

I started to miss the competitive battles inside corporate life. As a political junkie, internecine warfare actually fired me up—the CBS palace revolt was a punishing exception. And I agonized over RKO passing on the deal of the century. I still feel more than a pang from the successes of Imagine Entertainment that kept coming. The strange thing is that I'm so on their side for the remarkable, intelligent, beautifully conceived and produced cinema marvels that are family-friendly as desired by the head of RKO. Yet what mattered more was that Schiff-Jones Ltd. was flourishing. I had climbed my way up again after the assassination of my labor of love. Then something happened!

# PART 16

# I Had No Idea!

I remember the Italian Pavilion with Leila Maw.
I remember bragging about my thriving company.
I remember being in a hurry to get somewhere.
I don't remember where or why.
I don't remember any crash.
I don't remember any hospital.
I don't remember any coma.
I barely remember not remembering.

I knew nothing of the impact or what followed. The best I could do was put together a semblance of truths relayed to me by others, scattered notions that can't be relied upon, a kind of death. I'd been a camera with no film.

It scared me to think how lost I was, how alone. Dark, exasperating dreams came night after night. One stayed with me. *Gotta get up. Walk around and around the block—afraid to cross the street. Where do I go if I cross the street?* Never mind—try to think of something else to think about. I had to get up. Had to get dressed. Couldn't find anything. My big sister Judy reminded me that flattering stories had moved me to incorporate my company. She told me my executive assistant was doing the best she could, but things had slowed down.

My last real memory before the crash came to me. It took place outside the Italian Pavilion on West Fifty-Sixth Street in Manhattan on a clear, sunny day. I was with client Leila Maw of UK's Granada Television. We'd had lunch in a very authentic Italian ristorante. Artistically photographed segments of Michelangelo's David were set in unexpected places throughout. The great statue's right foot—or left foot?—was next to our well-placed table. We were in my favorite trattoria. It's not there anymore. After lunch, we stood on the narrow, noisy sidewalk talking. We raised our voices to be heard against heavy traffic and shouted every time a fire truck or ambulance blared by. Leila and I were scheduling another Concord flight to London for a meeting with Sir Denis Forman, Granada's CEO and founder. I looked at my watch to check on possible dates and saw the time! I shouted, "I'm late for a very important date with a new client." I ran toward my office, hoping the new client would still be there.

When I woke up in my own bed, my family told me the clear, sunny day was a long time ago. It was the day my life was ripped apart. It needed to be fitted back together piece by painful, jagged piece, like a giant jigsaw puzzle—out of joint, surreal, unreal, too real. I had no memory of any of what happened. They told me things. Judy said that after a horrific accident, I was taken by ambulance in a coma to Roosevelt Hospital and was there for a long time, close to death with a broken skull and broken body. My son David told me his brother Richard, sounding terrified, had called him in LA to let him know and said, "I thought she was dead… spread out on a gurney as still and gray as stone. Her face had no expression." Someone else told me Richard turned ashen when he saw me, my sentimental son whose strong feelings are private. I dreamed relentless dreams of moving in and out of a tunnel. A neurologist explained that they came from unconscious memories of CT scans to find and end life-threatening blood clots.

I have a vague memory of how lost I felt when I came out of the coma. My eyes opened. A hand clutched a wrist, and I felt a pulse, my pulse. My body was alive, but I felt inanimate, insensate, cold. The dark, exasperating dreams came back.

Recovery took more than finding my mind. When they sent me to a physical rehabilitation center, I entered a large space, and there stood a tall, muscular, hairless man who looked like Atlas without his globe. This man was known as Doc. I never knew his name. He shouted orders to me and all the people he was helping. His Dickensian demands became harrowing rigor. He imposed rules. Rule 1: no air conditioning, even when New York summer temperatures hit the high nineties. Rule 2: long sleeves and long sweatpants in winter and summer. Rule 3: heavy lead boots—yes, lead boots—for maximum effect from leg exercises.

The workouts were exhausting, yet I stayed sharp to abide by Doc's strict orders. The prize for laborious pain would be to cure me. After all, Doc may have been a crazy loon, but he was a genius to straighten me out as well as he did. I came to understand that his concept was centered on balance and alignment, and his fundamentals stayed with me to this day. My body never forgot what he taught me. I have no idea how or with whom I made it to his torture chamber almost every day for three years. Somehow my company's doors were kept open. My staff had been servicing remaining clients—RKO, Granada, MTV Networks—but there were no new ones. My assistant told me much later that I'd rarely come to the office or even place a call.

It was two years into rehab when at home, a strange voice on the telephone told me both bank accounts were empty. I panicked. Felt faint. Couldn't get enough air in my lungs. It seems my assistant Mikey had done her best to keep open Schiff-Jones Ltd., my thriving consulting company. I had given her the authority to write checks for the high rent, generous salaries, and my personal obligations to cover my travel absences. More money was going out than coming in. I had one option: dissolve the corporation and give up a superb suite of offices in the elegant Hotel Delmonico. No more looking at the naked lady, one of Botero's "fat subject" bronzes on Park Avenue's median strip outside my window. I loved my grand office, but its loss was a drop in the bucket compared to my sea of troubles.

Thousands of dollars in stock options from years in corporate America were gone. My winning entrepreneurial enterprise and my new house in the Hamptons flew away like confetti. Against the losses— mental, emotional, and financial—I tried to find a way to survive. What do I do? What's left? Friends must have come to commiserate, but I don't remember who. My sons were young men carving out their futures. Two of the three, David and Paul, were too many miles away, with Richard soon to follow. The price for being free of a troubled seventeen-year marriage had been my acceptance of no alimony or settlement. I was busted and alone. I wanted to die.

In the third year of recovery, lost words began to come back, along with the awareness of how far out of the loop I was. The words began to help my mind pick up on things that I could assess and react to with some reason. That felt good. Yet when I realized how broken I'd been and still was, despair hit me again. Getting out of bed in the morning was too much. How could I make it through the long day? Stay in bed. Try to sleep. Fitful sleep. Narcotic sleep. One day I woke up and didn't want to die anymore. I wanted to break something.

Somehow, I got myself to the office of my old friend, Dr. Richard Bader. He was tall, dark-haired, and otherwise aesthetically. But he was a genius. As soon as I saw his familiar, friendly face, I started to cry and couldn't stop. Nor could I catch my breath. I was breathing normally a cup of tea later, thanks to my doctor friend. He sat me down and said, "Charlotte dear, I want you to get out of bed tomorrow morning, take a shower, do your face and hair, dress in something you love, and go out…to the movies? A shopping spree? Maybe a museum you love." The next day I followed his advice to the letter.

I took the elevator down to the lobby and was greeted warmly by the surprised hall and doormen who hadn't seen me in ages. I stepped lively to the sidewalk where the sun shone bright and walked briskly to the corner. I stopped; I thought just to check the traffic. I saw no cars but could not cross the street. I was too terrified to cross the street. I stood at my own personal crossroads, not going left, not going right. I couldn't go straight back to the lobby. They would know. The hall and doormen would know. My sense of shame preposterous yet real. I walked around the block. I walked around and around the block. It hit me that I'd lost more than I thought. I'd lost myself. I waved for a cab to go back to Dr. Bader to confess I'd failed the experiment. His reaction was to fill out a prescription for an antidepressant. He gave me the first pill then and there and promised it would ease my "disability."

I raised my hands to my head and squeezed them to stop the pain. He gripped my trembling palms, held them still, and then sent me to the restroom for repairs. I looked into the mirror and saw myself. Or did I? "Mirror, mirror, on the wall, do you know this me at all?" Then, his word, "disability," came to mind and rang a bell. I rushed back to his office. "Richard, did you say 'disability'? I think I took out a policy. Mikey would know. Call her for me."

He talked to Mikey, listened a bit, and said, "Yes, I'll hold." He finally smiled at me. "Charlotte, you signed a contract with your broker two days before the accident. Mikey checked the policy with him. You will receive tax-free $4,000 every month until you're sixty-five."

Chicken Little was right. The sky had fallen. But a disability policy executed when I started my company fixed that. Mikey had validated what I feared was a crazy made-up idea. With a deep sigh of relief, Bader restated his personal prescription for a happy day in the city. I exited his Fifth Avenue office building, lifted my chin, and strode home smiling. I crossed one street, then another, street after street, still smiling. The next day I awoke early, showered, washed, combed my hair, and painted my face like a ballet dancer. I dressed in a favorite brown suit with a beige silk blouse tied with a soft bow. Then I sprayed Chanel's Mademoiselle on my neck and wrists, slipped into my ankle boots, and rode down to the lobby and out to the sidewalk where the sun was shining. I walked to the corner. The traffic light was green, and I crossed the street.

# PART 17

# Waking Up to the Future

You know now that what kept me whole were healthcare and disability policies that covered basic daily expenses and pretty much everything else needed. The accident came just as my venture in the cottage industry was thriving, which had helped me survive the murder of CBS Cable, my proudest labor of love. My mind started to function a bit again. Was I to look for a job? No! Should I restart Schiff-Jones Ltd.? Absolutely not! To find my way, I read cable trades to catch up, but I'd been out of the loop too long, and it didn't assist me. Before my lost years, communications wizardry was actualized in science fiction stories I'd been devouring from teen-hood, like the love story by Jules Verne in which the characters are video-chatting in the nineteenth century.

I'd awakened to a rate of change that was toying with the speed of light: DVDs, digital compression, communications satellites, addressability, Wi-Fi, internet, and all things wireless—life-transforming at high speed even before artificial intelligence and robots were implementing life functions. Could I re- enter a world feeling more like an outsider than a pioneer—handicapped, sidelined, and out of the game, out of the future. I woke from a long, fitful three-year sleep, too often wishing I hadn't. I faced an uncertain future at a critical time.

There seemed to be no ceiling, the sky not the limit anymore. Cable advertising had grown to a billion-dollar industry just a few years after I'd introduced it. HBO and Showtime were winning Emmys, no longer reduced to less-significant cable awards. I'd spent my life proving to myself, and to the world, that I was somebody. Three years after being knocked down and out, I still didn't feel I'd ever be me again. I was floundering alone to find out who I was and what to do.

# This Is Broadway

In the third year of my recovery, a man I didn't know named Bob Simonello, phoned. The multimedia artisan said he wanted me for "a Broadway project." My theater life flashed before me like images some see when about to die. For me, it was John Raitt singing "If I Loved You" in *Carousel*, Lee J. Cobb as Willy Loman in *Death of a Salesman*—forever embedded in my soul—chain-smoking with Murray Shisgal at *Fragments* rehearsals with Gene Hackman, and Noel Coward smiling as he says "little bitch" when I bust him for stealing a joke from a master. It was fun to ponder delicious moments I'd forgotten. I was getting a bit better and stronger every day yet still had a long way to go.

I agreed to meet with Bob at my place. Right on schedule, a small, thin, shy man stood at my front door. He looked as nervous as I felt. We started with random small talk. He cut himself off midsentence to get to the point. "I want to bring Broadway to the masses." He talked of a tourist attraction for the thousands of people who know about Broadway but have never been or can't get enough Broadway or might be drawn to theater simply by the high-tech display of its history. How did he know I was in love with theater? He wanted me to marshal marketing and management forces behind his creation. He went on about making high-performance art accessible for everyone. Bob showing up with this great idea was odd, as I'd come up with the idea to bring performing arts to everyone, which led to CBS Cable. It smacked of divine irony when Bob said that what he'd seen on that channel was precisely what brought him to me.

Doubts be damned! I said yes before fully committing. I needed to view the eighteen projector multimedia demo he'd created and read the script. Both superb, I was on board. I suggested we name the tourist attraction *This Is Broadway*. While wracking my brain to reawaken strategic thinking, a sidebar wrinkle surfaced. Bob confessed certainty that he carried the AIDS virus.

This was before the plague had a name or a proper test. He was in the fight to shake up a stubborn bureaucracy that stayed silent and did nothing to eradicate false hysteria about a sexually transmitted contagion. His fear became my struggle too. His friend, Larry Kramer, broke the AIDS silence with *The Normal Heart*, a brilliant play I'd seen. My friend Dr. Mathilda Krim started searching for a cure early. Since I'd only barely recovered from a near-fatal accident, I felt a connection with Bob that brought to mind Martin Buber's book about special relationships. His quote, "Inscrutably involved, we live in the currents of reciprocity." Those words gave me a way to define this new friendship. Men like Bob were dying, while homophobia and ignorant panic were decimating decency.

My new gay partner and friend faced a plague that rejuvenated the activist in me. Before my crash and long recovery, I'd done my best to help oppressed and ignored people who wanted to belong, to be respected and treated fairly. It was comforting that the theater world became a haven for homosexuals who were victimized by the outside world in those days. The chance to be in a new fight for justice lifted me from self-absorption with my own struggle. *This Is Broadway* became *This Is Your Life* for both of us.

We screened Bob's brilliantly conceived and executed multimedia demo for my friend, the Schubert Organization's Jerry Schoenfeld. He promptly offered the Belasco Theater. The head of the other big theater chain, Nederlander, also showed up to pitch the New Amsterdam Theater, a welcome metaphor of Coca-Cola competing with Pepsi. To top it off, we were endorsed by the League of American Theaters and Producers and by Fred Papert, who headed the 42nd Street Development Corporation. He was eager for us to choose a theater on that famous, heavily trafficked street of historic theaters busily gentrifying. With my financial life shattered, my boys came through to finance an even more advanced demo to attract an underwriter. Bubbling over with gratitude, I gave my sons equity positions in the venture. In what was hardly the first business plan I'd written, an excerpt from the promotion section declared, "Viewers will come as close as is technologically possible to experience theater in a multidimensional otherworld through sounds and images." The brochure contended, "The artistry will bring the audience inside the history of Broadway as if they're living it." Working on the project did that for me. But I did fear that my recovery was still in progress, and that filled me with uncertainty. Was I up to taking on a project of this magnitude? I loved it so. I had to try.

The script was outlined in the presentation. The first images simulate the 1849 Astor Place riot, then move through minstrels, vaudeville, burlesque, and on to the *Ziegfeld Follies*. The audience would find itself front row center on the opening night of *Show Boat*, Broadway's first interracial chorus in a musical play about a serious subject. Our show would include everything from *Oklahoma!* to *A Chorus Line*, from John Barrymore's *Hamlet* to Judith Anderson's *Medea* and Richard Burton's *Equus*, and then segue to mosaics of plays by Tennessee Williams, Eugene O'Neill, and for me most important of all, Arthur Miller's *Death of a Salesman*."

The tourist attraction was designed to flow through Broadway's history—the history of our country: *Porgy and Bess; A Raisin in the*

*Sun*, Lorraine Hansberry's post-slavery transition drama; *Our Town*, Thornton Wilder's twentieth-century classic. The show would end with clips promoting the current fare. *This Is Broadway* would be a sweep of theater at the admission price of $25 to bring costly Broadway to nearly everyone who wanted a taste. If we could pull this off, I might see my personal finances turn from red to black and keep climbing. My juices bubbled with hope and excitement. Of course, financing a new venture required projections backed by solid, relevant, empirical data. For this venture, *Time Inc.* would not be around to give me a year to validate my numbers. What sent me to Columbia University for my graduate degree in business had a lot to do with learning how to validate projections. Now I knew how to measure the correlation between low-priced tickets and robust attendance and how to factor in high quality. I'd have no shame getting rich from what would enrich everyone who experienced it.

Seven million dollars was the needed capital. Where does one go for $7 million? Maybe a credit card company. Value-added elements are obvious for a company that processes most of the tickets. I tried American Express. CEO Jim Robinson's response to my letter was to come to a screening with an associate. They were enthralled through the full twenty minutes. More meetings and viewings with their colleagues moved us to the fine-tooth- combing phase. Two days before signing on the dotted line, Robinson was fired and projects under his imprimatur were canceled. No discussion. Over and out.

Serendipity introduced me to Frank Marshal, the man whose client, Mobil Oil, was in its worst public image. Frank had conjured the plan for Mobil to sponsor Masterpiece Theater. A lightbulb in my brain shined on Texaco. Not a crazy idea. There'd been *Texaco Star Theater* on TV and operas in *Live from the Met* on radio. I made the pitch, and after weeks of promising discussions, they not only spoke of signing on, they wanted it in Houston and four other cities, agreed to a $20 million budget, and offered us the refreshment concessions saying, "We make our money from liquid gold, not popcorn."

Texaco was at full throttle to close the deal. About to sign the "Letter of Agreement," after loving the demo, the head guy answered his cell phone. The call over, in a whisper, he said, "President Bush gave Iraq two weeks to withdraw from Kuwait, or there'll be war." He then said, "We have two oil fields there and will have to wait to see what happens. Two weeks in a lotus position at the foot of the TV, selfishness and shame were my handmaids; I should have worried about my country going to war, but I was focused on *This Is Broadway*. With a drumroll at the podium backed by flags, President George W. Bush announced he would "defend the world from grave danger." The phone kept ringing. My life seemed locked in pockets of time between milestones outside my influence. The what-if scenario rattled my cage as thoughts of a fine future faded away.

*This Is Broadway* could be a forever turnstile to New York Theater. It might find a way one day, but I needed to find a job somehow, somewhere! The great Winston Churchill defined success as "the ability to move from failure to failure with no loss of enthusiasm." I think it's safe to say after all I've been through, I'm not easy to kill—and neither is my drive. I'd survived a near-death accident and a damaged brain and body. Bob's anguished state of mind had reconnected me to what really mattered. The next day, I joined ACT UP, the pre-eminent AIDS awareness organization. But in my third year of recovery, a search for work was to begin in Los Angeles. We put the venture on hold when I flew west for job interviews with major players with whom I had history. David, Lucinda, and baby Kaylie lived there, and Paul had recently moved there too. To be with them had me salivating.

I set up meetings with John Malone, CEO of American Television Communications (ATC), Harvey Shepherd and Bob Daly of CBS, and John Cooke, head of the Disney Channel—all superstars with whom I had history. Looking good helped. In my Calvin Klein olive-green pantsuit, luggage- brown leather boots, and shoulder bag with a muted plaid Missoni coat over my shoulders, I stepped out for the first time in nearly three years, with head held high and a mind riddled with worry. At the airport, the gate agent shouted, "If you have an assigned seat on the 8:00-a.m. flight and are willing to take the next, you get a free round trip." The flight was overbooked. I raised my hand for the free pass, which was an antidote for my decline to the cheap seats, the symbol of my losses. Tickets were reprocessed, and six of us moved on to a restaurant for breakfast. A stylish African American man named Hylan Booker started to talk to me. Judy Pfeiffer's name came up. That she happened to be a mutual friend relaxed me.

Engrossed in conversation, we found ourselves left alone at the table and rushed to the gate in fear of missing the flight. I stopped at a restroom for a quick pee. He boarded the plane. When I entered the cabin, the only vacant seat was the one next to him. The plane took off. The aroma of roasting mixed nuts hit me hard. In years of traveling first class on expensed business trips, I'd become addicted to those nuts. I sucked in a deep breath and stood up to break the rules. I opened the drapes and said to the cabin attendant for the privileged "Miss, I can eat plastic food from plastic plates and manage to straighten my legs out of a viselike seat, but I cannot fly cross-country without your lovely nuts." Her face screwed up as she shrugged, looking annoyed.

# PART 18

# Valentine

I continued to plead for mercy. Then with a smile, she handed me a portion. Hylan and I chomped away. And then he saw *The Philosopher's Pupil*, by Iris Murdoch, on my lap and said, "Iris is a dear friend of mine."

I gasped, "How does the one and only Iris Murdoch, the great novelist, poet, and philosopher, happen to be your friend?"

He answered that she'd been his philosophy professor at the Royal College of Art in London, where he earned his master's degree in fashion design. They became great friends and still were. Conversing with such a man was a very welcome surprise on what was a scary trip for me. I did not know what to expect. My seatmate had lived in London for twenty-five years. I was fascinated by his tales about the fashion world and even more impressed by his love affair with literature and his friendships with other great writers.

When the plane began its descent to LAX, the man I'd known for eight hours asked if we might have dinner one night. I liked this super-bright, very young man, whose smile could melt glass and who made no pass the entire trip. I'd often made friends with men David's age, so why not have dinner with this charming youngster.

Then a subtle shift in his body language moved me to ask, "Are you talking about a date?"

I was fifty-three, and he appeared to be in his early thirties.

Looking a bit wounded, he said, "Yes, I am."

I said, "My name is not Mrs. Robinson, but thanks for trying."

He pulled out his passport laughing, and pointed to his date of birth, August 2, 1938, to prove he was older than he looked. Well, that was different, but I had to know: "Why date a woman nearly seven years older when twenties and thirties are ready options?"

He said, "My ex-wife is older, so are my mother, sister, and most recent girlfriend."

I said, "I can't argue with that, but I've been upchucking a tale of woe and failure for hours. Why in the world do you want to go out with me?"

He paused, scratched his head looking puzzled, and said, "What are you talking about? Yours is the bravest, most heroic story anyone has ever told me. It was not about woe. It was about survival."

I agreed to have dinner that night at Rex in the Biltmore Hotel downtown where he would be staying. We collected our bags and took separate taxis to drive to our destinations under a relentless downpour. Mine took me to my friend Kelly Ross's Coldwater Canyon home. She was cavorting in her whimsical Virgin Gorda beach house a few feet from the surf.

The phone rang as I fumbled with the front door lock. I made it inside in the nick of time.

Hylan said, "No reservation anywhere. It's Valentine's Day. Should we reschedule?"

I told him my son David could secure a reservation if anyone could, and I'd call back. I didn't tell my son I'd picked up some guy on the flight. I lied, "David, I ran into a friend."

A reservation was made at Dan Tana's on Santa Monica Boulevard for 8:00 p.m. What was I to wear for a man who'd won the Yardly Best British Designer award and became head designer for the House of

Worth, the world's first haute couture establishment? Heebie-jeebies threatened to take over. I found black crepe pants and a white silk Armani blouse, but no dressy jacket. I slid open a closet and a Yamamoto jacket spoke to me. My exotic friend Kelly with boyfriends half her age? Of course, she'd have a knockout jacket, and it fit like a glove. I drove her Chrysler against a solid sheet of water falling from the sky. I reached Dan Tana's parking area at last, and a valet guided me into the restaurant with a huge umbrella.

Hylan was at the bar. David's clout had us cozied up in a quiet corner where we picked up where we'd left off. His London friends included more literary marvels: Ian McEwan, Martin Amis, Christopher Hitchens, Jonathan Miller. I mean, really! A black kid from Detroit who'd picked cotton and fed pigs on his grandparents' farm in Oklahoma from age nine to eleven, now hobnobbed with literary giants. I asked questions that moved him to talk of his designs featured in *W, Vogue, London Times*—all the fashion venues. And then he switched adoringly to W. H. Auden and recited a sublime poem from memory in a soulful voice. I was with a true romantic. We were barely able to swallow food with all the gabbing, so we took turns—one talked, and the other chewed. We leaned toward each other when the conversation moved to life intention and society's ills. My elbow was on the table, my hand poised upward.

His palm connected with mine and slid up, clasping my fingers. Earlier butterflies inside turned to firecrackers, then chills came mixed with heat spasms. My heart pounded so loud I was afraid the whole room could hear the thunder. Sensations cavorted through my nervous system that I hadn't felt for as long as I could remember. Frankly, I'd stopped expecting to feel them ever again. When tables were cleared and chairs turned up, we got the hint. He called for a taxi and then walked me to Kelly's car under a borrowed umbrella. He held me close against the rain and then kissed me good night. What a kiss! My knees buckled. Hylan helped me into the car as if we'd spent a long night making love and drinking too much wine. Yes, that's what I wanted, a night of lovemaking. Too late! The car door closed, and I was driving in a monsoon, a grown woman on fire! Why didn't I take him home with me? I probably would never see him again. Men are men. Could I believe any one of them after two marriages to serial womanizers? Damn it! Life works best when expectations are where they belong.

I was glad to know that my sensual self was alive. And as I pulled into the wet driveway, my inner voice was yelling, "You idiot!"

Once inside, the phone rang. "Can we have dinner again while still in LA?" he asked.

"Yes," I said.

"When?" he said.

"Tonight," I replied.

"Where?" he queried.

I said, "Here, come at six. I'll cook."

The snazzy house was mine for an evening with this dark Cary Grant. I compiled a list: candles, champagne, Billie Holiday, Courvoisier. I collected vases for the flowers I'd pick from the garden, then eased into bed. The next day, I shopped for filet mignon, onions, endive, radicchio, mushrooms, asparagus, fresh figs, and Perrier-Jouët. I gave my kids a trumped-up excuse for not coming over until Sunday. At six o'clock sharp, we hugged hello. He was thrown by the architecture of Kelly's house. It didn't surprise me. I'd been losing my way all day in rooms that seemed to move to another place every time I turned my back. With a bit of bubbly, we step out to a bougainvillea-filled backyard, the flowers I'd picked not noticeably absent. We strolled through the garden, then back to the sofa for more of my favorite foreplay, rich conversation. Another luscious kiss brought us to a mad coupling on the couch, the rug, against the wall. His satin velvet skin felt like my mother's wonderful evening cloak that I once loved stroking. His every touch created erotic magic filled with tenderness. I surrendered, feeling the love with every breath. We lay prone, the only sound our heavenly sighs.

I rose and put Kelly's apron on my naked body, and he watched me move from pot to sink to stove, cooking dinner. I must confess, cooking nearly naked in my lover's line of sight was a first. I don't think I ever felt so beautiful. Hidden aspects of my inner life were somehow revealed by this wonderful person with the weekend to take us where it would. I awoke Monday morning amazed that he knew me sexually better than I did, opening doors to feelings I never knew were there.

He left on Monday after breakfast. Would I see him again? Was he different? He'd just ended a fifteen-year affair, the logistics unresolved as she was in France. Same old, same old? Well, he'd gifted me his company and passion for two days. If I never saw him again, I would be sad but grateful for a most memorable weekend. I spent a marvelous Monday with Lucinda and darling Kaylie, lessening my trepidations about this job search in Los Angeles. Paul was working on the film *Streets of Gold* as associate producer, the start of his new career. And David rose from mailroom clerk to talent agent at William Morris. Both of them were too busy to hang with their mom before dinnertime.

Richard's first acting job was a couple of lines in *Bodyguard*, with much more to follow. On a lunch date with David on Rodeo Drive on a very hot day, I was struck by his heavy tweed jacket. It turned out he'd been gaining positive recognition as a talent agent with a wardrobe of one heavy jacket, a few shirts, and two pairs of pants. Well, that was not acceptable to me. We spent an hour shopping to advance my darling son's ambitions and lift his confidence. Back at Kelly's house, my mind was on meetings in a world that once had been proud of me. I set the alarm and slept soundly. The device never rang. I'd be late. I remembered on my way that Harvey had asked me to bring pilot properties for CBS. I apologized for forgetting. We chatted a bit and parted politely. It was a most disturbing episode. More meetings like that? I thought not. I canceled them, knowing I'd jumped the gun and there'd be no going back. I escaped to see Lucinda, who was swelling with her next child, and I reveled in baby Kaylie's adorableness.

Home on East Sixty-Eighth Street, I picked up my mail and was surprised to find a poetic letter from my new friend. Yes, I would see this terrific man again. It was a big mistake to fly to Los Angeles for interviews before I was ready, but I'd met a very special man on that flight.

I wrote a thank-you letter to the TWA chairman. His reply a week later was tangible, another round-trip ticket for two from JFK to LAX. Nothing tangible about my new guy, though. He was wary of a new attachment so soon after ending a long one. It so happens that having spent years married to fabricators, I relished a relationship without demand or presumption. But still in recovery, I didn't see things as they were. I saw them from new eyes and tempered aspirations. I'd just met a rare, proud man not threatened by his female sensibilities, a real man who enjoyed being tender! A caring, creative, decent human being who found happy endings everywhere, even in my tragedy. He said one day that he needed to confess so I'd have no wrongheaded ideas. Confess what? Was he ending us already? Had she come back and changed his mind? My body remembered the kiss in the rain that buckled my knees.

He explained, "My lovely, wonderful one... I had no idea that in the middle of ending a serious relationship, I'd find anyone like you so soon, too soon. I told Dee that she and I were done before she left for France, but I haven't moved out as yet. I'm told that she chose not to believe me. It would pain me to dishonor her before things are firmly settled." Dishonor her? I never knew of a man who used the word dishonor about a breakup.

With this guy, there'd be no games, no devious manipulation. On Saturdays, we spent hours over wine and infinite conversation about everything from Caravaggio to Jean Paul Gautier, from string theory to Iran Contra and our favorite operas. Background music was often La Traviata or Muddy Waters—in sensual ambiance with a whimsical twist. In New York, he wanted to wait until parting with his girlfriend was official. I liked that. I'd gone to LA for interviews before I was ready. I didn't want this thing with a great guy to end, but if it did, I'd still be glad of the time we spent together.

I stuck to reality. I'd spent glorious days with a splendid man and hoped it might continue for a while in some casual way. Still in recovery, I relished an affair with no presumption, demand, or regret. The best conceit when savoring a rich, fabulous meal is to balance out the calorie count on a couple of very lean days. I relished keeping expectations realistic. No more programmed failures!

His girlfriend returned, and their parting was official. He moved to Murray Hill near his job and not far from my abode. He saw his apartment as a place to ponder and create, with no TV to distract him from reading, writing, designing, painting, and most of all, thinking. That was the "activity" he'd committed to in grade school, starting with imagined conversations with Plato. In London, he was happy to find live thinkers like Martin, Ian, Jonathan, and Hitch—along with Iris, whom I was to meet at her home in Oxford. Getting to know all of them was a joy and an honor.

Hylan had me come to his lovely red apartment for an authentic Chinese dinner. Each course a work of art laid out in the raw and cooked with a stretch of time between each one. During the breaks with him in the kitchen, I investigated his living room to find out more about this guy. In a body of shelves in one corner, there was a collection of Jewish-related books—including many I'd read and a number of anthologies of Jewish lore and humor that I hadn't. I asked him what that was about. His answer was endearing: "One, I'm in the garment business. Two, I'm a big fan of Philip Roth. I've read every book he's written."

What a nice coincidence! So had I. And the music system playing blues had me dancing on my own between each course, the food looking as good as it tasted. I spent the night in his Korean bed, and after being loved again as never before, I fell asleep to Muddy Waters. Belonging came naturally to this friendly guy with no ax to grind. He didn't try to be taken seriously, as I was often driven to do. I think it had done wonders for him to pick cotton, plow fields, and feed pigs on the eighty-acre farm given to his great grandfather when freed from slavery.

I assumed walking four miles each way to school after doing chores begun at dawn had played a positive role in the development of his character. My friends didn't recognize the multidimensional magnitude of this black guy from Detroit who'd been a couturier in Europe, where fashion is true art. When I browsed through his portfolio, I saw comfortable, sexy creations that combined power, glamour, and femininity seamlessly. His sensuality was in his designs. And in our time together, it was clear that poetic tenderness was central to his very being.

My friend Ursula, who lived in the same building, asked me, "What in the world do you see in him anyway?"

I answered, "If you really want to know, he's a straight guy not threatened by his female sensibilities. He believes women are the greatest! And my sister Judy was his top favorite."

## This Is Broadway

Still with no job, I felt it a lucky break that Bob hadn't abandoned our project or me in the long stretch of time it had been before I'd come up with another good idea after two that fell from force majeure. I managed to weasel my way into Fujifilm Corporation. A strikingly handsome man with wavy blue-black hair, perkiness peeking out of his almond eyes, sauntered into the studio dressed like Dapper Dan—a camel-hair coat draped over his shoulders. Mid-screening, Kaito called the Tokyo head office, enthusing in Japanese. We didn't need a translator. For weeks, colleagues were crossing the Pacific to experience Bob's demo. Poring over the business plan, they declared

Tokyo and Osaka to be the sites and didn't raise an eyebrow at a $12 million investment.

Our Fuji representative scheduled a flight to Tokyo to obtain the head honcho's official seal of approval. The next day at dawn, a call came from Tokyo. I was told that Kaito suffered a heart attack on the plane and died crossing the Pacific. Enough was always too much. The show might find a way one day, but after so many defeats from forces beyond our control, it had to be put on hold. I needed to find a real job somehow, somewhere! I devised a strategy: I entered the office of my former boss at *Time Inc.* But I felt like Blanche Dubois lit by an unforgiving bare bulb. Thayer shook my clammy hand and motioned me to sit.

In a quivering voice, I said, "Thayer, you know about my accident and that I'm recovering from a head injury, right?"

He smiled and said, "Yes, of course. How are you feeling? You look great."

I didn't feel great, but I managed to say, "Well, Thayer, can I talk to you about an idea I have—"

He cut me off. "Are you telling me you're available?"

I mumbled, "I guess so. But let me explain. I'm not asking for—"

He interrupted again, "When can you start, Charlotte?"

He gave me no chance to pitch my plan that I'd work gratis for as long as it would take to catch up and be me again. He hired me as a consultant. My apartment became home on weekends for my dear one and me, at least when he wasn't in Hong Kong or other Asian territories on business for weeks at a time. I adored the poetic love letters he faxed to me. When back home, he wrote poetic letters to me from the next room.

Eddie and I married too young, but we produced three super sons who balance out any vestigial regrets or blame. And I've come to understand that my attraction to Clarence had been more politics than passion. Uprooting my sons from a place they loved haunts me, but somehow, they turned out to be honest, brilliant, beautiful men with high moral compasses. You may wonder why I'm so focused on the new man in my life, with many more stories ahead. My rationale is simple. A memoir is meant to be about the person writing it, and the thirty-eight years I've had with this marvelous man have been profoundly transformative in my sense of self, my love of life, my emotional and physical well-being. If I were to pare down his role of influence on the person I've become, this would not be my true story. A ferocious feminist then and now, it amazes me that romantic love was what freed me to finally find and be myself, the self I'd dreamed about. Every weekend was a honeymoon, my sex life a wonderland, and living separately, perfect. He came to know my family, and I was hot to know his in Detroit.

When the time came to meet them, I saw a tall modern building in a nice neighborhood. My mensch had organized and financed a move from the house they'd occupied for years, now old, neglected, and surrounded by decay and danger. I stepped into what looked like the apartment I grew up in—hand-crocheted doilies, vases filled with pussy willows and mostly muted colors. Mama wrapped her arms around me. "Oh Lord, aren't you the loveliest thing?" Her complexion was close to mine. Sister Fay and niece Kim arrived. I liked them at once. Fay was dark, beautiful, and dressed fashionably for her position at Wayne University. Kim, pretty, stylish, charming, and warm was the manager and entertainment producer for a fine restaurant downtown. Hylan's stepmom arranged a family brunch in my honor for the next day. The scent from her kitchen was different than what wafted from Bubbi's but every bit as lip-smacking.

The mostly female extended family gathered around a large portable table in the living room. Trays of cornbread, grits, bacon, sausages, scrambled eggs, and biscuits kept coming. With everyone calling one another mama or sista, I needed a who's who. I shouted, "Hey, guys, help me out! I can't tell who belongs to who." Mama's eyes twinkled. "Dahlin, listen up. Let me tell you how it's done in our family. Whoever is not working is everyone else's mama and everyone else's sista. Just go with the flow." In the evening, we went out to dinner at the restaurant that niece Kim managed and then to a jazz joint named Hippopotamus.

# Breakfast in Oxford

When in London again, we enjoyed breakfast in Iris Murdoch's home in Oxford. It was crowded with piles of books, papers, and manuscripts. For one of the very few times in my life, I hardly said a word—just soaked up every one of hers, wishing I could find a way to write them down. Later we had a lunch date at Ian McEwan's home a few blocks away. I have no words strong enough to describe this extraordinary day, and in the evening, it was dinner with Martin Amis, his first wife, Antonia, and their two sons, one is my darling's godson, Louis. The next day, I met the London side of Hylan's family. He'd been a single dad raising his daughter from age seven when he and her mother separated. I loved spending time with Alex, Ronnie (her husband), and their Lily, who has begun a brilliant career, as have her brothers Jo and Ronnie.

Hylan's twins and their children come even later. That spellbinding backstory deserves a telling, one that I've mentally outlined for another time, but I'll give you a hint: my husband met his twins, William and Edith, when they were thirty-six years old. The coming together of two grown children and their dad has been a beautiful love affair for nearly eighteen years.

I have a yen to add that where London is concerned, we miss Michael and Ludmila Boettcher and their great kids. We stayed in their mansion many Septembers until the pandemic. Their first generous welcome was sparked by their friendship with my son Richard and was repeated every year with expressions of love and sincere pleasure to have us there. And for Michael's seventieth birthday bash weekend in a grand hotel on the Riviera, we were sent plane tickets to ensure we'd be there. We're eager for our next London trip if and when this plague ever passes, and a flight to Sweden to be with Hylan's twin daughter Edith, Magnus (her husband), and grandchild, Iris. And we always include a visit to a countryside not too far from London to spend time with Edith's twin brother, William, and his wonderful wife, Vanessa. We've been vaccinated thrice and are hoping zealously for a trip to all of them and for many of them to journey to Los Angeles again when life is back to normal, if anyone still knows what normal is.

# PART 19

# Lost and Found in Paradise

Much joy came to me after lost consciousness, lost judgment, lost career, lost money, lost house, and lost reputation. I had found romance with a remarkable human being who helped me regain a semblance of my former self—I now think a better version of me. With abandon, we took off for three weeks in Italy. I came home calling it Lost and Found in Paradise, an experience so joyous that thirty-odd years later, I'm still dreaming of it.

Our first stop was Milan to rent a car. We flopped into bed for a rest upon arrival and hallowed the occasion by exploring each other's bodies as if they were new countries. We awoke from a dreamy sleep starving and quickly dressed to hunt for an all-night restaurant. Nothing was open anywhere until I spotted a dimly lit restaurant on a dark, empty street. It was closing, but I spoke Latin with an Italian accent and with a bit of charades that won entry. We started with carpaccio and melon, then osso bucco with mushroom risotto, all in a local cafe being swept and scrubbed for the next day. I felt ashamed to order hot water and lemon after such an elegant meal, but the waiter surprised me: "Ah si, signora, canarino, perfetto!" I'd never use the words hot water and lemon again.

I fell in love with Milan—from DaVinci's *The Last Supper* to men in bizarre costumes on streets in the fashion district. Shop windows filled with works of art had me think design should be every Italian's middle name—coffee pots and irons in hardware store windows were worthy of the Guggenheim. We drove to Bellagio's Hotel Florence on Lake Como and settled into a room with a terrace and a view of the lake. Our passions were sparked by the romantic vista that pulled us into each other's arms with magnetic force. Our eyes met, knowing we were on the same wave. My darling let me know by planting another magical kiss that buckled my knees. Our bodies meshed as one, his kisses and gentle strokes seeming to discover me for the first time every time.

At a string of magical cities and landscapes from Florence to Rome, Hylan became my private docent. Earlier when I had visited Ofizzi, I looked at glorious paintings but hadn't really seen them until Hylan described the artist, the art, and its history. In Venice, seeing a painter unknown to me, my darling's words brought the painting to life. He said, "This masterpiece is even more impressive when you consider his malformed hand, burned when he was a baby... the semi-tragic myth made somewhat winsome and a dreamy repose made stunningly present." It meant a lot to me to learn the meaning and the history of the beauty I was looking at.

I'd cabled friend Jackie in Rome to find us a modest-priced bed and breakfast. We arrived at the address given and climbed up to a gorgeous flat with frescoes on the ceiling and antique furniture throughout. It was a Contessa's palatial gift to her "friend's friends." Our price was to commit at least one full day to Jackie, no questions asked.

The Eternal City captured me with its contrast of ancient and modern, sanctified and pagan. Priests, nuns, and little schoolchildren scurrying in and out of cathedrals and tiny churches in their crisp uniforms, the ancient stone and brick structures speaking Rome's history. On the promised day, Jackie took us in the tiniest car I'd ever seen to her favorite haunt for lunch. Was this her surprise? Not yet.

We squinted in the blazing sun and entered a tiny church so black we saw nothing. A coin in a slot and a beam of light revealed a painting my art lover knew at once was a Caravaggio he'd never seen. He talked about the artist's huge body of work. He explained that it took time to be appreciated and, years later, began to inspire artists through time. Filmmakers strove to capture the magic of his chiaroscuro. The artist's street people inspired Scorsese's bar scenes in *Mean Streets*. The Jesus in Scorsese's film *The Last Temptation of Christ* was modeled after Caravaggio's paintings. Hylan was thrilled to see them all over Rome, church by church.

Then Jackie took us to a superb Rubens exhibit at a major museum. On the way out, my lover was bowled over by what he saw at the far end of a very long corridor. It was the Caravaggio he'd searched for at the Vatican but couldn't find. He thought the Vatican must have lent the painting for this exhibit because Rubens was influenced by Caravaggio. High from the exquisite surprise, my dear one needed to sit on the top step of the entrance steps to think himself back to earth. Jackie had remembered his passion for Caravaggio and planned this day for him, a loving gift.

On our last day, Hylan filled a Steuben glass vase with white lilies and orchids, put fine champagne in the fridge, and left the Contessa a letter of thanks for gifting us four luxurious days and nights in her magnificent abode. We prepared for the trip home from the most splendiferous vacation either of us had ever known, our connection to history, beauty, and each other felt boundless. The long road to finding where I belonged had been shortened. We landed at JFK, where our love affair was born and taxied separately to our respective apartments to ponder privately on our idyllic voyage. I started to unpack like a robot, my mind on the Italian dialectic between old and new. I held onto both, the past that informs the present, two time zones at once. I couldn't stay in Italy or bring it home, except for a few pretty things. But the me who came home from a romantic odyssey had learned a thing or two about herself. I thought of all I'd done and failed to do over the years and wondered how to unpack that.

It helped to know my sons were thriving privately and professionally. David was married to Lucinda and was already a dad. My other two sons were in love with beautiful, bright, and talented women. Richard and Sheila Kelley married after their son Augustus (Gussy) was born. At age two and in a white suit, he was the best man at their wedding. The Kelley clan filled the gorgeous space with the Irish cheer I always enjoy. Paul and Caryn tied the knot in 1997, her red-headed Scottish family filling a round table. It made me glad that three wonderful women were loved by and in love with my sons. My life bubbled with happiness. Joy comes in all sizes, shapes, and happenstance and sometimes unexpectedly. Caryn discovered her natural talent to paint magnificent portraits, and Hylan has taken his coutour design artistry to surreal paintings of stunning black women with touches of fashion positioned on their beautiful bodies.

And there was my seventy-fifth birthday in London, Paris, and most significantly, Berlin, a city in a country in which I'd sworn as a child I would never step foot. What happened? Dear friend Paula Holt happened. A special friend who'd been producing plays and owning a theater for decades arranged for us to see something very special. If Paris is the city of light, Berlin was correctly seen then as the city of darkness, at least from this Jewish girl's fearful, historical imagination. For me, the German thing sat where terror and tears soaked the very foundation of the buildings. This is where time stood still. And the darkness, like a spider's web, made the mere thinking of the place a black hole. A vortex of dark matter. A crime scene. Or at least this is what I thought. But fate and time are mysterious movers, and I was fortunate enough to face an invisible realness that only my imagination knew. I stepped off the plane, and just the familiar confronted me: lines, passports, direction, the same customs questions, the taxis, the hotel, a ridiculous flight of stairs where, as usual, I'd brought too many clothes—but relief came once the room door closed. I was in Berlin and yet not! Why did I expect the sound of jack-boots and clicking heels? We had come to see a musical play, a much-loved one.

By the time the taxis let us off at the park where the theater sat, it was dark. A slight white fog added to the density of the night on our path through trees. As if in a dream, Bar Jeder Vernunft, a round red tent, with lights that glowed or shimmered in the distance. This moment was like an entrance to the Weimar of the 1920s and '30s, some slippage backward to the real moment. Bewitchingly, we had left our world outside in the park and had entered the louche, crazy rictus drunken rage of a Berlin on the edge of its own gay but doomed nightmare.

Yet just as suddenly, we quickly fell under its spell. It was *Cabaret* that moved Mark Twain to say, "To get the full value of joy, you must have someone to divide it with. Joy is one of those treasures that paradoxically multiply whenever they are divided." He added, "When we share joy, we don't lose it. We watch it grow into happiness." Something I've experienced every day since the day I met the love of my life.

When I go back to feeling alone, lost behind the crib bars of childhood, Samuel Beckett's words came to me as the story of my life. Those I once trusted told me to "Give up, stay prone, live with failure. It's the way it goes." My inner voice resisted, insisting that I fight back, find a way to start all over again, and be able to go on, even if Beckett said, "Looking for meaning in life is a fool's errand."

Three oft-asked questions always haunted me: Who are you? What do you do? How are you spending your life? I never knew where to start, how far to go, how deep. Eternally vanquished by those queries, I hoped finally to find the answers by writing a memoir. But looking back actually did turn into madness—glimpses etched in half-remembered words. I dug into hard truths long-buried. Doors opened to full sentences and images that felt true. Philip Roth proclaims, "Memories of the past are not memories of facts but memories of your imaginings of the facts." What has been my life's nexus? Maybe it boils down to a deep sense of the future.

Perhaps that's what moved me to break barriers brazenly enough to climb high in the broadband communications universe. History came at me. Events and people unimagined spun around me, and I reacted. Hell-bent on turning the corner to find my place all these years, I had no idea the path would be so long and peppered with potholes. Finally, after a lifelong search to find my place, I came to understand that my place is wherever I happen to be. I raised a family and built a career I hadn't dared to dream of when such meanderings were rare for a female. Virginia Woolf may have been talking to all of us when she wrote: "Arrange whatever pieces come your way." Her way of saying, *You must go on.*

Judy employed that kind of thinking to deal with all the obstacles she overcame to succeed brilliantly in her career with consideration, especially when she moved on as a psychoanalyst. Hylan was quick to capture Judy's elegant intellect and humanity. A time came when his affection and respect for my sister became profoundly significant.

# PART 20

# My Judy

It was midnight. I'd dialed Judy's number many times. A premonition unnerved me. I'd spent much time at her side. Earlier, there'd been a mastectomy, glaucoma, high blood pressure, and diabetes-related amputation. I'd made her apartment ready for a wheelchair. Then the point of no return came when her doctor explained what had caused her diminished cognitive capacity. He said congestive heart failure brings significant loss of energy. What came of that was the absence of the elevated and complex thought process by which my genius sister functioned. This was not like her previous losses. When her vision faltered, she studied braille. When her foot was amputated, she reinvented her life to work around the disability she considered just an inconvenience. But a bad effect on her cerebral acuity was like a pianist losing a hand.

Richard told me he and Judy were there for me after the accident that had brought on my own cognitive disfunction. Her problems worsened as mine waned. She pleasured in my company every day at her home or at the Rusk Institute of Rehabilitation. Anxiety-ridden doubts about her future hung over me on every visit. Before she'd been stricken with congestive heart failure, she'd say, "Don't worry about me, little sister. I have it figured out. I retired with a pension and completed my PhD for psychoanalyst credentials. You helped me by having the place wired so I could buzz my patients in and out from a comfy chair, my prosthetic shoe resting on the ottoman."

Throughout the analysis required for the PhD, Judy kept asking me to validate her endless stories of mother's abuses, a subject I'd hidden in a dark closet with no light switch. I worried that her obsessive hatred for our mother might stand in the way of her new profession. She railed on about how Selma (never mother) intentionally tarnished or disallowed her every pleasure.

I said, "Judy, how can you, a feminist before the term was even in play, not forgive a classic female victim who was never allowed an identity of her own?"

After a perplexed pause, she said, "I'll think on this one and call you."

A few days later, she told me that our talk had inspired a therapy breakthrough, which became a strong theme in her analysis. She thanked me. The truth is, what I told Judy made me aware that what I'd said to her applied to me too, even if my mother's indifference was a less aggressive abuse than what Judy suffered.

What I told her led me to a forgiving awareness of my mother's limitations. A giant weight was lifted, and I had Judy to thank once more for saving me from a profound sadness.

Dr. Judith Grad was certified by the Metropolitan Center for Mental Health. Her flat wired, she rolled into her new career to do professionally what she'd done for me and others her entire adult life. She thrived helping people and was keen on writing essays on critical topics. She published many, some as chapters for books, others in newspapers and magazines. She wrote a perceptive, early AIDS essay against unsafe sex and another about the distorting effects of sexist language. Then came a ground-breaking essay entitled "The Politics of Fat," stymied by a loss of energy became one lost step too many for my brilliant sister. She reached out to find a doctor who might declare her weakened cognition correctable. No such luck.

My fear that she might take her own life intensified when she invited me for a Friday night dinner to "talk about something important." It was on the night before the dinner that I kept calling with no answer. Afraid to go it alone, I called Hylan and begged him to come with me. We arrived at Thirteenth Street near Fifth Avenue at her tiny, charming co-op flat at 11:00 p.m.

My new key didn't work. We called the police department. Two cops showed up and were able to open the door with an odd device. The younger one entered. Hylan and I stood helplessly still and silent in the corridor. We clutched hands and held our breath. The cop who looked too young to shave came out and said, "She passed." I dragged my hero to the end of the corridor and around the bend, away from them, and away from Judy. I gripped his collar with both hands.

"Why didn't she tell me? She was going to tell me… That's why the dinner for tomorrow tonight…to tell me. What changed her mind? Why didn't she trust me?" My darling held me tight. I was so angry I couldn't cry. He pulled my arms around his neck and almost carried me back to the open door. I sucked in a breath so deep it hurt my ribs, then I gritted my teeth.

Step by slow step, I felt my way into the apartment with my hands, like a blind person. My touch recognized the beautiful sideboard that we'd grown up with. It made me aware suddenly that Mom, Dad, and Sammy had died way too early too. A seismic disturbance rose up from the depths of my being. I was too young to have lost my whole family. My eyes shifted to the bathroom doorway I'd enlarged for her wheelchair. I looked at her chair and ottoman in the parlor as if waiting for her next patient. A dire need to be strong enough to walk into the bedroom was strangling me. I finally stepped in, and there she was, on her multiple pillows wearing one of her flowered moo-moos, almost smiling. My breath escaped in a burst as if I'd been holding it the whole time. Everything was in place. No pill bottles. No crusted remains of spaghetti in a bowl under the bed that used to make our mother scream. No contraband candy wrappers. A simple room with a huge flat-screen TV facing the bed, floor-to-ceiling books, and a few photos of her nieces and nephews. The room was not neat by accident or coincidence.

The scene was set and played to perfection. Judy's tranquil expression calmed me. This ending was her choice, an ideology she always supported. My Judy chose to end what was no longer tolerable. My sister, my friend, my buffer, and my mentor were my "Lucy of Peanuts cartoon-strip fame to whom I gave a nickel for every bit of good counsel she gave me. She's been gone for nearly thirty years.

I still miss her. I have never stopped asking the wind, "Judy, what should I do?" Her instructions about her death were made clear years before. No funeral. No memorial service. No burial. I honored her wishes, but she never said no to a celebration of her life. I chose to do that, and a great gift came from Norman Redlich, former dean of New York University Law School. He'd acclaimed Judy the best law student of his long career. He actually begged for the honor of hosting her celebration at NYU's elegant library. He asked to say a few words. He was the dean that had brought Judy with him to the Corporation Counsel's office when he accepted the top job. His reason: "I want the best for the City of New York." She became chief of opinions and legislation, wrote the very first gay rights bill, and wrote the amendments for the state-wide rape law, which we achieved together, and when raised as counsel to the Board of Ethics, she waged an anti-corruption sweep of the city's public servants.

I wanted to create a takeaway for everyone. I thought of a small book of her poetry to read and remember her by. Judy's poems are graced by her transcendent intellect that marries pain and humor in a way that best sums up her very essence. I searched for the emblematic ones, wrote an introduction, and used the lengthy obituary in the *New York Times* for the epilogue. The cover for the book I had printed featured my favorite photo of Judy at her city desk next door to Mayor

Koch, with a warm, intelligent smile on her face. Over her head is just a one-line caption at the bottom of a poster of Golda Meir. It reads, "But can she type?" I made it Judy's epitaph.

Sadly, I was the only Grad present in 1969, when at age thirty-nine, she graduated from law school. I choked up each time her name was called as the very top for both day and night classes in every single category but one— ironically, social justice. To be there for her final "graduation" was fitting. The historic, wood-paneled walls with portraits of academic and legal giants and beautifully bound books were the perfect setting in which to celebrate a multifaceted woman who beat all records as a student. I wish she could have been there to hear how heralded and loved she was, especially by Hylan, whom she adored. He read the poem "Law, Like Love" by W. H. Auden, a meaningful choice and a soulful read. My eyes swept the room and found Richard. He and Judy greatly mattered to each other. My sentimental son, in his reserved way, chose not to speak to the room. But he spent hours with my estranged cousins, daughters of my mother's sister. His loving and thoughtful gesture toward them touched me deeply. At the end, it was my turn—all eyes on me. My prepared remarks were off in space, but I didn't freeze.

What came out of my mouth was off the cuff. All that's left in my memory bank is that I talked about the different paths we'd taken. I think there were words about coming together in the sixties on the issue of rape, then staying together on a path for women's rights from that day until she left us. I confessed to the crowd that Judy had been annoyed by my endless strategies for her to lose weight. She resented the intrusions, but her love for her baby sister was unconditional. A part of me died with Judy. She helped me scale mountains by way of her very special place in my life—still does so and always will. Upset that she never told me, I do understand why. It would have been too hard for her to come to me with her secret. I forgave her, and I know that if she'd revealed her decision, she'd have added, "Don't worry, sister, you've got Hylan." And again, she'd be right.

The truth is, Judy was there for me when I was unhappy or afraid. In my mind and my heart, she still leads me to where I need to be. Her ghost is with me. We may have started out following different forks in the road, but we were close where it counted. Marriage and motherhood were taboo for Judy, yet I was her favorite "baby factory," and she was a Bronte aunt. And as my champion, she motivated me to convert blows to benefits, and it always amazed me that she could do that. And with her legal genius and my political chutzpah, we got the idiotic rape law changed. I love and miss my Judy, but at least Google has saved me from dialing her number in the middle of the night to ask some obscure question that no one but she could answer. But it isn't the same. Google is not as smart as she was.

## Wedding Bells

Judy had been at my black-tie sixtieth birthday party in January 1992, hosted by my love at friend Nikki's Central Park West duplex. In 1994, Nikki offered her elegant home again, this time for our wedding. How marvelous of her. But it pained me that Judy, who loved every moment she spent with Hylan and me, was gone from this world before the most special moment. Hylan captured the magic of our wedding day in a letter to his special friend, Iris Murdoch:

*Dearest Iris,*

*As we stood in that tall, elegant room on Central Park West under our gold fringed chuppah with a large embroidered Star of David at the center, its cloudlike mass held aloft by four male friends, Charlotte simply glowed in a silk ensemble of palest avocado mist. In the large, very high room with its mixture of eighteenth-century furniture and paintings alongside African artifacts, a room full of our friends and family standing at what seemed rapt attention, the joy and cheer was palpable like a hidden sun beating on the backs of our necks. A Hebrew cantor's haunting voice rang out blessings and proverbs followed by a Protestant minister's softly spoken version, led to our self-invented vows, alternating with ethereal tones in a mystical Hebrew while the earthbound spoken sensibility of the minister attempted to clarify something which had already passed into the vague, notional world of private myth.*

*I don't think anything more beautiful has ever happened to me. It was the grandest and finest of occasions crowned with a white lily encrusted cake and more champagne than we could drink. Somehow, something bubbled out of this dream state, an out-of-body experience, and I felt transformed. Yes, maybe this is the real celebration, an irresistible act of faith in romance and the redeemable heart.*

*All my love to you and John.*

In wedding photos and the video recorded by Jane Brill, everyone is smiling wide with eyes glistening. Our families and best friends filled Nikki's beautiful home with happiness. A joyous day for all! My grandchildren Kaylie and Mickey, ages eleven and eight, were intent on their respective assignments to spread flower petals and carry the wedding rings. The cantor sang like a Broadway star, and the minister's mixed marriage dissertation was divine, followed by our personal vows heard by each of us for the first time. We stood under a beautifully contrived chuppah in front of nineteenth-century master portrait paintings. The lovely interior design of the duplex was enhanced by an elegant flower display created by my artful genius groom.

Before we'd planned a wedding, we'd been commuting weekends to and from Miami, as Hylan had agreed to work there for a time with friend Bob Weinroth, a former boss. For us to be together as much as possible, he came north every other weekend in the summer. I did the same in reverse in winter. Bob pressed my guy to join the company as head designer and junior partner. A contract to buy the failing company was conditioned on meeting certain sales benchmarks.

Bob said, "I can't turn losses around without your designs."

Hylan said, "Sorry, Bob, my lady lives in New York. Can't do long-term Miami, but I'll stay until we get the revised Nikki Peters collection off the ground."

I helped him find a beautiful condo on Brickell Avenue to sublet on a month-to-month basis. My first weekend there, we stepped onto the three- sided terrace. We each held a glass of champagne and each other's hand. I missed hills and dales in flat Miami, but when I looked up to a three- dimensional sky with clouds in shapes suggesting all manner of exotic creatures, I was entranced. It would always be my favorite Miami view. We stood spellbound, still holding hands, bald eagles flying over the tops of tall palm trees. The golden sun turning to shades of orange as it appeared to move toward the horizon, the sky turning dusky. The gorgeous sunset made me want my man to say yes to Bob.

With a Time-Warner consultancy going strong, I asked Thayer if it mattered where I live. He said, "It's a virtual world now. If we need you here, you'll come, and for another city, you'll go. No problem."

I pressed Hylan to take Bob up on his offer. We'd had our wedding, and I was ready to move to Miami. Why is there almost always a hitch? Weeks later, Thayer named me executive creative director for a new upscale shopping channel that I had recommended, featuring Spiegel, Neiman Marcus, and other prized catalogues. It was time to go back to weekends until Catalogue One would be up and running. Months later, when Thayer and I called it a day, I was free to move to Miami with all my furniture, art, accessories, clothes, and memorabilia galore.

It was my eighth move, the one when Ed was in the Navy the only one that wasn't entirely my responsibility.

Not long after my arrival, I met an interesting woman named Nina Duval. She came for an interview at a temporary office I was using on Lincoln Road. A photo of Hylan and me caught her eye. "We have a lot in common," she said. "My husband, Eduard Duval Carrier, is an acclaimed Haitian artist. I met him in Paris some years ago." The next day, Hylan and I went to the Perez Art Museum Miami to see his work, a spectacular installation of his paintings and sculptures depicting the legends and myths of Haiti.

We were invited into their world of comrades from all over the globe. An intercontinental mix of talents, ethnicities, and attitudes brought a welcome flavor to what seemed largely an intellectually concave city. Their marvelous collection of personalities and the sky full of mysteries substituted for what was missing in flat Miami. And one night at an art walk in Coral Gables, we met Suzi, Lyn, and Miles, who, with dear Sam Blum, became our special, intimate, dearly loved friends, some forever. But I sorely missed my very dear Manhattan and Fire Island friends, and my man was sorry not to have his Saturday squash games with best buddies. All of them were at our wedding. Trips to the Big City were sadly becoming less frequent.

When we settled in our condo on Brickle Avenue, Sam Blum invited us to dinner at an elegant Coconut Grove restaurant. He's a gracious, fashionable, successful, good-looking friend of our dear Sonya Hamlin. She'd asked him to welcome us. He did so with warmth and again many more times in his fabulous home. He made it clear that his world was our world whenever we wanted it to be and became our attorney for our condo purchase and to codify our Living Wills and advance directives regarding medical care. A truly great guy with a stimulating and charming cadre of terrific friends who added so much to the big change of place and people.

In Miami, there was IWF, the International Women's Forum. Way back in the seventies, Peggy Guggenheim, philanthropist and champion for women and children, had asked me to join the new organization she'd founded. She described it as a group of exceptional women considered preemptive in their respective spheres. I felt honored and thanked her, but with first marriage over, career rising, sons growing, politics and causes prevailing, I deferred. Now situated in Florida, my dear friends Sonya Hamlin and Carol Hyatt connected me to the South Florida chapter at a time when I was more than ready to be part of a forum that included women like Sondra Day O'Conner, Madeleine Enright, Maya Angelo, and Barbara Walters. And in the chapter, multigenerational Floridians enlightened me about the state's history, many of them heirs of principal Florida founders. The global IWF runs an annual conference, and one held in Jerusalem brought me to Israel for the very first time, a spectacularly enlightening experience. My plan was to take my dear granddaughter Kaylie, but she had exams. I regret missing the opportunity to share one of the most amazing experiences of my life with my darling granddaughter. My thrill began when I was still in the jet, thirty thousand feet high. My eyes fixed on the miles and miles of nothing but sand, and then a wavy green oasis appeared in the barren desert like a mirage. I could feel my pulse quicken.

When in the plush oasis, I saw and felt the wonder up close. In Masada, I marveled at the engineering that collected and piped water to the top of a steep mountain, the flow plentiful enough to fill a swimming pool and bathhouse. And in the year 73 CE, when the Jews were overrun by the Romans. In Jerusalem, Shimon Perez tried to convince to think of peace in Israel as a possibility.

At Hebrew University, I witnessed a debate between two 18-year-old women, one an Israeli, the other Palestinian. Their anger and pain were different, but their feelings were the same, and a bond began to develop. To observe a mutual metamorphosis from rabid blame to honest debate made pacification actually look at least plausible. It saddens me deeply that it was just another short-lived hopeful moment.

On the bright side, though, I loved time spent with my pals from the Manhattan chapter and to befriend Paula Holt and Betsy

Hailey from the Southern California Trusteeship, the place where our friendships would deepen. The time spent in the miracle of Israel was a long-overdue thrill, as I was learning that IWF members from all over the world are ready to welcome me or any sister member—friends without borders! When a conference was held in Miami, I hosted a Dine-Around for members from Canada, London, Singapore, New York, and California, and I've been getting to know their worlds better at Dine-Arounds ever since, which are wonderful.

I enjoyed blessings in Miami, like a ritual 6:00 p.m. splash in our condo's warm swimming pool. One night a super intellect in her eighties, Miriam Ritvo, nicknamed Mikki, joined me. She'd raised the study of human behavior in management to PhD level at Harvard and was a Bell Atlantic consultant retained to ready the huge corporation for the twenty-first century. We swam, exercised, talked, and then turned into prunes in the jacuzzi every evening.

"Tell me about yourself" was her mantra.

Mine was, "What would you do if…?"

Her curiosity was insatiable about cable television, Public Access, the Houston Women's Conference, and me. Her generous Judy-style genius gave me the strength to forgive myself for failures. I loved picking her brilliant brain. A few years later, she died. Her prescient wisdom still stirs in my mind.

A big question came to me. Would Judy, Mikki, and Dorothy help me reach my holy grail if I channel memories of their wise counsel? My three graces did believe in me. And now my wise counsel is my husband, whose love of poetry, philosophical thought, art, women in general, and me in particular, combine to make him a mentor extraordinaire, just as his adoring fan, Judy, predicted.

Ready for a honeymoon and wondering where it should be, Jim and Marie Brill's wedding present made the decision. They'd given us all the time we'd need in their pied-à-terre in Paris. It was great that my groom had spent many summers in Provence and a great deal of time in Paris, scouring art museums more avidly than fashion runways.

His time spent there would surely improve on my long-ago Paris *vue touristique.*

The first morning, we hunted for breakfast by following the perfume that drew us to a patisserie. Standing on shiny cobblestones at its window, we saw infinite delicacies. How would we choose? Inside we pointed and said, "Ceci, cela," and carried the selections up four flights. It reminded me of Dad's Sunday breakfast feasts. We washed down our gluttony with coffee. Our honeymoon had begun, and Picasso was waiting for us in a mansion built in the seventeenth century. My eyes, my heart, and my brain were boggled by the most thrilling display of the master's work I'd ever seen. It made me swoon. I was dazed by the paintings and uplifted by my art lover's revelations. We walked the sculpture-laden garden path to the street in dumb- struck silence. Our first words were a duet, "I'm hungry."

We found a café, its sawdust-covered floor reeking of garlic and olive oil. We sat by the window. Soupe-repas aux pommes de terre et aux saucisses frites seemed safe choices, the only items on the menu we understood. With wine from Provence, we had a divine experience in a local haunt. We arrived at the Louvre. It would take a month to see everything. We waited in the crowd to get up close to the Mona Lisa and then to see the "the Dying Slave" painting, a time immemorial horror that was a giant stab to my heart. We returned to the flat in the evening to sit outside on its ledge. We gazed at the lights and listened to the silence—two Americans romanced by the beauty of this well-planned, immaculate city. Yet I missed the chaos, noise, and messiness of New York, London, and the Italian cities. In any case, we dined in fine restaurants and walked the streets of the fashion district. Maybe Italians left me spellbound by their friendship, unlike the aloofness of Parisians. My first time in Paris on a business trip in 1965, I kept a dinner date with a French Screen Gems colleague. After a day of rudeness and rain, and at the restaurant, I asked him why Parisians hate Americans so much.

With a wry smile and in a deep French accent, he said, "Ma Cherie, we do not hate Americans—we hate everybody!"

Things got better and better in Paris with the groom at my side. The truth is, we are fine together wherever we are and whatever we're doing—reading, giving dinner parties, talking about Nabokov or Nixon, exploring a foreign country, discovering each other and ourselves in bed, on a couch, or whatever catches our mood. The sexy sun always breaks through the menacing clouds of what-if and if-only haunts. We left Paris full of good cheer and more in love than I thought possible. Going home now meant returning to Miami, the strange city in a redneck state with a political history that would not fly any welcome flags for me.

The wonderful Maya Angelou said, "The ache for home is the safe place where we can go as we are and not be questioned." I hoped the Imperial on Brickell Avenue would deliver such serenity.

At home at last, our art, antiques, and furniture blended so well they looked as if they'd always lived together. And in a city that to me felt as foreign as Paris, the wonder began. Hylan's designs for the dress company that had drawn us to Florida brought sales up higher than the benchmarks established to codify the purchase. The unexpected achievement aroused greed in the elderly owner's sons. They persuaded their dad to renege on the sale. The conflict went to court. Legalities kept my man from engaging in anything competitive for the duration of the trial, expected to take no less than a year. What could we do about that in Miami?

A sleepless night raised an idea. I didn't know if it would fly with my man. It did take some doing to persuade him that we should go into business together. He'd go back to couture, this time privately, and I'd incorporate HB Couture Inc. and run it. Hylan Booker would do what he'd sorely missed since leaving Europe. There was a hitch, though. Fashion was not my métier, except on my back or in my closet. It was *Business Week* that highlighted me as one of the top corporate women in America, not *Vogue*. I sold ideas and strategies, not dresses.

I'd have to bring my producing and marketing skills to a not entirely unrelated medium.

# More Miami

My couturier began drawing gorgeous gowns, dresses, and suits and hired Heather Davis, a fine model, to be his muse. His first collection was on its way. When she came to our condo, the third bedroom originally meant for guests had been converted as a dressing room for models and customers. The artist needed to see his designs the way playwrights need to hear their words before an audience does. I escorted Heather to the dressing room. My couturier entered with the three gowns he wanted to test. Heather casually dropped her clothes down to a thong in one stroke. It shocked the hell out of me. They both rushed to let me know that to a couturier. Heather is a model, not a woman. I was told that given his profession, he looked at bodies the way a surgeon does. The pleated silk organza gowns looked fabulous on her. Greg Nye, a multitalented guy, was the graphics and location genius who helped me produce fashion shows in fine restaurants, hotels, and theaters in Miami, South Beach, Boca Raton, Coral Gables, and Palm Beach. Our first show was on the romantic terrace of the Carlyle Hotel in Coconut Grove. I turned it into a French outdoor cabaret with raised runways threaded through the tables, palm trees, and filigree. The models in elegant ball gowns were coiffed Marie Antoinette style and with fantasy makeup like the ballerinas in the film *The Red Shoes*. The music was a haunting mix of opera and jazz. It was a pleasant surprise that my skills transferred well to the fashion world. Comme c'est merveilleux!

With his artful designs back on the runway, our first show was a hit. I hid my private goals mentally under a mass of tulle and taffeta.

Yet I was glad that producing fashion galas revived creative genes. Let's call it a right turn, not one too far off the beaten track.

The Booker buzz spread to Neiman Marcus. We ran trunk shows in their Bal Harbor store and won a place in the Palm Beach salon of famous Martha's of Park Avenue. Full pages with photos of gorgeous models in his magnificent creations appeared in the *Palm Beach Journal* with banner headlines like "His Majesty Comes to Palm Beach." High sales and acclaim were great rewards. Producing hit shows of a new kind and gaining good press were my joys. The haunting aftermath of my near-death accident hung over me in spite of irrefutable evidence that I was making it happen for HB Couture. What was missing for me in Miami was a political climate with which I could connect. Always an incurable activist, living in Florida made me feel like an Eskimo trapped in the Everglades. Such malfeasance as favoring Cuban immigrants with goodies in all aspects of life while putting Haitian refugees in jail, or letting them drown, was infuriating. And it upset Katherine Dunham severely. We got to know each better when we met in Miami. In her eighties, as magnificent as when we first met, she was there to fight for Haitian refugees.

Then the 2000 presidential election was upon us. I needed to find a way to help keep W from winning, even if all I could do was make phone calls to expand Al Gore's turnout. At a booth in my station on voting day, I couldn't punch a hole in the ballot. "Need someone here!" I shouted. No answer. I shouted again, louder.

An elderly volunteer walked over and said, "Just press again, dearie, if it doesn't go, through don't worry about it. A dent is fine."

I shrieked, "Get in here and fix it!"

She yelled, "No one but the voter can be inside the booth. It's a rule."

I said, "Lady, I'm not leaving until someone fixes this machine!"

A man approached, scowling. He examined the device and said there'd been a mistake. The ballots had not been properly installed. He fixed it. I voted and marched out of the building feeling victorious.

The next day Florida's politics hit the fan. There was confusion with the West Palm Beach ballot that fooled elderly Jewish voters and probably lots of other folks. Throughout the system, "hanging chads" were voided. It looked like the fix was in to produce voidable votes. A recount was started, and I joined a group to pitch in. Florida's sorry secretary of state, Katherine Harris, also chair of Bush's campaign, and possibly even with help from Governor Jeb Bush, achieved a Florida Supreme Court decision to stop the count and declare W the winner in Florida, then the US Supreme Court did the same. A hell of a way to win an election. But George W. Bush became the president of the United States. Machines likely tampered, ballots made to confuse, blacks excluded, under-punched votes voided, the recount stopped prematurely, and Al Gore too decent to challenge the ruling.

I was living in the dystopian capital of the country. I watched an election for president stolen by Florida and the Supreme Court right in front of my bloodshot eyes. It was while I was counting ballots that the winning vote for W was declared. The ballet box experience left me with a regret I will take to my grave. If only I'd raised a larger red flag about Florida's voting machines that possibly were engineered to spit out voidable chads. I thought maybe voting rights would not still be under attack. But the last two presidential elections have been so corrupted by our former so-called president and his minions, my concerns have magnified beyond measure.

We made friends in Miami whom we still love, but I missed walks around the block that are like a trip around the world in the place where I love the people, the energy, the noise. I came alive in New York, and so did my boys. Miami was sweetened when David, Lucinda, Kaylie, Mickey, and Henry spent a week with us. We took them to the Parrot Jungle, drove to Disney World in Orlando, spent days on the beautiful beach, and swam and splashed in the warm ocean and our condo's pool. Time with them was divine and exhausting. Later with Richard, Sheila, and baby Gus, heaven hit the ground. And we were close to the Carolinas to visit Paul producing a film there. Caryn and their infant son, Elliot, were there too. And then my daughter-in- law Alex, Ronnie (her husband), and their daughter Lily arrived with two cases: one with clothes and toiletries, the other filled with two-year-old Lily's books. Visits by our kids are always delicious. I yearned to be their neighbor, not a visiting guest. I was not a fan of Los Angeles, but that was where my growing family lived and where I wanted to be. My adult life was a permanent paradox between career and children. As a woman, it seems that these conflicts breed unnecessary and yet universal land mines. In spite of my sons often getting the short end of the stick, they and theirs turned out beautifully. I wanted to see the third-generation bloom face to face. I could not tolerate being a visitor from so far away any longer.

# PART 21

# Westward Ho!

We feasted on a series of farewell parties hosted by our dear Miami friends. Leaving them saddened us, as did selling our beautiful condo where we'd enjoyed hosting great festivities for friends, family, and clients galore. I knew I'd miss standing on our balcony holding hands with my sweetheart and following the romance of the magnificent sky.

We moved to Los Angeles in 2001. It felt great to satisfy what had become an obsession. We'd be neighbors with our family. And I was glad to be leaving a political scene that sickened me. My man was not eager to live in Los Angeles, but he agreed to make a move if we could expect to keep our company alive there. I wasn't nuts about Los Angeles either, and in all the years when my career was bi-coastal, the dividend was being with family. On my first business trip, when the taxi dropped me off at the Beverly Wilshire Hotel, I looked around to get a feel of the place. I knew that a whole lot happened in Hollywood and its surroundings, but I felt I was on a movie set still standing after the filming was done. But now I'm with my family and have fallen in love with the weather and many very nice people, the major player being the International Women's Forum's superb membership and valid purpose.

David and Lucinda had graciously offered their spacious home in the Pacific Palisades for a trial trunk show to help us ascertain the viability of HB Couture in LA. We needed to find out if the land of jeans and T-shirts contained some women who dressed elegantly. Our favorite Miami models flew in to bring his gorgeous designs to life. The two-day show was a great success. In the mezzanine of generous new friend Brenda French's knitwear factory, at her generous invitation, we set up an attractive atelier, and my man started his first collection.

Since Kaylie was at NYU, we moved into her bedroom suite until we could find a place of our own. Eager to experience the blossoming of my children's children, especially living with some of them, we'd visit my husband's family in London, no longer needing to decide which way to go on holidays. And thanks to daughter-in-law Sheila, the HB Couture launch would be in Somper Furs, her friend Donna Papas's elegant fur salon in Beverly Hills. There would be a five-page *In Style* magazine article about Hylan, with photos of movie stars in his gowns taken at the home of Richard and Sheila, who'd engineered the whole deal. The story would be in the August issue. Invites were out to all our guest lists, including Somper clients. The *Instyle* article with its huge circulation meant a solid turnout. Hylan dressed the Somper windows showing his ball gowns and cocktail dresses. I hired and rehearsed local models. Excitement was in the air.

At 6:00 a.m., the telephone rang, and I picked it up. In a quivering voice, Kaylie said, "Nani, there's been an explosion. I'm taking pictures, but there's too much smoke."

I said, "Go back to your dorm. It could be a gas main…more explosions might follow. Swear to me you'll get back inside."

She swore, and I was asleep in seconds. The phone rang again at 6:30. "Nani, I'm on the roof, and I just saw an airplane crash into a World Trade Center Tower… and the other one is burning!"

Shaking as if in Hurricane Andrew, I said, "Kaylie, darling, how awful! Go back to your dorm and see what there is to see on TV. Stay in touch. I'll wake everyone."

The throbbing in my head brought me back to my accident, my body remembering what the brain could not. For the rest of the day, we were all in televised horror, seeing the first tower already collapsed to the ground, rubble, and bodies covered in smoke. Then we watched as the other building crashed down into demonic dust. We crashed with it. The whole world was crashing. America's illusion of safety was lost—and so was its innocence. From her dorm building's roof, Kaylie had seen a plane dive into the second tower with her own eyes.

Who would comfort her in her first week away from home, a freshman in a city that would be reeling for her entire tenure? In Los Angeles, we stayed close where we felt safe. I kept reassuring my family and myself that Kaylie was safe. We were so grateful that her cell phone stayed alive. She kept calling. I worried that the air she was breathing was filled with toxic debris. In the course of that awful day, we stayed with and in touch with our family and friends and begged former husband Ed in Manhattan to watch over and comfort our grandchild.

David was a calming influence helping us get through the terror and our fears of the consequences we might be forced to face. Living can be such a weird thing, full of light and darkness, an endless cycle of lessons somehow never learned. At midnight, half-asleep, I was jolted awake by a wholly different bolt of lightning. I shook my head to make the bad dream go away. Our launch was in two days. It really was. We were ruined. All that work, money, support, and amazing good luck blown away. It was our own private crash and burn in the face of a murderous attack on our home city, our country, our world. It was too late to cancel or reschedule. Models had rehearsed in the salon filled with his artful creations. Feeling ashamed to be wallowing in personal despair at such a time, we simply had to be there in the unlikely chance somebody might show up.

It was eerie to be almost alone in a Vogue-worthy display of couture artistry. Hylan had worked around the clock conceiving and drawing the designs, making the patterns, cutting the fabric, overseeing the dressmakers, and fitting his muses. What happened was positively Shakespearean. In King Lear, Kent says, "Good night, Lady Luck. Smile and spin your wheel of fortune again." Remembering those bitterly ironic words brought back shadowy, tortured moments. Our dear friend Betsy Hailey did show up to console us, a lovingly empathetic gesture that touched me profoundly. It still does. When it came to busting through barriers created by external forces, they were immune to my efforts to get them out of my way. I thought, here we go again. One more time to make my way through rotten reality. But I go on!

We did everything we could think of to get back on track but to no avail. The hot moment had frozen, and we stayed cold. Then, at last, something good did happen. We were invited to present a fashion show in San Diego for the Red Cross annual event on January 7, and dear friend Loni offered her superb estate in La Jolla for a trunk show to follow the nearby Red Cross event. We worked overtime for weeks to be ready.

Then, a powerful force erupted like another deadly explosion. A tumor as large as a lemon was found in Lucinda's brain. A craniotomy was booked for January 7, the very day of our fashion show. My heart was beating so fast, my lips trembled, and then I burst out crying. It was a must that I be with Lucinda, David, and the kids in this crisis. But it would end HB Couture and us. The uncanny conflict choked the will out of me. As Lucinda's "mom" for over twenty years then, how could I not be at her side at a time like this?

When my dear husband walked in, I ran to him as if he'd just returned from a war zone. "Oh, darling, you're here at last. Lucinda's having brain surgery on the day of our Red Cross show. I don't know what to do." He pulled me close. Sobbing in his embrace, I didn't want him to let go.

I said, "If I don't produce the show, we'll be dead in the water forever."

He said, "Dearest, take a breath while I bring you a glass of wine." He brought the wine and sat at my side. "If you can't accept missing Lucinda's surgery, we'll cancel the show. I'm with you."

The crisis was ripping me apart, but in the end, reality made the decision. I justified the hard, necessary choice with the rationale that Lucinda would be surrounded by family, and she'd likely be sedated until I got there anyway. My cellphone would be my lifeline to what was happening.

On the fateful day, I called David every fifteen minutes for hours and never reached anyone. I went through the motions of producing the fashion show. There were thunders of applause in spite of the entire experience feeling abstract. We had help moving fifty couture garments back into the van. As we arrived at our friend's house for the planned trunk show that was meant to be the payoff, David called at last with the news. Dr. Black had "removed the tumor fully without disturbing any gray matter." My body collapsed as if I'd been shot. As I slumped over a chair, my eyes dripped with tears of relief, a stirring rose from the pit of my stomach all the way up to my throat. I cried thank you to the heavens and to Lucinda for having had the smarts and the will to fight for a proper diagnosis after rounds of dismissals like, "Take two aspirin and go to bed, you'll feel better in the morning." I'm no stranger to what was then typical tepid treatment of women by the largely male doctor universe. Later on, the surgeon team's resistance to her repeated questions of worrying symptoms was infuriating.

Fear and shame for not being there for this ordeal were not only about her. It was also about not always being there for my kids and grandkids. I was making mommy mistakes again, this time with my defenseless "adopted" daughter. I hoped she'd accept that I'd have been there if possible. I made a private pledge to be with her when she needed me from that day forward.

The trunk show for me had been as surreal as the fashion show but oddly successful. A woman dealing with a hostile divorce ordered many dresses and outfits for which he'd have to pay to serve her need for revenge. After moving the garments into the van, we left for home as quickly as possible and went straight to the hospital. There Lucinda was, her head wrapped in bandages looking helpless and still. My heart skipped a beat as I wondered if I had known where I was when I'd come out of the coma. I didn't think so. Would she know where she is and why? I had my answer when her eyes opened, and then her mouth was spewing a run-on sentence. She knew the names of nurses, aides, interns, janitors, attendants, anesthesiologists, surgeons, and volunteers. She knew about their children and all manner of private information collected before she'd gone under. We were told her tumor had been surgically removed completely and didn't find out until months later that it wasn't true. Her next craniotomy was conducted by the highly respected surgeon who had taught the famous specialist who performed her first surgery. He told us that he had not been able to completely avoid affecting the gray matter.

In time, recovery began to build. The Lucinda we knew was returning, but slowly. Knowing her deep sense of abandonment from a stressed childhood, I was sure that my not being there was felt profoundly. It was. But she was suffering the monstrosity of satanic luck.

I researched convex meningioma. The odious adjective "recurring" was omnipresent for her particular brain tumor. I searched to find a site absent of the deadly nomenclature, and failing that, I looked for one that spoke of a way to limit recurrence. We were doing our best to deal with her agony. I was getting to know and love my daughter-in-law Caryn for her caring and her wonderfulness as a mother who left a high-end position in a major film studio, the dividends very high from her concentration on raising Elliott, the epitome of a fine young man with a brilliant and spiritual understanding of the human condition.

Being with Lucinda in crisis was complicated. To escape seizures, she had to swallow venomous meds. Their toxicity, combined with brain damage- caused diminished mobility, fear, rage, and loneliness. Her recovery was what mattered. At her side a lot for fourteen years helped me to forgive myself for not always doing or saying what was best for her. I refocused on my old, dusty memoir pages, but my imaginings didn't stand up against her relentless nightmare. I wanted to understand, but I didn't know what she knew or feel what she felt. I couldn't find the right words, the right tone to comfort her. She listened daily to Pema Chodron's Buddhist meditation tapes, and at her side in bed, I listened with her. Pema spoke with wisdom for the patient and the caregiver. I learned how to express true compassion and mean it, which benefited both of us. And through her wisdom, I recognized that I knew more than I had realized about Lucinda losing her memory, judgment, and awareness. I understood and identified with what she was going through because I'd lived without words or wisdom for what seemed a lifetime.

Lucinda was a warrior, but five craniotomies and eighty radiations over time brought her down, and the toxic meds to reduce seizures made it worse. But she was determined to enjoy any day in which she awoke feeling alive. I'd take her to a friend's wedding, a luncheon, a fundraiser for a cause she cared about, physical therapy sessions to which she was committed, and the flea market for fresh food and flowers—her favorite outing.

Lucinda's dear friends came to her sixtieth birthday lunch at their wonderful house in the Palisades. Twenty-five women showed up, and her dear friend Beth brought all the food and her chef. In advance, I had asked each one to tell a story about their friendship with her. I was not surprised but deeply moved by each anecdote revealing a powerful, often life-changing effect Lucinda had on each and every one of them. A few weeks later, she said again how much she loved every moment, every word, and she asked if we could do it again. At this point, she was in a wheelchair, not up for physical therapy and losing ground every day. Hospice made it possible for her to be at home with David, the children, and eventually a caregiver whose smile never left her face.

We were all broken-hearted that Lucinda died three weeks before her first grandchild would be born. After grieving and honoring her with beautiful memorial Shivas for two days at their house attended by hundreds of friends and family, we came to believe at the end that it was best that she'd been beyond awareness. That she'd never know her first grandchild hurt us all. It helped, though, to recognize that she was too far gone by then to even be aware of the baby. We were all in the birthing room at Cedars Sinai Hospital. The young, charming, and kind obstetrician sat at the foot of her bed as her contractions were building. His mobile phone rang.

He answered and said, "Okay, don't worry about it. Take care." He closed the phone, turned to me sitting in a chair at his side, and asked if I would help.

I said, "Me, help? How? Why?"

He told me his nurse had a crisis and couldn't come and had asked if I would help. Somewhat taken aback, I responded, "What do I do?"

He answered that at the beginning of every hard labor, I move her knees up to her chin and keep them there for the duration of each hard contraction.

Hours later, my bad back's cry for help was heard only by me. And then my gorgeous grandbaby slid into our world just inches away from my eager hands. Our family, sadly missing Lucinda, were struck simultaneously with the idea she will carry Lucinda's legacy into the future. Our grief gave way to celebration spontaneously, as if it had been planned.

# PART 22

# Erotic Creature

In the last years of comforting Lucinda, David, and the kids, I was asked to help my bright and beautiful daughter-in-law, Sheila, with her new business, a fitness program conceived and choreographed by her to empower women's bodies, minds, and spirits. Convinced I needed to see it to believe it, Sheila arranged for me to observe a class, and here's what I experienced.

I heard Nick Drake singing "Pink Moon." Mats were down, the women's eyes closed as they listened to Sheila's whisper, "Stretch out your body... pull your arms up over your head... breathe as you slowly move your right hand down your left arm and across your chest and breasts, over your belly, your thighs, and around your hips and butt."

The only one in the room not on the floor, I watched them follow the sitting spine circles, the open leg stretch, the brain massage—Pilates and yoga moves I knew well. The music became Coldplay's "Yellow" and then "We Never Change." After kneeling hip circles, the tired class rose for standing ones. The music heated up with Muddy Waters and Miriam Makeba that, for me, always generated bursts of vigor, the same music that has me dancing as I sit in a chair if there's no place to do so standing. Students moved their hips with wild abandon, but their focus never waned in the demanding two-hour fitness program. Sheila says in her book that, "There exists in every woman a hidden erotic creature, a center of sexual power and self-knowledge." In my young years, I was afraid to let go; I'd often stay hot until my husband snored with a smile on his face.

Aroused and hot to trot in those days, I did not like ending up on a bridge to nowhere. Watching these nubile young women sensuously move their bodies to a whisper reached my heart and my pudenda. I wanted to dance and fly with them. Their heavy breathing started to sound like a storm brewing, but Sheila's whisper and Madonna's "Material Girl" recaptured the intimacy and bonding. Each student took a turn around the pole for the "Firefly," then the sultry "S Walk" practiced around the room. I was struck by their radiant smiles. Being no stranger to hip circles, I yearned to be a part of this. But a seventy-two-year-old woman with a bad back? What a shame! I'd been dancing since I learned to walk. My whole life I'd stop worrying about belonging or being taken seriously when I let the music have me. And now, my dear daughter-in-law Sheila wanted me to watch the class to capture the essence of what I'd been helping her translate into a business. I'd listened to her stories and descriptions, but now I saw it and felt it. I knew in my bones this was no everyday fitness class. I didn't need to pull up an imaginary string from my head to stand and walk tall, so I'd feel the sensual fitness in my body and mind. Feeling the power by just observing the magic made me want in on its full force.

It all began in Sheila's and Richard's former guesthouse, then turned into a gym/studio. Sheila taught friends her high-concept choreography. Female empowering was its central purpose. Seventy-five paying students and two newly trained teachers later, it began to look like a business. Legal and real estate steps needed to be taken. Sheila asked me, her mother-in-law with the MBA, to translate what for her were indecipherable meetings with the "suits." Empowering women having been my mission for decades, I agreed to help.

We named it Sheila Kelley's S Factor and moved it to a building on La Brea and Wilshire. In the funky space, there was a reception area, office, and large studio, now with hardwood floors, soft lighting on the four corners, and eight poles installed. Sheila's intention was for each student to fall in love with herself with no mirror image. I wondered about that. Would women work out without seeing themselves? Then I asked myself—what is a mirror anyway? Maybe just a two-dimensional third person that haunts us all, a distortion. Sheila wanted her women to be captured by the movement, the music, the whisper, their eyes often closed. She didn't know that I'd spent my adult life empowering women in and out of the workplace. I didn't think Richard had told her that his Aunt Judy and I had changed the New York State rape law or that I'd worked with rape victims. Living in our patriarchal society, women have only recently turned tough against all manner of abuse. We are energized by the power of the #MeToo movement and the budding cultural and legal changes on the subject. I'd be thrilled if women reading my book or taking S Factor's class, if and when harassed, will look fierce, stand firm, say, "Get outta my way," and mean it!

My marketing and political brain warned me that it must be made clear broadly that S Factor's two-hour class made demands on every muscle. Getting on the pole came as an earned dessert in the last fifteen minutes of what was the first fitness program I ever knew that aimed to enliven female sensuality. We fully expected there'd be misplaced male chauvinist objectification and tabloid misogynist gossip triggering the inevitable rash of crass copycats focused only on pole dancing to titillate men. Sheila choreographed a movement that was a sensual, empowering discovery that brought the love of self for women—those whose erotic creature was lost, hidden, or never known, with much benefit even for women whose erotic creatures were alive and well.

I'd imagined ancient women's hip circles that spoke to nature, to men, to women, and to children. In ancient Sumer, only wellborn women lived with men in harmony under the *"Queen of Heaven."* Then came the story of Adam and his so-called sinful rib, Eve. His lust blamed on her led to fertility rituals of hip circles to be seen as scornful. In our patriarchal society, pole dancing, even as a private female enterprise, was sure to raise false ire.

At S Factor, an adrenaline rush from women finding their true selves helped me to remember early inklings of truths unknown, and this nubile female world of self-discovery made me feel thirty-five again. Eager to help, I sat in on meetings to translate business and legal lingo for Sheila and hung out and watched classes. The S was changing me. Sheila described what launched her in this direction.

She told me, "When studying stripper moves for a movie role, I was mesmerized by the slow, undulating movements emanating from somewhere deep inside…a place of power and knowledge… I was haunted by something unbelievably beautiful." It inspired her to write and coproduce the film *Dancing at the Blue Iguana* and to costar as one of five strippers. Sheila transformed moves at S Factor dating back thousands of years. Her mission was to help us honor our femaleness. Her power hit me like a blood transfer.

The S began to tear down random vestigial bars still standing in my seventies. I yearned to be a student, but my bad back kept saying, "No way." Or maybe I was just afraid. The sight of new students coming out of class with eyes blazing, cheeks flushed, looking happier than when they'd entered, my desire to truly belong grew stronger. I wondered at what age a woman says adios to her sensual side. Who decides? Husband, sons and daughters, society, or just a look in the mirror? My love life was up high these days, but I still wanted to find out.

The idea came to me to form Gentle Splendor, a one-hour version instead of two, for older and/or broken gals like me. Women signed up. I knew why I joined that class, but I wasn't sure what the eight others were seeking. Was it that sex was hiding while they'd raised babies and hadn't returned? Or maybe they just hoped to unleash the erotic creature locked inside, to feel the power of self-love, to be strong. Or was it just fear of feeling old?

When the time came for my first class, I stood at the studio door wishing Scotty would beam me home. My back was much better than I could remember. What the hell was scaring me? My classmates gently prodded me across the threshold. I picked up a mat, positioned it for a clear line of sight to the instructor. I lay down and wait. Soft, sexy, languid music, whispers to "feel your body, love your body, get to know your body," carried me to a safe and serene feeling. The rigor turned strenuous. When I raised myself onto my feet to start the hip circles, the thinking world wafted away. We were each alone in the music with a sense of wholeness. Then the Firefly. A few whirls around the pole, for me just a couple of inches off the ground, but hey, at age seventy-three, I was on the pole. I'd broken one more barricade. With my back straight as a laser beam, I walked out, or better still, I put each foot out with the opposite hip accentuated as in the S Walk I'd just learned, feeling like my darling's models on the runway, sexy and powerful. After class, my mates and I gabbed about personal glories and blunders. One by one, truths came out—a loneliness, a deep frustration, a divorce, a widowhood, a bewildered angst for never having felt an erotic creature. Was it the men and boys in our lives, or was it our perception of ourselves—thickened waists, graying hair, wrinkles around the eyes, the flesh of our arms flapping along with our heavy breasts? Never mind. Let it go. We were on each other's side without judgment, unsure of what would follow but eager to find out.

Feeling free and fit, my sleep was sound. But I would awake in a state of penetrating sadness that men still held the power to scorn and stop us. Obstacles to marketing S Factor, or even looking for new studio space in other cities, took me back to the regicidal treachery of the CBS "broadcast mafia." Tired of Paley, the aging King Lear, and me, the crazy bitch, they concocted a mutiny and drove him to retirement so they could shoot CBS Cable in its head and in my head too. They certainly slowed me down. But they couldn't stop me the way my broken skull had done for three years, and that happened during the flourishing Schiff-Jones Ltd., my entrepreneurial venture that began after the murder and ended with the crash.

And now, even after the HB Couture launch was crashed by 9/11, something made me feel strong again, a return to feeling that nothing was going to stop me. Whoever might try would find that I was now holding my own to get trouble-makers out of my way. And in spite of much time spent out of town finding locations and building studios, I hardly ever missed the weekly Splendor class or time with Lucinda in the evening.

One night at home, my husband looked at me queerly and asked, "What's going on?"

I said, "Nothing, what do you mean?"

In an unfamiliar tone, he asked, "What are you up to?"

I turned to crunch the dried rosemary. "I don't know what you mean."

His hands on his hips in a commanding stance, he said, "Well, Charlotte, you were sexy the first time I saw you at JFK twenty years ago, but it's different now, mysterious."

I sour-creamed the butterflied hens and sprinkled the rosemary on them, turned my head to the Jasper Johns on the wall, and asked what I'd never asked a man before: "So tell me, darling, what do you think makes a woman sexy, anyway?"

In a flash, he said, "Confidence!"

I sighed. "Ah, well then, I'm taking S Factor classes and have fallen in love with myself. How's that for confidence!" Dinner would have to wait.

In November, 2003, on *The Oprah Winfrey Show*, the camera moved in on a closeup of Oprah's beautiful face and hair as she said, "The Sheila Kelley fitness movement does a lot more than tighten your tush." Then a video of Sheila teaching class and an insert of my handsome son Richard, his wicked smile hiding a sexy secret he showed no intention to spill. Cut then to Sheila, saying, "The S unlocks the erotic creature inside our bodies. She may be hidden or afraid, but she's always there."

The screen then cut to a mom in a pumpkin-colored sweater, messy hair, sloppily slumped like she never knew what sensuality meant. After a few hours of being taught by Sheila the previous day, she was reintroduced. Slick and sultry, she hip-circled and did the Firefly. The audience went wild, her husband among them. Watching the program alone, I leaped to my feet, cheering. The next day, the telephone and electronic systems crashed from an overwhelming rush of calls, texts, and emails. The show was successful.

Oprah chose to do another one with Sheila and replayed it six times, again crashing the system. I was promoted to executive vice president, my responsibility was to further studio expansion. Time was needed to learn about locations, architects, leases, contractors, carpentry, and lighting design. I'd gained some knowledge the hard way when enlarging and reconfiguring our Los Angeles studio. I'd added two studios in tangential spaces effectively, on budget, and ahead of schedule. For expansion nationally, I scouted locations, found sites, negotiated leases, hired architects and contractors. I oversaw the building of studios in Encino, Costa Mesa, San Francisco, and Chicago. I'd managed to get every hindering obstacle out of my way until Houston. There I obtained the most perfect site. It was in a posh enclave of high-end boutiques. But the largest and most prominent Southern Baptist Church in Texas pulled out all the stops to keep us from the finest shopping center in the best location. I'd signed an excellent lease and had begun meetings with the architect and contractor for what was to be our flagship studio. Things were moving along brilliantly when, out of the blue, the landlord called to cancel.

What I was unable to get out of my way was the powerful church that had scared off the support with all the proprietors in the posh shopping area by flooding them with leaflets calling us a "sleazy strip joint." The irony of ironies was that two blocks away, there actually were oodles of topless strip clubs that apparently didn't bother them at all. I had to and did find a site free of selective objectification after an exhausting search. The site was not as well situated but clearly the best possible substitute. Working closely with Todd Blitzer, the architect, our flagship turned out to be gorgeous and utterly functional.

To create a buzz in each new studio area, I organized workshops for local women to try out "the bubbles for a sweet or acid taste," as Emily Dickinson put it. Our best salespeople were students. The changes in their physicality and state of mind inspired future students. Enthusiastic word of mouth made for the best promotion possible, and with keen help and free press, the word continued to spread. All of this brought me back to when my advocacy for women had started—and now the same quest in different guises. I was part of it again. My private and professional lives were whistling the same tune. I was being taken full cycle back to when my consciousness started to be raised about being female.

On the cusp of 2006, weeks before my seventy-fourth birthday, my sweetheart and I followed a customized New Year's Eve ritual—black-tie party for two. Streamers, balloons, party hats, favors, and with Hylan as chef, every dish a work of art. On my knees, I dug through an old chest of memories. I found Mom's monkey fur jacket, Bubbi's crystal beads, and my playsuit from childhood. Buried under other vintage remnants, I came upon a crumpled ball of black lace that opened to a full-length bodysuit. Was it mine? I didn't remember wearing it, but I made it my New Year's costume. Over the lace, I draped an off-the-shoulder, long-sleeved top and a leopard silk print wraparound skirt made by Hylan, my personal couturier. In the history box were high-heeled silk shoes that my bad back wouldn't let me wear, with which I'd not been able to part.

Candles lit, Miles Davis set the mood with "Sketches of Spain." Dinner prepared by my darling Hylan was duck a l'Orange with cherries, wild rice, and sautéed asparagus. Dom Perignon and chocolate mousse cake covered in raspberries were desserts. After dinner, I switched the music to Carmen McRae's pure jazz and summoned my dear one to the den. As he settled into the cozy club chair and I filled his glass with more bubbly, backed by Streisand's "The Way We Were," with my arms over my head, I slid down the wall moving hips side-to-side. I eased down to the rug, raised my pelvis, then lifted one leg at a time while running my hands over my breasts and belly, down my thighs, calves, and ankles, and up to my throat. Then I turned onto my knees, sensuously rose, butt out and back arched, and with hip circles as danced in ancient times to cultivate the land, I began to strip out of my wrap-around skirt, turned round and round until it dropped to the floor, and removed my top one sleeve at a time, tossing the things to my wide-eyed husband.

Neck to toe in black lace, I exaggerated the hip circles as if on stage at the Hudson Theater in Union City. I slunk to the floor onto hands and knees, then crawled toward his chair, with my eyes fixed on the wry but happy expression on my dear one's face. While Billie Holiday, in her fragile, raspy voice, sang "Ain't Nobody's Business," I lifted my left knee onto the chair at his right side, my right on his other, and gave my man the lap dance of his life. Although sexually aroused, of course, we almost never stopped giggling. I danced for my darling privately, my childhood bars gone forever. Confinement for women has been a long-suffering absolute, being locked in worse than being locked out. Sheila found the last avatar of old matriarchal structures, a female renaissance. The critical first step for me, and for any of us, always will be to find the key to any confinement and use it to unlock the cell without punishment or humiliation, free to choose a path.

I followed a chosen path assiduously, even had my fifteen minutes of a kind of fame. I admit I always wanted another bite of the apple, drug-like. I don't anymore. Now I wake up and go right to the mirror. The sunspots and wrinkles are there. In fact, more than yesterday. I pick up the makeup mirror and turn my back to it to see if any more hair has vanished. It has. My hair used to be my trademark. Now it has a fake piece to hide the bald spots. Growing old and then older has its rewards, but not feeling or looking like a glamour puss once admired can be kinda kinky. When asked my age, I told the truth every time. I loved that the response would always be, "Give me a break. Who do you think you're fooling?"

But I keep trying. "Putting on my face" and a smashing outfit overshadows the wrinkles. I walk into a room filled with stunning women and am greeted with "Hey, gorgeous, you look terrific!" Darn it, when I hear that, my juices bubble up. At the end of the evening, I feel ashamed that I allowed flattery to matter so much. What I really care about is knowing that what's great about my getting older is having more time to tell the special people in my life what they mean to me. That's what fills my heart with love these days. My young self has been an echo that never leaves me. There were dumb things I said and did way back that I still regret. And as I write this memoir, some of what I've created and experienced in my life feels like it might elicit a compliment or two. Getting obstacles and misguided people outta my way has been good for me. And I'm still thriving along with my expanding family.

# Life Does Go On

Serendipity shined on my son, David, one day. Mickey asked his dad for guidance in a project he was conducting with Assia Grazioli, a very accomplished Italian woman. The meeting took place in David's office. He came up with excellent advice—a lunch or two and, on one evening, a private dinner with Assia.

The casual connection between my widowed son and a woman, who was outstanding in more ways than I can count developed into a budding romance. Assia is a bright, beautiful, loving, and loveable woman. She's an ambitious, hardworking entrepreneur who has delicately eased her way into our family and is loved by all of us—especially Edi Lou, David's first grandchild born into my arms on my birthday.

When my great grandbaby was age three, her granddad's casual meeting with Assia became a magical love affair, and not too long ago, a marriage—a treasured match made in heaven. Thanks to my son's magnificent love and generosity toward his mom and my darling husband's poetic devotion to me, our love affair keeps young in its fashion. We have such a good time together despite the pandemic and political madness that have been, and still are, serious dangers to our country. We must prevail!

# Swan Song

My grand and great grandchildren are the source of joy I will continue to relish in my life's last chapter. David and Lucinda's first child, Kaylie, who's my first female, looks like a Rembrandt, maybe Mona Lisa. She graduated NYU, married, had a baby on my birthday and soon after courageously ended a marriage not working. She's a marvelous single mom engaged in ventures with energized ambition and effervescent creative imagination. Years ago, on a visit to LA, the family ushered me to a sandy place where my unusual female grandchild in middle school was on the football team. Next day I escorted her to a cotillion at a country club. Holding the hand of my pretty girl in a flowered chiffon dress, white lace gloves, and lace anklets in patent leather shoes, it hit me that my granddaughter didn't yet know she was a feminist but was headed for a surprise. At that moment I thought it best to keep it to myself for a while.

With her brothers Mickey and Henry, a 21ˢᵗ Century Three Musketeers emerged—adventurous, brave, creative, witty, and as bright as clouds in the sky of a setting sun. Mickey juggled his *White Arrows* band as composer, guitarist. and lead singer. The band's star drummer, younger brother Henry, whip-sawed between his passion for fine art and music, good at both. Mickey moved on to develop projects. A recent screening of his first film spoke to a winning future. He's sharp. Henry is a private, independent person with a high moral compass. He is a self-aware young man who is carving out his future while composing and recording music and drumming for good bands like Pink Ariel. He never stops drawing, painting, or riding a bike as his main means of transportation. His value system includes refusing to eat anything that had a mother. He cares about all living things.

The first in son Richard and Sheila Kelley-Schiff's clan was Augustus, called Gussy. His early passion focused on ancient mythologies. I pleased my video-game-playing super-smart grandson by sending him Greek and Roman mythology video games I uncovered at the Metropolitan Museum of Art. A Latin scholar still in high school, he was invited to college graduate level Latin conferences in DC. And then at University of Chicago, he spent Saturdays at Second City studying improv comedy. Our bond started when he was very young. As a child, he had issues. Good therapy and a big heart released his affectionate, ambitious self. Fascinated by history and writing improvisational comedy replaced quantum physics. When I was invited to address the media freshmen at the university, he arrived dressed to the nines, proud of his grandma. Now at UCLA graduate school to perfect his writing skills. He's reached a promising stage of edgy scripts. I'm waiting with baited-breath for him to join his dad as an Emmy Award winner, or maybe even an Oscar.

His sister Ruby and I are discovering each other anew. Watching her fearsome fury on the Marymount High School basketball court took me back to my tomboy childhood. She liked the memoir chapters about my grandma, and my mom and dad, her great grandparents she never knew. Ruby sent me the start of a short story she was working on after she'd finally unwrapped the joy of reading and writing. She's good at both, her work edgy and sophisticated. She enjoys an adorableness of personality that becomes more and more endearing as she grows into an intellectual, curious, and caring young woman. After three years at Pace University studying both performing and fine art, she moved on to an acting conservatory.

Paul and Caryn's son, Elliot is as smart as my sister. We visited his boarding school in Ojai, a small city not too far. In his Chinese class we heard him hit the tones and dialect with ease as he translated what to us looked like wavy gobbledygook. He'd already spent private time learning Japanese and at age 12, he built his own computer. And there's more. Every first-year student has a horse for the year. They must bathe, groom, feed, shovel slop, ride, and do all sorts of incredibly difficult tricks. Elliot had never seen a live horse. Yet he won prizes galore at the gymkhana amidst practiced equestrians. In his dorm room, he shared his hand-written, impromptu analysis of Afghanistan's history written in class with no notes. I was floored. Elliot is funny, handsome, kind, and elected by the student body and faculty to be the school's Senior Chair. Then he loved the intellectual environment at Harvard University. Elliot, like Gus, is in the improv comedy world. The irony that tickles me is that they were both brilliant in math and science. Four years apart, the awakening came to both, independently and at the same time. Elliot's essays are often among the most brilliant pieces of writing I've ever read, and Gus's witty masterpiece on gravity was just the beginning.

And then there is my first great grandchild who entered our world into my arms on my birthday in 2016. We now have double birthday bashes for her friends and mine, every year. On my 85th birthday I was taken by my whole family to the Women's March against Trump's inauguration, with one-year- old Edie Lou in a baby sac on her mother's chest. It was a thrill to be one of a million people expressing horror at the election of an ignorant, dangerous fool as president of the United States of America. What meant so much to me was that my family chose an historic political protest to celebrate my birthday. It felt safe to surmise that my kids know and respect the political junky grandma who never stopped caring deeply about making the world a better place.

What pleases me most about my progeny is that they are such fine, caring, deep-thinking people. I see their futures in my dreams and awake with confidence they'll come true. Evidence is there and keeps getting stronger. It softens my worries about their future in a polarized battle between cult madness and decency. I'm proud that my children believe in democracy and fairness. I know they will do their best to make a difference that matters.

# Afterword

It is said that there are two great days in life—the day we're born and the day we discover why. I'm just an ordinary person who grew up with some ideas that put me on a path. But no quest for equality is casual. It is an unraveled riddle. Now I'm a young old broad, looking back to justify my pursuits, accolades like Wonder Woman dolls, stock options, and feature stories—all gestures of affection and regard. But nobody ever raised a flag or pinned a medal to my lapels. Nothing I could ever do would catch up to my genius sister Judy, and even she wore no crown. I'm still wondering. Are better people waiting online for the same rewards or forgiveness? Does it always boil down to male versus female, white versus color, rich versus poor, gay versus straight, and us versus them? Why does this unanswerable, existential question persist? And how old do I have to be before I stop worrying about it? It's all in the finish, isn't it?

Maybe not. The finish can be the beginning—the real prize— beautiful children, grand and great grandchildren's turn, their turn to create a brand- new world to find new things and unravel old riddles. Of course, they're speaking a new language about players unknown to me and using devices and processes that are a mystery—an odd mystery for a cable television pioneer who demonstrated *satellite*-distributed television in 1971. And an odd mystery for a woman who lost words for nearly three years—words I'd read, written, spoken, or pondered, words that had been my life. And now there are emojis, supposedly to serve when emotions and words are not enough! Communication's future is the skinny on what I think my life's been about, focusing on free speech for the voiceless and forgiving failures as I approach my ninth decade.

I'm a feminist whose lens of history was seen and lived through a woman's narrative. Focused on the future, I knew that time is linear, rushing forward, unable to reverse, though my fantasy would have it otherwise. I've tried to take detailed notice of each moment, small or large, good or bad. I came to see *time* as a vast stream we swim and, like all good clichés, unshakable. Yet I came to swim in a new stream, wireless information. I flowed through to see and interpret the world, which whirled around with a million other valuable things like family, social justice, human rights, and the intrinsic chaos that comes with the flow forward. Wi-Fi made the world into something larger and smaller. It was where I came to the edge. I had to step into the technology that was given in this life. To understand where one lands is a wonder, and for a woman, doubly so, for most of history has been seen and realized through the male lens; it's a seemingly natural conduit. I spent decades hoping to be able to say one day, "*Not anymore!*"

My feminist consciousness began its rise in 1960. The slogan then, "We have come a long way, baby," was clever but apocryphal. We've moved closer to our respective holy grails, but the march is far from over. *But not close enough.*

My sister Judy's poem written for me in 1986:

*Woman*

*They call her indomitable,*
*say she's an inspiration, that nothing fazes her.*
*They do not know,*
*even she scarcely knows,*

*that she's been scared*
*the whole time.*
*But it is written*
*that courage is no lack of fear.*
*It's moving ahead, afraid.*
*Maybe she is indomitable.*

Age 5 with my mom, dad, sister, and Brother

Me at Age 13 Summering in the Catskills

Sister Judy's high school graduation

Brother Sammy in the NAVY in World War II

My High school graduation

Mom, Dad, Judy, and me happy that my brother is safe

The Grad family celebrating my marriage at age 19 to Ed

My handsome parents honoring the wedding day.

Ed and I at Richard's Bar Mitzvah

My three sons: Paul and Richard with David at his wedding

I was having fun with David's growing family on vacation

A photo of my Grandchildren Henry, Richie (ex-husband), Kaylie,
Mickey, Elliot and Castro, the family pet

Ruby and Gus, Richard's kids

Grandson Gus gets ready for college

Hylan painted this portrait of David's beautiful late wife who sadly
left us much too soon

# Career

Bill Wilson, long-standing romantic friend escorted me to a black-tie People event that honored my promotion to assistant publisher of the magazine

Co-produced "Androcles and the Lion" on NBC starring the brilliant, witty, Sir Noel Coward,

A Dinner date with Clarence Jones, Martin Luther King's attorney
and civil rights hero

Supporting my super activist friend, Bella Abzug, on her campaign
to win a U.S. Senate

With Phyllis George and Willie Nelson on the People TV Series I
created and produced

*Time, Inc* magazine division conference in Bermuda, President
James Shepley on the right.

Invited to Cannes Film Festival by Steve Ross, Warner
Communications Founder and CEO, his intention that I be there
for the corporation's spectacular gala for its 50th Anniversary.

At my launch of CBS CABLE network I founded under the aegis of
William S. Paley, known as the King of Television who founded and
ran CBS, the first national network,

Me with Geoffrey Holder, multi-talented great friend with amazing creative spirit

David, Lucinda, me, and Paul at my 60th black-tie birthday party made by Hylan who also created the gown I'm wearing.

A glorious photo of me and the man who'd become the love of my life

Our marriage was attended with cheer by both families—children, grandchildren, cousins, aunts, uncles, sisters, brothers, and friends

We're at a charity auction show with the gown Hylan provided that
drew the highest price

Kaylie's first child named Edie Lou, was my first great grandchild, a
joy to behold at every turn.

Assia and me

Film Star Helena Bonham Carter and me

David and his new bride, Assia—a heavenly match loved by
everyone

The gown Hylan created for me to wear at my granddaughters'
Kaylie's wedding.

# About the Author

Charlotte Schiff-Booker was born and raised in Brooklyn. She finished elementary school at P.S. 137 a year early and did the same at Tilden High School, where she was hyperbolically seen as a Latin scholar. She earned a bachelor's degree at Brooklyn College, majoring in political science. Her confrontation with racist policies launched her into an activist life that didn't slow down until she was in her eighties. Her passion for dance began at age seven and for human rights in her teens. Both remained in her heart and mind to this day.

Charlotte started her career the only way a female could in 1963, married and mother of three. She moved on from secretary to higher positions in communications future and earned an executive MBA at Columbia University at age forty-five. *Time Inc.* then appointed her assistant publisher and general manager of *People* magazine. Later she created and produced a TV series on CBS based on the magazine and went on to found a cultural, performing arts cable channel with William S. Paley, founder and CEO of Columbia Broadcasting System. They named the network, CBS Cable.

Charlotte raised her sons, David, Richard, and Paul, to follow the paths they favored and gave them her full support. They've reached pinnacles of achievement and recognition as professionals, husbands, and dads. And they brought to life and raised her six superb grandchildren and one marvelous great-grandchild.